NTH EDITION

OFF THE BEATEN PATH®
ILLINOIS

A GUIDE TO UNIQUE PLACES

LYNDEE JOBE HENDERSON

gpp®
travel

Guilford, Connecticut

All the information in this guidebook is subject to change. We recommend that you call ahead to obtain current information before traveling.

To buy books in quantity for corporate use
or incentives, call **(800) 962-0973**
or e-mail **premiums@GlobePequot.com.**

Editor: Amy Lyons
Project Editor: Heather M. Santiago
Layout: Joanna Beyer
Text Design: Linda R. Loiewski
Maps: Equator Graphics © Morris Book Publishing, LLC

ISSN 1540-871X
ISBN 978-0-7627-5025-2

Printed in the United States of America
10 9 8 7 6 5 4 3 2 1

To Jacob and Bryce

About the Author

Lyndee Jobe Henderson has been digging up history—literally—ever since she was a little girl accompanying her father on archaeological digs. As a free-lance writer and lifelong student of Pennsylvania and Illinois history, she has authored books on her favorite topics, including *Johnstown, Pennsylvania* and *More than Petticoats: Remarkable Illinois Women*.

Contents

ILLINOIS

Rockford

Waukegan

CHICAGO AREA

NORTHWESTERN ILLINOIS

Chicago

NORTHEASTERN ILLINOIS

Moline

Peoria

Bloomington

WESTERN ILLINOIS

Urbana

CENTRAL ILLINOIS

EASTERN ILLINOIS

Quincy

★Springfield

SOUTHEASTERN ILLINOIS

SOUTHWESTERN ILLINOIS

N

Carbondale

Harrisburg

Introduction

The diary of a settler arriving in northern Illinois in 1818 described the land in nautical terms, referring to the tallgrass rolling in the wind like waves on the ocean. Settlers even compared their wagons to ships, dubbing them "prairie schooners."

Although it was first nicknamed the "Prairie State," Illinois isn't just a flat expanse. Iceage glaciers ripped, dug, and tore at the land, creating a dynamic landscape. Throughout its borders the land boasts beautiful hills, mountains, and gorges as the flat terrain rolls into unexpected mountains, wetlands, and beautiful natural lakes.

From east to west, and tip to top, Illinois is a land of diversity. And as colorful and interesting as her landscape is, so are the people who've called this place home: four U.S. presidents, humanitarians, Pulitzer and Nobel Prize–winners, scientists, civil rights leaders, inventors, athletes, lawyers, gangsters, entertainers, and industrial visionaries that have formed the culture, laws, and charities that have touched the nation and beyond. Add to that the heart of the state: the everyday people who work, serve, farm, mine, teach, struggle, create, and achieve. Illinois feeds the world in more ways than one.

The Land of Lincoln might well be known as the land of surprises. This book will guide you to some unique and quirky places. So fill up your tank, break out your comfortable shoes, and get ready to make some lifetime memories.

Welcome to Illinois!

Illinois Facts

TOURISM CONTACT

- Official Illinois Tourism Web site—www.enjoyillinois.com

MAJOR DAILY NEWSPAPERS

- **Aurora**—*The Beacon News*
- **Champaign**—*The Champaign News-Gazette*
- **Chicago**—*Chicago Sun-Times* and *Chicago Tribune*
- **Peoria**—*Peoria Journal Star*
- **Quincy**—*Quincy Herald Whig*
- **Rockford**—*Rockford Register Star*
- **Springfield**—*State Journal-Register*

READING

- *Frontier Illinois* by James Davis, Indiana University Press, Bloomington, Indiana
- *Nature's Metropolis: Chicago and the Great West* by William Cronon, W. W. Norton & Company, New York, New York
- *Chicago Then and Now* by Elizabeth McNulty, Thunder Bay Press, San Diego, California
- *Paddling Illinois* by Mike Svob, Trials Books, Boulder, Colorado
- *Remarkable Illinois Women* by Lyndee Henderson, Globe Pequot Press, Guilford, Connecticut

READING FOR KIDS

- *Dragon of Navy Pier* by Kate Noble, Silver Seahorse Press, Chicago, Illinois
- *Illinois from A to Z* by Betty Kay, University of Illinois Press, Urbana, Illinois

PUBLIC TRANSPORTATION

For bus, subway, and elevated train information, contact the Chicago Regional Transit Authority at (312) 836-7000 or www.rtachicago.com. Remember that Chicago Transit Authority (CTA) buses require exact change. Commuter trains

Fun Facts

- The state's name originates from the language of the Algonquin tribe. Their word *Illinois* translates to mean "tribe of superior men."

- The first French explorers described the land as *prairie,* which means meadow grazed by cattle. However, the early distinctive landscape was created through three factors: grazing, climate, and fire.

- The official state slogan was formally adopted in 1955 when the Illinois legislature voted to display the phrase "Land of Lincoln" on every automobile license plate. However, many long-time residents still refer to Illinois as the Prairie State.

- The state has been home to four U.S. presidents: Abraham Lincoln, Ulysses S. Grant, Ronald Reagan, and Barack Obama. Ronald Reagan was the only true "native son," having been born in Tampico and reared in Dixon.

- The official snack food of Illinois is popcorn, as designated in 2003 by the Illinois General Assembly in honor of its major crop.

Climate Overview

Illinois weather is unpredictable, and that's almost an understatement. As the old joke goes, "If you don't like the weather, just wait a minute!" From the Windy City to the ominous tornado alley, Illinois gets its share of bad weather press.

The summers are hot, but even with temperatures hovering in the eighties, there's an active wind pattern that tempers the heat. Winters are bitter, but with less snow than you might imagine, averaging at about 38 inches; it's the zero or below-zero temperatures in January and February that tend to wear on folks. According to climatologists from the University of Illinois, the state averages five major snowstorms a winter. When put in those terms, it doesn't seem too bad. But add in the stubborn frigid air and sub-zero temperatures that linger for days in a row and you have one brutal package. What the state does feature is bright blue skies on many of those snow days, giving residents a sense of a sunny, "glittering like diamonds" day.

And talk about wind! The state experiences windstorms as well as tornadoes, particularly throughout the summer and fall. So when you visit, bring more clothes than you think necessary, because it's more comfortable to remove sweaters than freeze; but don't forget to pack your sandals and swimsuit, too!

to Chicago and suburbs are provided by Metra (312-322-6777). Amtrak trains travel throughout the state. Contact Amtrak at (800) 872-7245. The customer service hotline for both O'Hare International Airport and Midway International Airport is (773) 686-2200.

POPULATION

- **Illinois**—12,901,563
- **Chicago**—2,836,658
- **Aurora**—170,617
- **Rockford**—155,138
- **Naperville**—142,901
- **Peoria**—113,107

FAMOUS ILLINOIS NATIVES

- **Jack Benny**—comedian
- **William Jennings Bryan**—politician and lawyer
- **Chris Chelios**—hockey player
- **Clarence Darrow**—lawyer
- **Everett M. Dirksen**—U.S. senator
- **Walt Disney**—entertainment genius

- **Wyatt Earp**—lawman
- **John Hope Franklin**—historian
- **Ulysses S. Grant**—U.S. president, general
- **Charlton Heston**—actor
- **Ernest Hemingway**—writer
- **Wild Bill Hickok**—lawman
- **Jesse Jackson**—civil rights leader
- **Mahalia Jackson**—gospel singer
- **Abraham Lincoln**—U.S. President
- **Edgar Lee Masters**—writer
- **Bill Murray**—comedian, actor
- **Barack Obama**—U.S. president
- **Ronald Reagan**—U.S. president
- **Carl Sandburg**—poet
- **Studs Terkel**—writer
- **Oprah Winfrey**—media mogul

CHICAGO

History, Houses, and Towers

While you're surrounded by towering skyscrapers, it's possible you might miss this landmark unless you think to look down at your feet. **Fort Dearborn** was built by the federal government in 1803; at the time it was an outpost in the far western wilderness. There are various plaques, a relief sculpture, and a miniature model of the fort that are listed in city brochures and considered tourist stops, but the **Fort Dearborn sidewalk markers** are often overlooked because they're not at eye level, but embedded into the sidewalk and the street at the intersection of Wacker Drive and Michigan Avenue. Pause a moment (on the sidewalk, please) to look at the brass monuments, and as your eyes take you to the surrounding modern buildings, think of the log fortress that once sat along these inscribed lines.

Formerly Chicago's first library building, the 1897 **Chicago Cultural Center** now houses a visitor center as well as numerous exhibits and events, and there are architectural features of this building that make it worth a stop. In keeping with the themes popular in the Gilded Age, this structure

CHICAGO AREA

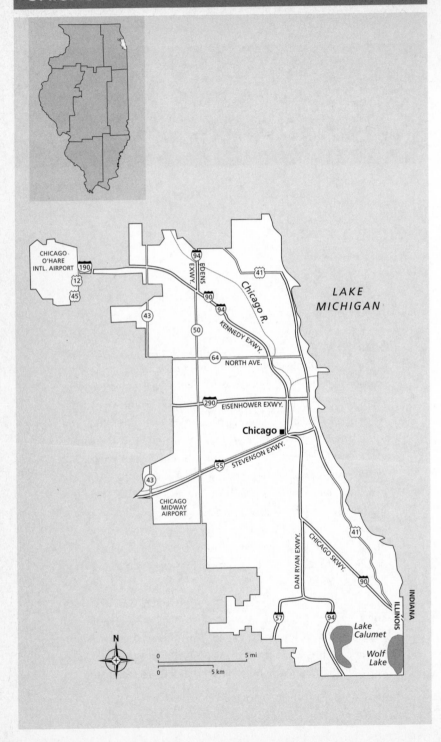

boasts exquisite materials, from imported marbles and hardwood to mother-of-pearl and mosaics of precious glass. The largest verified **Tiffany Dome** reigns above the south side of the building, with its restored 30,000 pieces of glittering cut glass spanning 30 feet in diameter. At the south end is the **Healy and Millet Dome,** which is even larger and more complex with over 50,000 cuts of stained glass forming a 40-foot dome. The building is open Mon through Thurs from 8 a.m. to 7 p.m., Fri from 8 a.m. to 6 p.m., Sat from 9 a.m. to 6 p.m., and Sun from 10 a.m. to 6 p.m., with building tours Wed, Fri, and Sat at 1:15 p.m. from the Randolph Street lobby; admission is free. 77 E. Randolph St.; (877) 244-2246; www.chicagoculturalcenter.org.

During the industrialist boom, Prairie Avenue became the place to live: Marshall Field, Philip Armour, and George Pullman added gravitas to this street's nickname of "Millionaire's Row." Today, visitors are welcome to visit the **Prairie Avenue Historic District** and tour one of the remaining vestiges of that era: the **Glessner House Museum.** Mr. Glessner earned his wealth in the farm-tool industry. In 1886, he hired architect Henry Hobson Richardson to design his 17,000-square-foot, thirteen-bedroom residence. The home appears to have a bit of a dual personality as it looks like a cold stone fortress from the exterior, but inside it's actually a comfortable family home with Arts and Crafts decor. Tours are given Wed through Sun at 1 and 3 p.m.; admission is $10

AUTHOR'S TOP TEN PICKS

**Wicker Park/Bucktown
neighborhoods**
(773) 384-2672

Richard Crowe's Supernatural Tours
Includes summer boat tours
(708) 499-0300

**Chicago Hauntings Ghost Tours by
Ursula Bielski**
(888) 446-7891
www.chicagohauntings.com

Lincoln Park Zoo
(312) 742-2000
www.lpzoo.org

Mexican Fine Arts Center
(312) 738-1503
www.nationalmuseumofmexicanart.org

Green Mill Lounge
(773) 878-5552
www.greenmilljazz.com

**International Museum of Surgical
Science**
(312) 642-6502
www.imss.org

**Lincoln Park/Lakeview
neighborhoods**
(773) 880-5200
(773) 472-7171

Buckingham Fountain
(312) 742-7529

Second City Theatre
(312) 337-3992
www.secondcity.com

for adults, $9 for students and seniors, and $6 for children ages five through twelve; admission is free on Wed. 1800 S. Prairie Ave.; (312) 326-1480; www .glessnerhouse.org.

An example of early settler life can be seen at the **Clarke House Museum,** located in Chicago's oldest remaining home, within the grounds of **Chicago Women's Park.** Built in 1836, well before the Civil War, it's said that the residents could see plumes of smoke rising from the campfires of Indians living nearby. Considering it is well over 170 years old, the restored exterior of this Greek Revival–style home is startlingly beautiful and gives the house the appearance of a government building. Tours are arranged through the Glessner House and held Wed through Sun at noon and 2 p.m.; admission is $10 for adults, $9 for students and seniors, and $6 for children ages five through twelve; ask about the combination ticket to see this and Glessner House; admission is free on Wed. 1827 S. Indiana Ave.; (312) 745-0041; www.clarke housemuseum.org.

customerservice

Retailer Marshall Field is said to be the first merchant to coin the phrase "Give the lady what she wants," a forerunner of the retail axiom "The customer is always right."

Possibly the most prestigious residential area of Chicago is the **Gold Coast;** this is where socialites and the very wealthy settled in the late 1800s, and where Potter Palmer built his daunting Lake Shore Drive castle. In 1892, this is also where James Charnley commissioned Louis Henry Sullivan and his draftsman and protégé, a young Frank Lloyd Wright, to build his personal residence. The **Charnley-Persky House Museum** is considered the first modern home in Chicago. The stark brick and limestone exterior and the straight lines and rich wood interior demonstrate the early architectural influences that would become Wright's design signature. The museum is open for tours from Apr to Nov on Wed at noon and Sat at 10 a.m. and 1 p.m., and Dec through Mar on Wed at noon and Sat at 10 a.m. Saturday admission is $15 for adults, $12 for students and seniors, and $8 for children ages five

lincolnlog architecture

While his father, Frank Lloyd Wright, toiled at the Tokyo construction site of the Imperial Hotel in 1916, son John Lloyd Wright toyed with pieces of redwood and developed one of America's most popular building toys: Lincoln Logs. The notched logs were reminiscent of the building techniques used in the construction of the hotel's earthquake-proof foundation.

through twelve; admission is free on Wed. 1365 N. Astor St.; (312) 915-0105; www.sah.org.

There's something quirky at the **Tribune Tower,** and if you've ever wanted to travel the world, a walk around this prized Gothic skyscraper might satisfy your longing. In the 1920s *Tribune* owner Colonel Robert McCormick sent his correspondents on a side mission, requesting that while they covered stories worldwide, they should find and return artifacts of note to be incorporated into the building's construction. Today, as you walk around the stately structure you're bound to notice the unusual **Tribune Tower Stone Collection,** which includes relics and ruins from famous sites with accompanying identification markers embedded into the tower's foundation walls. The Tribune Tower is located at 435 N. Michigan Ave.

whoops!

Although the Chicago World's Columbian Exposition was intended to celebrate the 400th anniversary of Columbus's founding of America in 1492, the fair actually opened on May 1, 1893. To deflect criticism, the commissioners issued a "cover the mistake" statement explaining that they planned the delay so as not to upstage the October 1892 celebrations of other communities.

One of the landmark events in Chicago's grand history was the 1893 **World's Columbian Exposition.** This was Chicago's opportunity to demonstrate its recovery from the devastating fire of 1871 and show the world that it was a first-class city. The buildings of the exposition's "White City" were covered with a mixture of materials and deemed temporary except for the Palace of Fine Arts, which required higher construction standards to protect the artwork and antiquities displayed there. At the conclusion of the fair, many of the other buildings were destroyed by fire, but the Palace remained, though crumbling, until 1926, when philanthropist Julius Rosenwald's plan to turn it into a science museum became reality.

The **Museum of Science and Industry** opened in 1933, and the fourteen-acre campus remains a silent monument to its remarkable place in Chicago's history. So the next time you visit, take time to admire the structure and picture it in the 1890s as it was enjoyed by women in long, bustled dresses and men decked out in their fine top hats. The museum is open Mon through Sat from 9:30 a.m. to 4 p.m. and Sun from 11 a.m. to 4 p.m. Admission is $15 for adults, $14 for seniors, and $10 for children ages three through eleven; inquire about free days and the City Pass for discounts. 57th Street and Lake Shore Drive; (773) 684-1414; www.msichicago.org.

Between the Chicago Fire of 1871 and the razing of buildings for urban renewal, many of Chicago's classic structures are lost for the ages. With that in mind, consider visiting the *International Museum of Surgical Science,* but not to see the displays of 4,000-year-old Peruvian trepanned skulls and early medical instruments. Instead, take the opportunity to enjoy the rich ambience of the restored 1917 mansion that houses these unusual displays. Patterned after Louis XVI and Marie Antoinette's chateau *Le Petit Trianon,* it's one of only a few such homes still standing, and the only Chicago lakeside mansion of the era still open to the public. The museum is open May through Sept, Tues through Sun from 10 a.m. to 4 p.m., and Oct through Apr, Tues through Sat from 10 a.m. to 4 p.m. Admission is $10 for adults and $6 for students and seniors; free on Tues. 1524 N. Lake Shore Dr.; (312) 642-6502; www.imss.org.

In this city filled with landmark skyscrapers, there's always a new building or attraction in the works. In 1973 the tallest building in the world was the Sears Tower; today that same building has experienced a few changes. The name is now the *Wills Tower,* it's the tallest building in the nation, and

Building R-E-S-P-E-C-T

Unlike the 1876 Philadelphia Exposition, which featured women's sculptures carved in butter, the philosophy of the *Chicago World's Columbian Exposition Women's Building* was to showcase women's contributions beyond traditional homemaking.

Initially, planner Daniel Burnham informed the president of the Board of Lady Managers, Bertha Palmer, that a male architect would be at the committee's disposal to design and oversee the construction of the Women's Building. Mrs. Palmer refused any suggestion that might compromise the philosophy of the Women's Building, and interjected that a contest should be held to select a woman architect for the project. Burnham took a deep breath. At that time in history, there was only a handful of qualified women architects from whom to select.

One such woman was former Massachusetts Institute of Technology honors student *Sophia Hayden,* who in 1890 had become the first American woman to graduate with a professional degree in architecture. Hayden's contest entry of a three-story Italian Renaissance structure with projecting pavilions was selected the winner. Her detailed drawings showed skylights, a 200-foot-long main hall with a two-story cathedral ceiling, exterior column terraces, and repeating arches.

Hayden's award included about $1,500 in prize money and international recognition as the first woman to design a major American building. The honor came with more than she bargained for: unexpected building problems, lack of control over the project, and a rumored nervous breakdown. Hayden was so devastated by the politics surrounding the construction that as soon as possible, she removed herself from Chicago and retreated to her New England home, away from the fuss and fury. The experience, which should have made her a star in the field of architecture, ended her budding career, as she retired shortly after the end of the exposition.

Windy City

Having transformed itself from a city of fragile wooden structures to one of impressive stone and brick fireproof buildings after the devastating Great Chicago Fire of 1871, Chicago vied to be host of the World's Columbian Exposition. The competition included bids from other well-established cities including New York, St. Louis, and Washington, D.C. Heated debates on the merits of each city were fought among the respective newspapers and ended with Chicago earning a new moniker when the *New York Sun* editor, Charles A. Dana, sternly suggested the nation ignore the "nonsensical claims of that windy city."

there's one scary addition for daredevils who want to stand on air, called *The Ledge.* Four clear enclosures constructed of tempered glass and an invisible support system jut 4 feet from the building to allow visitors to stand 103 stories above the city, suspended in the air a la Superman. The Wills Tower is open Apr through Sept daily from 9 a.m. to 10 p.m., and Oct through Mar from 10 a.m. to 10 p.m. Admission is $15.95 for adults (age twelve and up) and $11 for children ages three through eleven. The entrance is located at Jackson Boulevard. Call (312) 875-9447 or (312) 875-9696 for more information, or visit www.theskydeck.com.

One of the newest additions to the Chicago skyline is an eighty-two story hotel/apartment/condominium building that's known by one name: *Aqua.* This tower is the world's tallest superstructure built by a female-owned architectural company, and depending on the angle from which you're observing it, the building's balconies, or lack of them in some cases, give a rippling effect that tricks the eye into feeling a sense of movement. The building is located at 430 E. Waterside Dr.

Toddlin' Tours

Whether they're run of the mill or downright unusual, city tours are popular ways to discover the real Chicago. There are so many of these junkets around town that you can spend your vacation just trying to select the best. Here are some that fall into two categories: old tried-and-true and the unexpected.

If it were a perfect world, the Cubbies would win the World's Series yearly and it would be a snap to score cheap tickets and attend every game. Well, if you can't get tickets, how about stepping into the on-deck circle instead? Enter ninety-plus years of history by visiting the stadium through *Wrigley Field Tours.* Get the perspective of an insider: See the clubhouse, press box, mezzanine suites, and the Official Cubs Gift Shop. Cameras are allowed, so snap away. Tours run from Apr through Sept; tickets cost $25 and go on sale in late Feb until they're sold out. Wrigley Field is located at 1060 W. Addison St. Call (773) 404-2827 or visit www.cubs.com for more information.

You can be one of only a few to take the one-hour **Soldier Field Tour;** this is the only time the public is permitted to explore the Visitors Locker Room, the Colonnades, the Skyline Suites, and the playing field, so your experience will be unique as space is limited. Tickets are $15 for adults, $7 for seniors, $10 for students age ten and up, $4 for children ages four through nine, and free for children under age three. 1410 S. Museum Campus Dr.; hotline, (312) 235-7244, or direct, (312) 235-7000; www.soldierfield.net.

Although Michael Jordan retired from the Chicago Bulls in January 1999, memories of "His Airness" linger, not only in the hearts and minds of Bulls fans but also in the form of an extraordinary statue that memorializes Jordan's

Spit and Tarnish

Chicago White Sox owner Charles A. Comiskey was known for skimping on player's salaries and once announced they'd be charged 25 cents to clean their uniforms. The club balked, choosing instead to take the field in filthy uniforms and suffer the nickname the Chicago Black Sox. The atmosphere was ripe for corruption, coming to a head when a bookie approached several players with promises of a big payoff if they threw the *1919 World Series* against the Cincinnati Reds. It appeared that eight Sox took the bait when the Reds won the Series handily. Indictments were issued and after a court trial in September 1920, all were acquitted.

Probably the most sympathetic character caught in the scandalous turmoil was *Shoeless Joe Jackson,* a colorful man who named his bats, collected rusty hairpins, and held just about every record in the book. He'd earned his nickname "Shoeless Joe" after he once ran the bases in his stockinged feet because his ill-fitting shoes had caused blisters. He joined the Sox in 1915 and immediately wowed fans with his amazing outfield performances and lifetime batting average of 0.356.

When word of the game fixing broke, many of the fans and press felt that authorities had railroaded Jackson, especially after team owner Comiskey testified three times that he did not believe Jackson was guilty of throwing the Series. Certainly, Jackson's Series hitting average of 0.375 indicated he was there to win.

Unfortunately, baseball was undergoing a transition with a new commissioner who felt it necessary to make an example of the accused players, and despite their acquittal, each was banned from baseball for life. Considering his statistics, Jackson would have been a shoe-in as a member of the Cooperstown elite. Throughout the rest of his life, Jackson maintained his innocence, saying, "When I stand before the greatest umpire of them all, I know he'll call me safe at home."

trademark *Dunk in Flight.* The 12-foot-tall bronze image connects with its black granite base by just one knee, providing an uncanny airborne realism with its human subject. Fans make the pilgrimage to the front entrance of the United Center sports arena to have their photographs taken with it. For most, it's the perfect way to commune with the former basketball superstar who helped lead the Chicago Bulls to a remarkable string of six NBA champion-ships. The statue is located at 1901 W. Madison St.; (312) 455-4500.

For a goosebumps-raising adventure, hop aboard a ghost tour. Chicago has two options for those who search for things that go bump in the night. If you see the Black Ghost Bus roaming around town, you can be sure that Ursula Bielski, author and student of all things haunted, is behind the micro-phone, running her *Chicago Hauntings Ghost Tours.* Choose from several adventures, including one dubbed "Haunted by Holmes," which was inspired by Erik Larson's best-selling novel about the 1893 Chicago World's Columbian Exposition, *The Devil in the White City.* Brave participants can opt to disembark for close-up viewing of eerie sites. For reservations call (888) 446-7891 or visit www.chicagohauntings.com.

The *Supernatural Tour* is led by Chicago ghost buster Richard Crowe, who claims to have seen all kinds of spooky spirits and is willing to share them with you, from creepy cemeteries to doppelganger-filled houses. He also runs *Crowe's Supernatural Cruise,* a two-hour boat trip along Chi-cago's waterways in which he shares tales of organized crime, the sinking of the *Eastland,* and the phenomena of the Lake Michigan Triangle. If you dare to be scared, place your reservation at (708) 499-0300 or visit www .ghosttours.com.

For other, more sedate boat tours, give your walking shoes a break and sail along Chicago's waterways aboard a tourist boat. Three generations of the same family have owned and operated *Wendella Boats,* which offers tours daily from Memorial Day to Labor Day. Riders enjoy several tour options, from Sightseeing, to Chicago at Sunset, to a combined Lake and River cruise. The highly touted, hour-long *Architecture Tour,* presented by a knowledgeable docent, gives a new perspective of Chicago's recognizable skyline. Or try the ninety-minute *Fireworks Tour,* in which you get a front-row water seat for the city's fabulous pyrotechnic display held every Wednesday and Saturday evening, weather permitting. Wendella Boats is located at 400 N. Michigan Ave.; (312) 337-1446; www.wendellaboats.com.

Chicago Line Cruises also offers a favorite architectural tour; consider booking the *Architecture Cocktail Cruise* that traverses both the Chicago River and Lake Michigan. The glittering views of the city's lights are breath-taking. The cruises also coordinate with the *Chicago History Museum* to provide fascinating historical tours. The boats dock at the Ogden Slip; tickets are sold at 465 N. McClurg Court; (312) 527-1977; www.chicagoline.com.

broadcastmajor?

WTTW Channel 11 in Chicago was the first television station in the nation to broadcast college-level courses for credit. The 1956 show was called *TV College*.

You can tour the town by foot, car, or boat, but how about by way of an antique fire truck? The **O'Leary's Fire Truck Tour** is owned and operated by "Captain G," a retired fire captain with thirty years on the force and longer as a Chicago resident. Besides the novel ride, you'll be treated to all the highlights around town and maybe learn something new. Reservations are required; board at 505 Michigan Ave. Tickets cost $20 for adults and $10 for children age twelve and under. Contact them at (312) 287-6565 or www.ole arysfiretours.com.

So, how about a food tour? Check out **Eli's Cheesecake World,** where you can tour the factory during the **Eli's Cheesecake Sneak-Peek Tour,** which admits walk-in visitors without reservations Mon through Fri at 1 p.m. The cost is $3, and children under age five are not permitted. Note: The factory line might be idle, but you can get an idea of how things work. The **Week-end Tasting and Traditions Tour** is first come, first served, and samples of several different products are included. Held Sat and Sun at 1 p.m., this tour is free. Regular store hours are Mon through Fri from 8 a.m. to 6 p.m., Sat from 9 a.m. to 5 p.m., and Sun from 11 a.m. to 5 p.m. 6701 W. Forest Preserve Dr.; (773)-736-3417 or (800) 354-2253; www.elicheesecake.com.

Not Your Typical Museums

Entrepreneur George Pullman's heart was probably in the right place when he devised the concept of an all-inclusive factory and city space on 4,000 acres outside of Chicago. As owner of the Pullman Palace Car Company, he speculated that if his employees worked close to home and had comforts that other laborers didn't, then perhaps his workforce would produce more and forgo unionizing. The result was a community that included everything from residences to places of worship, but the utopia fell on hard times and the inequities in Pullman's housing and treatment of workers led to the town's downfall. Today the thirteen-acre site of the Pullman Factory is managed by Illinois as the **Pullman State Historic Site.** Of the more than 1,300 buildings that once graced the land, a few, such as the clock tower of the administration building, the Hotel Florence, and a factory shop have been restored. The site is open

Mar through Dec, Mon through Fri, from 11 a.m. to 3 p.m.; in summer add Sat and Sun from 11 a.m. to 3 p.m.; closed Jan and Feb.; admission is free; 11111 S. Forrestville Ave.; (773) 660-2341; www .pullman-museum.org.

expositionflyers

During the Chicago World's Columbian Exposition, Pullman renamed his coaches "Exposition Flyers." Riders glided along the tracks at the then mind-boggling speed of 80 miles per hour.

About a mile down the road, also in the **Historic Pullman District,** is a tribute to the Brotherhood of Sleeping Car Porters and its leader Asa Randolph, who fought for equal rights for African-American porters. In 1937, under the leadership of Randolph, the union won a landmark battle in collective bargaining from the Pullman Rail Car Company. The **A. Philip Randolph Pullman Porter Museum** chronicles that struggle and victory. The museum is open Apr to Dec 1, on Thurs from 1 to 4 p.m. and Fri and Sat from 11 a.m. to 4 p.m.; admission is $5. 10406 S. Maryland Ave.; (773) 928-3935; www.aphiliprandolphmuseum.org.

Across the street from downtown Chicago's **Grant Park** is the 155,000-square-foot **Spertus Museum of Judaica,** where more than 15,000 artifacts tell the story of Jewish culture and history, including the Holocaust. The museum is open Sun through Thurs from 10 a.m. to 5 p.m.; admission is

First Presidential Railcar

The private presidential railcar, named "United States," was a Pullman Sleeper built in Chicago. Records are unclear regarding who ordered its construction. Lincoln preferred other modes of transportation; in fact, due to security concerns and the need for flexibility in his schedule, Lincoln usually traveled by water. Rail travel was rigidly timed, and a Civil War president could not risk being a prisoner of the tracks.

Elaborately appointed, the three-room Pullman featured etched-glass windows, upholstered walls, and rich woodwork. Sixteen extra-wide-tread wheels insured comfort for riders and compatibility with railroad tracks commonly used in both the North and South. Since the presidential seal had not been created at the time, a United States crest was painted on the exterior.

Ironically, Lincoln's first official ride was scheduled for the day he died. Instead, several days after his death, Lincoln's body was transported for the first and only ride by any president in the official presidential railcar. After the journey to Illinois, the car was removed from service. One account reports it was first sold to the Union Pacific Railroad and later to various entrepreneurs who displayed the car as a commercial venture. Due to lack of interest, or maybe the lack of taste surrounding the exploitation, it was placed in storage in Minnesota, where it eventually burned in an accidental fire.

$7 for adults, $5 for students and seniors, and free for children under age five. 610 S. Michigan Ave.; (312) 322-1700; www.spertus.edu/museum.

Chicago's Polish community is said to be the largest anywhere in the world outside of Warsaw, and that makes the city the perfect place for the *Polish Museum of America.* Visitors can see paintings, writings, exhibits on notable Polish kings, soldiers, and Pope John Paul II, and sculptures and handicrafts from Poland. The museum is open Fri through Wed from 11 a.m. to 4 p.m.; admission is $5 for adults, $4 for students and seniors, and $3 for children under age twelve. 984 N. Milwaukee Ave.; (773) 384-3352; www.polishmuseumofamerica.org.

Each summer the community hosts the *Taste of Polonia Festival,* which is filled with fantastic Polish food, live music, and general revelry. The event is held over Labor Day weekend from Fri at 6:30 p.m. to Mon at 4 p.m. Admission is $7 for adults, $3 for seniors, and free for children under age twelve. For more information, contact the *Copernicus Cultural and Civic Center* at 5216 W. Lawrence Ave.; (773) 777-8898; or visit www.copernicusfdn.org for more information.

Ensconced in the *Hyde Park* neighborhood, the *DuSable Museum of African American History* was founded in 1961 and is the nation's oldest museum dedicated to African-American history. The varied displays feature art, sculpture, writings, and film. The museum is open Mon through Sat from 10 a.m. to 5 p.m. and Sun from noon to 5 p.m.; admission is $3 for adults, $2 for students and seniors, $1 for children ages six through twelve, and free for children under age six. 740 E. Fifty-Sixth Place; (773) 947-0600; www.dusable museum.org.

The centerpiece of Chicago's north side *Andersonville* neighborhood is the *Swedish American Museum,* which depicts the Swedish-American experience through fine arts, textiles, glass, and traveling and permanent exhibits. The museum is open Mon through Fri from 10 a.m. to 4 p.m. and Sat and Sun from 10 a.m. to 4 p.m. Admission is $4 for adults and $3 for students, seniors, and children; a family pass costs $10, and admission is free on the second Tues of each month. 5211 N. Clark St.; (773) 728-8111; www.samac.org.

Also on site is the *Brunk Children's Museum of Immigration,* which is suitable for young and old alike and features interactive exhibits about the lives of Swedish immigrants in Chicago in the 1800s. The museum is open Mon through Thurs from 1 to 4 p.m., Fri from 10 a.m. to 4 p.m., and Sat and Sun from 1 to 4 p.m.; admission is included with a ticket into the Swedish American Museum. 5211 N. Clark St.; (773) 728-8111; www.samac.org.

To see traditional crafts, dolls, and folk art, visit the *Ukrainian National Museum,* where the life and culture of Ukraine is taught through the artifacts of its people. The displays of costumes alone are worth the trip, until you see the intricate Easter eggs, which will amaze you even more. The museum is open Thurs through Sun from 11 a.m. to 4 p.m.; admission is $5. 2249 W. Superior St.; (312) 421-8020; www.ukrainiannationalmuseum.org.

One of the highlights of the **Balzekas Museum of Lithuanian Culture** is the stunning stained-glass window titled *Spring Time* by native artist Adolfas Valeska. This **West Lawn** neighborhood museum also contains medieval artifacts, including armor and crossbows. Cross the bridge at "Castle Quest" and enter the **Lithuanian Children's Museum of Immigrant History,** which transports visitors into medieval Lithuania. The museum is open daily from 10 a.m. to 4 p.m., except Christmas, Easter, and New Year's Day; admission is $5 for adults and $2 for children twelve and under. 6500 S. Pulaski Rd.; (773) 582-6500; www.balzekasmuseum.org.

At the **National Hellenic Museum,** visitors will meet "Homer," an interactive art exhibit in the **Frank S. Kambero's Oral History Center** that plays the stories of Greek-American immigrants as told in their own words. The exhibits include art from antiquities to modern, and articles of early immigrant life. The museum is open Tues through Fri from 10 a.m. to 4 p.m., Sat from 11 a.m. to 4 p.m., and the second Thurs of the month from 10 a.m. to 7:30 p.m.; admission is $5 for adults and free for children under age twelve. 801 W. Adams St., No. 400; (312) 655-1234; www.nationalhellenicmuseum.org.

Thousands of pages have been written about the successes of Hull-House, the settlement founded by Jane Addams and based on a similar operation at Toynbee Hall in England. At Toynbee, well-educated, upper-class men lived in a communal setting and taught the local poor about the finer things in life. Addams organized a similar facility in Chicago, but staffed by women. The project changed the lives of many immigrants and working poor, and in 1931 Addams became the first woman in history to receive the Nobel Peace Prize. The **Jane Addams Hull-House Museum** sits on the campus of the **University of Illinois at Chicago.** The brick building had been restored, and many

Land Baroness

Helen Culver is considered Chicago's first female real estate magnate. Culver's cousin, Charles J. Hull, built the home used for the Hull-House Settlement in 1856 as a summer retreat for his family when the surrounding area was mostly rural. Once the city began to encroach on the countryside, he lost interest in the property and rented it to a variety of people and groups. When he died, Helen Culver inherited all of his real estate holdings, making her one rich lady.

of her personal artifacts and her office can be viewed, as well as traveling and permanent exhibits about the settlement. The museum is open Tues through Fri from 10 a.m. to 4 p.m. and Sun from noon to 4 p.m.; admission is free. 800 S. Halsted St.; (312) 413-5353.

Food Wars

Chicago is home to some of the most fantastic five-star restaurants in the nation, but for most of us, it's not the white tablecloths and pricey menus that suit our tastes, but something a bit less civilized, like hot dogs, pizza, beef sandwiches, and an occasional super-thick pork chop thrown in for good luck. Our Chicago–style dogs are far from those mushy-meat, ketchup-topped dogs in a plain bun. In fact, here are the rules: The all-beef hot dog has a snap when you bite into it; yellow mustard and pickle relish must smother the dog; the toppings will include tomato, cucumber, hot pepper, diced onions, a quarter of a dill pickle, and a good dousing of celery salt, all resting comfortably in a nice poppyseed bun. That said, here are the candidates for the city's best Chicago dogs in random order.

Portillos started out with a single hot dog cart on a street corner. Today they own over thirty restaurants in and around Chicago. The theme here is 1930s gangster, and the dogs are perfect, but don't miss the crinkle fries and homemade chocolate cake that tastes like Ma's. Portillos is located at 100 W. Ontario St.; (312) 587-8910; www.portillos.com/portillos.

Superdawg Drive-In is an old-time favorite since 1948, and people rave about the dogs and the Superfries, too. The service is hands on, with carhops doing the honors so your food is hot and ready to eat on the spot. Chicago icons *Maurie and Flaurie Superdawg* are 12-foot fiberglass hot dog characters that welcome the hungry from atop the restaurant rooftop. Superdawg is located at 6363 N. Milwaukee Ave.; (773) 763-0660; www.super dawg.com.

Hot Doug's in the *Avondale* neighborhood serves The Dog smothered with all the trimmings. At this hallowed "Encased Meat Emporium," don't forget to order a side of the duck-fat fries, too. This is the kind of place where you expect to stand in line. The restaurant is located at 3324 N. California Ave.; (773) 279-9550.

Now we move to the Pizza Wars. Here it's about *real* deep dish, which means it takes an hour from order to serve, it requires silverware to eat, and the sauce is on top of the cheese, not underneath. At least four pizzerias claim to be the best-loved pizza in the city, but that's not just positioning. Years of newspaper and magazine readers' polls agree that these restaurants are the city's best. These places are listed by longevity.

The first **Pizzeria Uno** restaurant opened in 1943, and shortly afterward introduced Original Deep Dish Pizza as a bar food; it remains on the menu today. The specialty became so popular that they opened two additional restaurants within blocks of each other to accommodate the lines of hungry patrons. This is considered to be the first iteration of deep-dish fare. The restaurant is located at 29 E. Ohio St.; (312) 321-1000; www.unos.com.

Gino's East opened its doors in 1966, and before long word of its deep dish attracted capacity crowds including well-known political figures and celebrities. Besides the delectable tender crust, the sauce is really rich. Guests sign their names to the stucco walls while they wait for their pie. Gino's is located at 633 N. Wells St.; (312) 943-1124; www.ginoeast.com.

Lou Malnati's has expanded to thirty Chicagoland locations, but for old times' sake, start at the flagship restaurant that opened in 1971. You'll love the fresh chopped tomatoes in the sauce. The wafer-thin, butter-crust pizza is also "knock your socks off" good. The restaurant is located at 6649 N. Lincoln Ave.; (847) 673-0800; www.loumalnatis.com.

Based on the recipe of their Italian mother, the Boglio brothers opened their first Chicago pizza restaurant in 1974, and fittingly named it after their mother. Today **Giordano's** has nearly forty restaurants around the Chicago area. Their deep dish is super-stuffed with cheese, and the pie is taller and the crust thicker than its competition. Giordano's is located at 1040 W. Belmont Ave.; (773) 327-1200; www.giordanos.com.

For famous eateries, rub shoulders with fans of old *Saturday Night Live* episodes at the **Billy Goat Tavern.** There are several locations around town, but head to the original if you want the true "cheezborger, no Pepsi" experience. The restaurant is located at 430 Michigan Ave., Lower Level; (312) 222-1525; www.billygoattavern.com.

To sit at Booth One when you enter the **Pump Room** at the **Ambassador East Hotel,** you'll have to prove your stardom. Starting in 1938, this was the table reserved for stars and dignitaries. Frank Sinatra, Bette Davis, and Humphrey Bogart frequented those chairs, and when the old Hollywood guard

sweetfailure

No matter how hard the candy makers at Milton J. Holloway tried, they were unable to form a perfectly round caramel center, so the oddly shaped balls were called "duds"; hence the name Milk Duds. The company manufactured the popular treats at its Chicago location from 1928 until 1986.

passed, Robert Redford, Eddie Murphy, and Sting sat there. Truth be told, today it's probably the nostalgia, not the food, that draws stargazers to this

Chocolate Heaven

Milton Hershey, a Pennsylvania caramel maker and former Chicago resident, attended the World's Columbian Exposition just to be a part of the experience. However, what he found there so enthralled him that he changed the course of his business. A chocolate machine demonstrated by a German businessman solved the chocolate tempering problems that Hershey had encountered. He insisted the man sell him the display machine on the spot, and a heated discussion broke out between the men as the inventor wanted to keep the machine on display at the fair so he could take orders from other businesses. But Hershey made a sizable monetary offer to ensure exclusivity and had the machine shipped to his Pennsylvania shop. Within a week his confectionary began producing those beloved trademark chocolate treats.

Gold Coast landmark. And don't forget the dress code: jacket required. The Pump Room is located at 1301 N. State Parkway, Ambassador East Hotel; (312) 266-0360; www.pumproom.com.

If you're in the mood to be verbally abused by your waitress, eat at **Ed Debevic's,** where you'll get a meal with an attitude and the terse theme is "Eat and Get Out." The food is family favorites: burgers, fries, chicken strips, nachos, and milk shakes. And while you're eating, keep watch for the entertainment; you never know when someone will dance on a tabletop. The restaurant is located at 640 N. Wells St.; (312) 664-1707; www.eddebevics.com.

Although they're students-in-training, the chefs at the **Dining Room at Kendall College** offer top of the line culinary fare featuring international fusion, French, and American contemporary cuisine. Both your mouth and your pocketbook will be glad you stopped here; the average tab for a multicourse meal runs $18 for lunch and $29 for dinner, and the food is amazing. Reservations are required. The Dining Room is located at 900 N. North Branch St. (yes, that's *two* norths in the address); (312) 752-2328; http://culinary.kendall.edu.

This next place is like eating in Paris. At **La Creperie** the place to sit is the patio dining area. That's because once you pass through the back door, you'll feel as though you've been magically transported from Chicago's streets into a private garden of a quaint French restaurant. The authentic French crepes are tender and well stuffed—consider trying the buckwheat or wheat version. Even with reservations, you may have to wait. The restaurant is located at 2845 N. Clark St.; (773) 528-9050; www.lacreperieusa.com.

Long popular with celebrities, **The Rosebud** is fun to visit just to see the autographed photographs of Hollywood patrons along the wall. Since 1977 this family Italian eatery has been famous for its chicken Vesuvio dressed in a delicate white wine sauce and homemade square noodles, but the menu contains an array of fine choices. The Rosebud is located at 1500 W. Taylor St.; (312) 942-1117; http://rosebudrestaurants.com.

For a favorite sweet treat, head to the *Magnificent Mile,* where you'll find *Hershey's Chicago.* At this combination candy and bakery shop, professional "Hershey-izer" bakers transform all things Hershey into a bounty of yummy treats. The shop is open weekdays from 10 a.m. to 10 p.m.; 822 N. Michigan Ave.; (312) 337-7711.

If you're driving by *North Avenue Beach,* you might notice what seems to be the hull of an old boat. This is the *Beach Boathouse* and it's a combination snack bar and restaurant. On the first level you'll find a concession stand that sells typical summer fare that's suitable for the kids, too. Upstairs is the *Castaway's Bar and Grill,* which is geared toward adults and features live music on weekends. Seasonally the restaurant is open daily from 11 a.m. to 11 p.m. 1603 N. Lake Shore Dr.; (773) 281-1200; www.castawayschicago.com.

Starting in 1885, *Charles Cretors* was like a permanent fixture on Randolph Street, selling fresh roasted peanuts from his custom-built cart. More of an inventor than a food connoisseur, Cretors's true genius was in his ability to design and construct machine parts from an artist's rendering. The machines he made were of the highest quality, featuring beveled glass, highly polished nickel plating, and gold-leaf striping. To expand sales, Cretors invented and then incorporated the world's first popcorn popper as an additional accessory for the peanut cart.

Prior to Cretors's popper, popcorn was not typically a big moneymaker for street vendors because the process was cumbersome and time consuming. Patient customers, who waited for the kernels to pop in a wire basket held over a fire, often rejected the soggy snack after it was covered in butter. But Cretors developed a seasoned cooking oil that infused the popcorn with a buttery fresh flavor during the popping process. Finally, in 1893, just before the World's Columbian Exposition, Cretors patented the first popcorn machine as well as the method to pop the snack in his butter-oil and leaf-lard mixture. The aroma alone brought customers to his exposition demonstration stand.

In 1919 he invented the first "self-propelled and self-contained" popcorn wagon. Built on the chassis of a Model T Ford, this broadened the service area for vendors who could now drive to events. Today, *C. Cretors and Company* manufactures popcorn poppers at its Chicago factory (Note: The factory is not open for tours). Chances are that if you have purchased popcorn from a movie theater, store or concession stand, it was popped in a Cretors popper.

Mix and Match

There are numerous offbeat businesses and sites throughout this town and its near-suburbs. Here are some places to occupy your time.

Resurrection Cemetery in *Justice* is the center of a debate. First, there's the argument that the *Public Mausoleum's* stained-glass window is the largest in the world, with over 22,000 square feet of glass spanning four sides of the entranceway building. It just might be true, since its strongest competition was removed from New York's Kennedy International Airport and discarded in 2008.

The second discussion surrounding the cemetery relates to the woman known as *Resurrection Mary*—well, if she's a woman or a ghost, that is. The story revolves around one of those urban legends of the disappearing hiker. Although there are variations, in a nutshell a woman hitchhiker is picked up along the road or at a nearby dance hall, and when the driver nears the cemetery entrance, "Mary" announces that it is her stop and disappears from the vehicle without opening the car door. Moral to the story: If you visit Resurrection Cemetery to see the stained-glass window, don't pick up any hitchhiking women along the way! The cemetery is located at 7200 Archer Ave.

Another cemetery that is frequented by believers is the *Queen of Heaven Catholic Cemetery,* where a *life-size crucifix* is said to bleed and turn rosaries into gold. The first apparition of the Virgin Mary appeared in 1990, and when word of the incident spread, pilgrims converged on the scene, requiring the cemetery to move the cross to another larger location on the left side of the entryway. The cemetery is located at 1400 S. Wolf Rd., *Hillside.*

In the early morning of June 22, 1918, the Hagenbeck-Wallace Circus train sat idle on the track outside of Hammond, Indiana, when the unthinkable happened. A speeding train on the same rails failed to stop and struck it from behind, killing more than eighty circus performers and personnel. Fifty-six of the victims were laid to rest at the *Woodlawn Cemetery* west of Chicago. A granite elephant sits atop the marker in the cemetery's section called *Showman's Rest,* and the circus members are honored with individual gravestones. Since many were roustabouts with unknown identities, they're remembered by their talent, such as "4 Horse Driver." The cemetery is located at 7600 W. Cermak Rd., *Forest Park.*

Remember the little red wagon you were so fond of when you were a kid? If the thought gives you warm fuzzies, check out the *Radio Flyer, Inc.* headquarters to see that little wagon times nine. The *World's Largest Wagon* sits in front of the main building and is patterned after the Coaster Boy model, which was unveiled during the 1933 World's Fair. It's 27 feet long, 13 feet

TOP ANNUAL EVENTS

JANUARY
Chicago Cubs Convention
(773) 404-2827

MARCH
St. Patrick's Day Parade
(312) 942-9188

South Side Irish St. Patrick's Day
Parade
(773) 393-8687

Maple Syrup Festival
(312) 742-7529

JUNE
Printers Row Lit Fest
(312) 527-8132

Chicago Blues Festival
(312) 744-3315

Taste of Chicago
late June–early July
(312) 744-2400

JULY
Venetian Night
(312) 744-3315

AUGUST
Chicago Air & Water Show
(312) 744-3315

SEPTEMBER
Chicago Jazz Festival
(312) 744-3315

Celtic Fest Chicago
(312) 744-3315

OCTOBER
Chicago International Children's
Film Festival
(773) 281-9075

DECEMBER
Lincoln Park Zoo's ZooLights
early Dec
(312) 742-2000

high, and weighs 15,000 pounds. You could fit a lot of stuffed animals into that wagon! Radio Flyer is located at 6516 W. Grand Ave.

Along North Beach you'll find the *Chess Pavilion,* where over twenty boards are painted on concrete and ready for action. All age groups play here. Maybe you can get in on a game, but beware that chess pieces are not provided, so bring your own. And, before you leave the area, check out two sculptures by Boris Gilbertson titled **Chess Queen** and **Chess King.** These oversized limestone pieces have seen some weathering as they were installed in 1957 and sit unprotected on pedestals near the pavilion. The Chess Pavilion is located at 1600 N. Lake Shore Dr.; (312) 747-0832.

You're not in Kansas; you're in *Oz Park* and face to face with Dorothy, Toto, and pals. This thirteen-acre park is a memorial to the author L. Frank Baum, who wrote *The Wonderful Wizard of Oz* and lived in Chicago for many years. The grounds include a lot of open space where dogs play and joggers jog, but there's also a nice children's castle–like gym plus flower beds in what is called the Emerald Garden. The park is located at 2021 N. Burling St.; (312) 742-7898.

Gigi's Dolls and Sherry's Teddy Bears is a perfect stop if you're hoping to acquire antique, modern, or artist's dolls or bears. They also carry miniatures, clothing, and accessories for all your favorites, plus there's a Doll Hospital on site. Because these are collectables, remember the "look, don't touch" rule. The shop is open Tues, Wed, and Sat from 10 a.m. to 5 p.m. and Thurs and Fri from 10 a.m. to 5 p.m. 6029 N. Northwest Hwy.; (773) 594-1540; www.gigisdolls.com.

If you're into history, perhaps the *Abraham Lincoln Book Shop* will have items of interest. This is said to be the largest Lincoln bookstore outside of Springfield. Whether or not that holds true, it is a remarkable place that's been in business since 1938 and carries first edition and rare books, Lincoln autographs, and Civil War collectibles and memorabilia. The shop is open Mon through Wed and on Fri from 9 a.m. to 5 p.m., Thurs from 9 a.m. to 7 p.m., and Sat from 10 a.m. to 4 p.m. 357 W. Chicago Ave.; (312) 944-3085; www .alincolnbookshop.com.

And now, to finish this section with an explanation of the book's front cover. You might be wondering why Italy's Tower of Pisa is featured on the jacket of a book about Illinois. Blame it on water. Since 1934 the city of *Niles* has been home to *America's Leaning Tower,* which is a cleverly shrouded water tower dedicated to Italian physicist and "Father of Astronomy" Galileo Galilei. The building is about half the size of the original and stands in front

SELECTED VISITORS BUREAUS AND CHAMBERS OF COMMERCE

Chicago Convention and Tourism Bureau
2301 S. Lake Shore Dr., 60616
(312) 567-8500

Mayor's Office of Special Events Hotline
(312) 744-3370

Chicago Fine Arts Hotline
(312) 346-3278

Illinois Bureau of Tourism— Travel Information
(800) 2-CONNECT

Illinois Tourism
www.enjoyillinois.com

The Mayor's Office Official Tourism Site
www.explorechicago.org

Chicago Park District Events Site
www.chicagoparkdistrict.com
(312) 742-PLAY

of the YMCA. It's surrounded by a fountain and green space, making it the perfect place for a photograph that will confuse your friends when you show them what you did on your Illinois vacation. The tower is located at 6300 Touhy Ave., Niles.

Places to Stay in Chicago

The Avenue Hotel Chicago
160 E. Huron St.
(877) 283-5110
www.avenuehotel
chicago.com

Chicago Marriott Downtown
540 N. Michigan Ave.
(312) 836-0100
www.marriott.com

Conrad Chicago Hotel
521 N. Rush St. at
Michigan Avenue
(312) 645-1500
http://conradhotels1
.hilton.com

Doubletree Hotel Chicago Magnificent Mile
300 E. Ohio St.
(312) 787-6100
http://doubletree1
.hilton.com

The Drake Chicago
140 E. Walton Place
(312) 787-2200
www.thedrakehotel.com

The Fairmont Hotel
200 N. Columbus Dr.
(312) 565-8000
www.fairmont.com/chicago

Four Seasons Hotel
120 E. Delaware Place
(312) 280-8800
www.fourseasons.com/
chicagofs

Hilton Chicago
720 S. Michigan Ave.
(312) 922-4400
www1.hilton.com

Hotel InterContinental Chicago
505 N. Michigan Ave.
(312) 944-4100
www.icchicagohotel.com

Hyatt Regency Chicago
151 E. Wacker Dr.
(312) 565-1234
www.chicagoregency.hyatt
.com

The Inn Lincoln Park
601 W. Diversey Parkway
(866) 774-7275
www.innlp.com

Marriott Chicago Downtown Medical District/UIC
625 S. Ashland Ave.
(312) 491-1234
www.marriott.com

Palmer House Hilton
17 E. Monroe St.
(312) 726-7500
www.palmerhousehilton
hotel.com

Ritz-Carlton Chicago
160 E. Pearson St.
(312) 266-1000
www.fourseasons.com/
chicagorc

Sutton Place Hotel
21 E. Bellevue Place
(312) 266-2100
www.suttonplace.com

Swissôtel
323 E. Wacker Dr.
(312) 565-0565
www.swissotel.com

The Tremont
100 E. Chestnut St.
(312) 751-1900
www.tremontchicago.com

The Westin Hotel
320 N. Dearborn St.
(312) 744-1900
www.westinchicago.com

Places to Eat in Chicago

Ann Sather
909 W. Belmont Ave.
(773) 348-2378
www.annsather.com

Berghoff's
17 W. Adams St.
(312) 427-3170
www.berghoff.com

Charlie Trotter's
816 W. Armitage Ave.
(773) 248-6228
www.charlietrotters.com

Chicago Diner
3411 N. Halsted St.
(773) 935-6696
www.veggiediner.com

Ed Debevic's
640 N. Wells St.
(312) 664-1707
www.eddebevics.com

**Frankie's Fifth Floor
Pizzeria**
900 N. Michigan Ave.
(312) 266-2500
www.leye.com

Frontera Grill
445 N. Clark St.
(312) 661-1434
www.fronterakitchens.com

Gino's East
633 N. Wells St.
(312) 988-4200
www.ginoseast.com

Green Door Tavern
678 N. Orleans St.
(312) 664-5496
www.greendoorchicago
.com

**Healthy Food
Lithuanian Restaurant**
3236 S. Halsted St.
(312) 326-2724
www.healthyfood
lithuanian-chicago.com

**Harry Caray's Italian
Steakhouse**
33 W. Kinzie St.
(312) 828-0966
www.harrycarays.com

Hub 51
51 W. Hubbard St.
(312) 828-0051
www.hub51chicago.com

Lou Mitchell's
565 W. Jackson Blvd.
(312) 939-3111
www.loumitchells
restaurant.com

Pump Room
1301 N. State Parkway
(312) 266-0360
www.pumproom.com

Reza's
5255 N. Clark St.
(773) 561-1898
www.rezasrestaurant.com

Wishbone
1001 W. Washington Blvd.
(312) 850-2663
www.wishbonechicago
.com

NORTHEASTERN ILLINOIS

West Suburban Collar Counties

As far out as you can be and still be considered a Chicago suburb—that's how the collar counties see themselves—well, if as much as 40 miles away can be considered close proximity! With an easy train ride, and in many cases a reasonable car commute into Chicago, these suburbs have thrived as bedroom communities for the movers and shakers, and the regular worker bees that keep the big city running. Despite the economy's expansion and contraction over the years, *DuPage County* has maintained a rapid population growth. The explosion of research and technology is partly behind this surge.

It was a far different place when miller Frederick Graue arrived in America from Germany and purchased land in what is now *Oak Brook*. Using clay from his farm for the fired bricks and local timbers, along with four one-ton grinding burrstones imported all the way from France, he completed construction of his new mill in 1852. *Graue Mill and Museum* is the only Illinois structure to receive the American Society of Mechanical Engineers award as an Illinois Historic Mechanical Engineering Landmark. Be sure to stop by the museum store to purchase

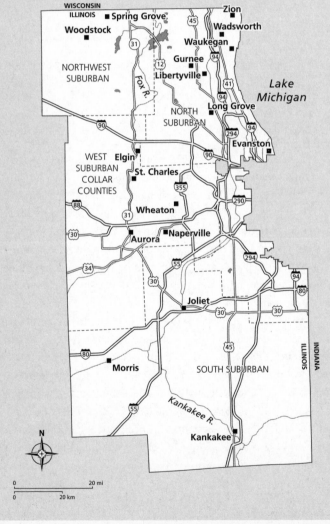

WISCONSIN
ILLINOIS
■ Spring Grove
Zion ■
Wadsworth ■
■ Woodstock
45
Waukegan ■
31
Gurnee ■
94
NORTHWEST
SUBURBAN
12
Libertyville ■
41
Fox R.
94
Lake
Michigan
NORTH
SUBURBAN
Long Grove ■
90
294
94
Evanston ■
WEST
SUBURBAN
COLLAR
COUNTIES
Elgin ■
90
St. Charles ■
355
290
88
Wheaton ■
31
30
Aurora ■ ■ Naperville
34
55
294
30
94
Joliet ■
30
30
80
80
Morris ■
ILLINOIS
INDIANA
SOUTH SUBURBAN
45
55
Kankakee R.
N
Kankakee ■

0   20 mi
0   20 km

some fresh-ground cornmeal, and ask for their free recipes for cornmeal muffins and griddle cakes. The museum is open mid-Apr to mid-Nov, Tues through Sun from 10 a.m. to 4:30 p.m.; closed on Mon; admission is $3.50 for adults, $3.00 for seniors, and $1.50 for children ages four through twelve. For more information call (630) 655-2090 or visit www .grauemill.org.

museumcountry

There are thirty-four museums thriving in DuPage County. The DuPage County Historical Museum is housed in the former 1891 Adams Memorial Library, which was a gift to the community from Wheaton resident John Quincy Adams, a cousin of the U.S. president who shared the name.

Possibly the biggest winner among the western suburbs is the town of **Naperville,** which is ranked forth in population in the state. In national business and lifestyle magazines, Naperville has garnered more mentions than any other Illinois town as the best place to live and raise a family.

On the north side you're sure to notice the life-size angel statues standing guard throughout the front lawn of a big pink house near the corner of Washington Street and Ogden Avenue. This is home to **Angelic Creations Doll and China Restoration;** parking is located in the alley behind the store. Inside you'll find popular and porcelain collectible dolls and accessories, and the angels in front are for sale, too. The store is located at 816 N. Washington St.; (630) 369-2522; angelicascreations.tripod.com.

Charm abounds along the brick trails of the **Naperville Riverwalk,** which was built to commemorate the city's 1981 Sesquicentennial Celebration. The path skirts the meandering banks of the **DuPage River** and passes through downtown past restaurants, parks, gazebos, covered bridges, an amphitheater, eatery, picnic pavilions, and sculptures. Take note of the **9/11 Memorial Wall** exhibit along the south side of City Hall; it features a piece of a beam from the Twin Towers site in New York City. Stop for a concert at the **Moser Tower and Millennium Carillon,** view the artwork along the **Century Walk,** or get your legs into shape peddling a boat on **Paddleboat Quarry.** There's even a public swimming quarry called **Centennial Beach.** For more information call the Naperville Park District at (630) 848-5000 or visit www.napervilleparks.org. To find the Riverwalk on your GPS use 188 W. Jackson Ave. as the starting point.

There's prime shopping along Chicago and Jackson Avenues and Jefferson Street, and unusual restaurants and small shops, too. And if you're feeling tired, take a break with a ride on the **Historic Trolley Tours of Naperville,** which starts and ends at the Trolley Stop on West Jackson Avenue at Eagle Street. Chances are that Annette, the "Trolley Chick," will be your driver. Reservations

AUTHOR'S TOP TEN PICKS

Goose Lake Prairie State Natural Area
Morris
(815) 942-2899
http://dnr.state.il.us

Six Flags Great America
Gurnee
(847) 249-4636
www.sixflags.com

Garfield Farm Museum
La Fox
(630) 584-8485
www.garfieldfarm.org

Morton Arboretum
Lisle
(630) 968-0074
www.mortonarb.org

St. Charles
(630) 377-6161
(800) 777-4373
www.visitstcharles.com

Kane County Flea Market
St. Charles
(630) 377-2252
www.kanecountyfleamarket.com

Fermi National Accelerator Laboratory
Batavia
(630) 840-3000
www.fnal.gov

Midewin National Tallgrass Prairie
Wilmington
(815) 423-6370
www.fs.fed.us/mntp

Naper Settlement
Naperville
(630) 420-6010
www.napersettlement.org

Waukegan Charter Boat Association
Waukegan
(847) 244-3474
www.wcba.info

are recommended; the fare is $8 for adults, $5 for children ages four through seventeen, and 1 cent for children three and under; (630) 420-2223; www.napervilletrolley.com

History comes alive within the **Naper Settlement,** where visitors can explore early Illinois life on the prairie as demonstrated within the walls of seventeen historic buildings on a thirteen-acre site. Costumed interpreters provide tours in this re-created nineteenth-century village, which features a working blacksmith shop, printing press, one-room school, and one-room log cabin. Stop at the gothic **Century Memorial Chapel** and the 1883 **Martin-Mitchell Mansion,** which has been restored down to the smallest detail, even to the accuracy of the wallpaper. The Naper Settlement is open Apr through Oct, Tues through Sat from 10 a.m. to 4 p.m. and Sun from 1 to 4 p.m.; admission is $8.00 for adults, $7.00 for seniors, and $5.50 for children. 523 S. Webster St.; (630) 420-6010; www.napersettlement.org.

Naperville hosts two award–winning festivals. At **Ribfest,** thousands treat their taste buds to four days of world-class barbecue from twenty competitive professional barbecue masters. There are concerts by nationally known performers, a carnival, and fireworks. Ribfest is held for five days over the Fourth of July holiday from noon to 10 p.m.; admission is $10 for adults and free for children age eleven and under; parking is limited so take the free shuttle (watch for signs). The festival is located at Knoch Park, at West Street and Hillside Avenue; (630) 848-5000; www.ribfest.net.

And as summer fades, the town turns out for the **Last Fling** celebration featuring a two-hour parade, a street full of carnival rides, and concerts in two locations. The celebration is held over Labor Day weekend; concert fees range from $10 to $12; (630) 961-4143; www.lastfling.org.

While in the south suburbs, drive down to Bolingbrook and have a meal at **Francesca's at the Promenade,** a restaurant that specializes in handmade northern Italian food. Even the menu is handwritten and changes every two weeks. Francesca's is located at 641 E. Boughton Rd.; (630) 739-6300; http://miafrancesca.com.

After your meal, visit the **Illinois Aviation Museum at Bolingbrook,** located at Hangar One on the grounds of the **Clow International Airport.** The 6,000-square-foot building houses replicas as well as restored and "in the process of being restored" planes, plus educational displays. The museum is open Sat from 10 a.m. to 2 p.m. or by appointment. 130 S. Clow International Parkway; (630) 771-1037; www.illinoisaviationmuseum.org.

The museum group sponsors an annual **FlightFest** that is a combination Oktoberfest and tribute to aviation. The event features free airplane rides for youngsters, the dramatic arrival of classic War Bird planes, great food, and a craft and car show. Visitors are invited to arrive by plane, car, or foot. The event is held the first Sat in Oct; admission is $5 for adults and $2 for children under age twelve. (630) 378-0479; www.bbclowairport.com.

If you're into chicken, try the family-style helpings at **White Fence Farm** in **Romeoville.** Owned and managed by the Robert Hastert family since 1954, the original restaurant was established in the 1920s. Twelve rustic dining rooms serve as the backdrop for serious down-home cooking, but the lines of hungry guests can be almost oppressive. To help you get through the wait, you can browse the eclectic collection of antique cars, hood ornaments, dolls, clocks, and more. In fact, you're liable to become so engrossed that you may forget why you came in the first place, until the hostess calls your name over the loudspeaker and directs you to your table. In the interest of your waistline, you should know that the chicken is fried, and if you want seconds it'd probably be the amazing corn fritters, but there are healthy selections available, too. No doubt, no matter what you choose, you won't leave this place hungry. The restaurant is located at 1376 Joliet Rd.; (630) 739-1720; http://whitefencefarm-il.com.

Next take the Stevenson Expressway (I-55) east and exit south at Lemont Road on your way to the *Hindu Temple of Greater Chicago.* The entrance arch welcomes you onto the grounds of this astonishing and beautiful white multibuilding complex, which blends ancient and modern architecture and overlooks the Des Planes River valley. Ninety-minute tours are available for a minimum of three people via appointment beginning at 10:30 a.m.; admission is free. 10915 Lemont Rd.; (630) 972-0300; www.ramatemple.org.

Driving into downtown *Lemont* you'll cross the Des Plaines River and discover the quaint river town's shops and cafes next to the canal off Front Street. Note the hand-painted murals that dress the sides of the old brick buildings. This town features many interesting types of architecture. The *Old Stone Church* is one such beauty that is listed on the National Register of Historic Places and currently houses the *Lemont Area Historical Society.* Visitors can peruse memorabilia, war artifacts, and exhibits of an old general store, one-room school, and stable. The Old Stone Church is open Tues, Thurs, and Fri from 10 a.m. to 2 p.m., Sat from 10 a.m. to 1 p.m., and Sun from 1 to 4 p.m. Admission is $1 for adults and 50 cents for children ages five through twelve. 306 Lemont St.; (630) 257-2972; www.township.com/lemont/historical/index.htm.

During the summer, the chamber of commerce hosts the *Lemont Legends Cruise Nights,* in which classic cars are displayed to the tunes of favorite oldies; there's entertainment, food, and a friendly atmosphere. Cruise Nights are held from June to Aug, Wed from 6 to 9 p.m.; 101 Main St.; www.lemontchamber.com/cruise_nights.php.

Then get back on I-55 and head to the Cass Avenue South exit, where you'll find the *Argonne National Laboratory,* a 1,500-acre facility, run by the U.S. Department of Energy, where more than 3,500 scientists conduct research vital to the nation's environment and security. Individuals over the age of sixteen are welcome to tour the grounds and laboratory, which includes the world's most requested research venue, the Advanced Photon Source. Tours run twice a day on Sat only, from 9 to 11:30 a.m. and 1 to 3:30 p.m.; call (630) 252-5562 for reservations.

At the *Argonne Information Center,* the younger set (under age sixteen) can view displays suitable for their age group, and no reservations are required. The laboratory is located at 9700 S. Cass Ave.; (630) 252-2000; www.anl.gov.

Back on the road, head north on Cass Avenue and then take North Frontage Road into *Darien,* where you'll find a fifty-acre estate that's the home of the *National Shrine of St. Therese.* Inside the St. Therese Chapel you'll be treated to the most exquisite carving, which graces an entire wall and is

Nuclear Deer

Legend has it that Argonne's Lemont site was purchased from several local residents, including industrialist Erwin Freund, the inventor of "skinless" casing for hot dogs and owner of a nationally revered boxer dog kennel. A herd of rare white fallow deer, which Freund had acquired from Chicago clothier Maurice L. Rothschild, roamed his 200-acre property. When it came time to close on the deal, Freund attempted to relocate the deer to game parks, but the nocturnal animals were not cooperative and several escaped the roundup. Argonne inherited the renegades, and today the herd numbers about one hundred and fifty.

The deer are petite and their fur is stark white, causing locals to joke that the critters must have suffered accidental exposure to nuclear experiments conducted at the lab; hence the nickname "nuclear deer." If you're driving anywhere in the area, not just on laboratory property, you might see the small deer scavenging a meal near the roadway, so use caution.

thought to be the largest wood fresco in the world. An antique rose case contains sacred relics, and Carmelites maintain the extensive collection of St. Therese's personal items, including toys and drawings from her childhood. Pilgrimages are available at varying prices, which include hours of study, mass, a meal, and private prayer time. The chapel is open at no cost to visitors every day from 10 a.m. to 4 p.m.; 8501 Bailey Rd.; (630) 969-3311; www .saint-therese.org.

Next, take 75th Street west to the *Chestnut Court Shopping Center,* where you'll find a cake maker's nirvana at the *Wilton School.* Here serious students of everything fondant and buttercream can prefect their skills at classes taught by skilled cake decorator artisans. If you just want to pick up an unusual cake pan or decorating accessories, stop in at the *Wilton Store* next door. The school is located at 7511 Lemont Rd. at West 75th Street; (800) 772-7111, ext. 2888; www.wilton.com/classes/wiltonschool.

Across the street at the *Grove Plaza* is the largest hobby store in Chicagoland. It's *Oakridge Hobbies and Toys,* and be forewarned, if you don't have a hobby before you arrive, you're going to have one by the time you leave! Everything is here, from dollhouse kits and HO slot-racing cars to Lionel trains and traditional craft kits to make puppets and paper dolls. The shop is open Mon through Fri from 10 a.m. to 8 p.m., Sat from 10 a.m. to 6 p.m., and Sun from noon to 5 p.m. 1510F W. 75th St.; (630) 435-5900; www.oakridgehob biesandtoys.com.

Following north on Lemont Road, you will enter the village of *Downers Grove,* and if you like an old-fashioned downtown, this is the place for you.

Hidden behind the quaint storefronts are high-quality shops and restaurants that will keep you coming back. For more information visit www.visitdowners grove.com.

To experience how midwestern Victorians lived, visit the Park District's **Downers Grove Museum,** where more than 10,000 items are on display inside the 1892 **Blodgett House,** a renovated eleven-room mansion that was once the home of one of the village's early founders. Knowledgeable docents will answer your questions. Tours run Sun through Fri from 1 to 3 p.m.; admission is free; 831 Maple Ave.; (630) 963-1309; www.dgparks.org.

If you're into architecture, take the **Sears Catalog Home Tour,** a self-guided walking or driving jaunt that highlights twenty of the two hundred Downers Grove properties that were once sold as kits from the pages of the *Sears Catalog* and assembled by homeowners on site. Most kits contained about 30,000 pieces, but some models could be built in a weekend. This collection is one of the largest documented pockets of original *Sears Catalog* homes in the state. For maps or information call (630) 729-0380.

atthemovies

The 1928 *Tivoli Theatre* in Downers Grove is a vintage restored movie house that was the second theater in the nation converted to show "talkies" back in the day. The theater is located at 5021 Highland Ave.; (630) 968-0219.

There are two major events hosted by Downers Grove, one in the summer and one in the winter. For more than twenty years during the second week of August, the **National Championships of Cycling** and the **USA Cycling Professional Criterium Championship** have overtaken the village's scenic streets in a strikingly American version of the Tour de France. Internationally known professionals fight for the prestigious Stars and Stripes jersey, while nonprofessionals and even kids on big wheels have the opportunity to race in fifteen events over the two days, which includes a festival atmosphere and $40,000 in prize winnings. Call the special event line for updates at (773) 868-3010. To garner a hint of the best places to stand along the route, view the official Web site, www.dgcycling.com

Then, don your parka and mittens for the **Ice Sculpture Festival.** When the weather cooperates, more than fifty ice carvings line several downtown streets and the Main Street train station. If you're too cold to walk, view the spectacle from the free trolley, and treat yourself to a hot chocolate from local vendors. The festival is held in early Feb on Sat from 9 a.m. to 4 p.m. and Sun from 9 a.m. to 3 p.m.; (630) 434-5555.

The crown jewel of nearby **Lisle** is the 1,700-acre **Morton Arboretum.** Start your tour at the visitor center, where you can ask questions, collect informative brochures, and arrange a ride on the **Acorn Express,** an open-air tram that traverses the grounds. Or stay in your car and drive the paved road to view the lush trees, shrubs, and plants that thrive in this meticulously maintained haven. The **Children's Gar-den** is a place where the youngsters can climb, splash, and slide amid manicured landscaping. Active people might enjoy the 16 miles of trails suitable for walking, biking, and skiing. Then relax and have a fine meal by the two-story glass windows overlooking the grounds from the dining room of the **Ginko Restau-rant,** or try the **Ginko Café** for lighter fare. The arboretum is open daily in the summer from 8 a.m. to dusk, and in the fall daily from 9 a.m. to dusk; admission is $11 for adults, $10 for seniors, and $8 for children ages two through twelve; special discounts are offered on Wed. 4100 Illinois Rte. 53; (630) 968-0074; www.mortonarb.org.

kithousingboom

When Sears unveiled its first catalog exclusively for the sale of kit homes in 1908, there were twenty-two styles ranging from $650 to $2,500. By the last catalog issued in 1940, there were 450 ready-made designs available.

One of the state's most heralded festivals is sponsored by Lisle's active community clubs and supported by more than three hundred volunteers. The award-winning annual **Eyes to the Sky Festival** combines Fourth of July festivities with the dramatic liftoff of more than three dozen hot-air balloons, weather permitting, of course. The event starts early in the morning, but it's well worth braving the dawn to see these majestic and sometimes comical character balloons lift into the soft morning breezes. When possible, a second launch takes place in the early evening, and glowing tethered balloons cap off the night. Plus, there's a carnival, live music, a hundred-booth craft fair, an old-fashioned hometown parade, and fireworks. The first balloon launch of the day runs from 5:30 a.m. to 6:30 a.m., and carnival hours are 11 a.m. to 11 p.m.; admission is $10 for adults, $3 for children age six and up, and free for children age five and under; parking costs $5 per car. Consider taking a free shuttle from satellite locations around town. The festival takes place at Lisle Community Park, 1825 Short St.; (630) 541-6095; www.eyestothesky.org.

Heading next to **Glen Ellyn,** you'll discover a safe haven for injured, orphaned, or rehabilitating native Illinois wildlife at the **Willowbrook Wildlife Center.** Founded in 1952, the center encourages visitors to take a self-guided nature tour of the grounds, butterfly garden, and exhibits of animals, such as eagles, foxes, opossums, and threatened sandhill cranes that are unable to return to their natural habitat due to permanent injuries. The center is open daily from 9 a.m. to 5 p.m.; the trail closes at 4 p.m. in winter; admission is free. 525 S. Park Blvd.; (630) 942-6200.

If you're into purple flowers, plan to spend time in **Lombard** during the famous **Lilac Festival.** It's a fragrant affair, with a nice scent pouring from the 1,200 lilac bushes spread over eight and a half acres of **Lilacia Park;** plus there are about 25,000 tulips thrown in for extra color! Droves show up for the parade, food, and music. Check the "Bloom-O-Meter" on the park Web site, which is updated daily so you will know when the lilacs are at peak. The festival is held the first two weeks of May; admission is free. 150 S. Park Ave.; (630) 620-7322; www.lombardparks.com/lilactime/lilactime.html.

If you're into stones, check out the **Lizzadro Museum of Lapidary Art** in **Elmhurst.** Opened in 1962, it was the vision of Joseph F. Lizzadro Sr., who turned his humble hobby of cutting and polishing stones into an extravagant collection of some of the world's most precious carved art specimens of jade, ivory, and amber, to name a few. The building sits in Elmhurst's popular **Wilder Park** and was cleverly designed to resemble a woman's jewelry box. The museum is open Tues through Sat from 10 a.m. to 5 p.m. and Sun from 1 p.m. to 5 p.m.; closed on Mon; admission is $4 for adults, $3 for seniors, $1 for children ages seven through twelve, and free for children under seven; Friday is "free day." 220 S. Cottage Hill Ave.; (630) 833-1616; www.lizzadromuseum.org.

Wheaton is the DuPage county seat and a place of independent spirit. Prohibition ended nationally in 1933 but not until 1992 in Wheaton. If you love politics, there's nothing like **Wheaton's Fourth of July Parade,** long a magnet for national and state politicians of all parties, who bravely stump for votes to a chorus of loud boos or quick applause; the people of Wheaton will let you know where they stand.

For generations, a core member of the community has been **Wheaton College.** Founded in 1853, it might be best known for its most famous gradu-ate, the Reverend Billy Graham. In association with the college, the **Billy Graham Center** provides a history of Christian evangelism, clarifies the story of the Gospels, and highlights of the life Billy Graham. The center is open Mon through Sat from 9:30 a.m. to 5:30 p.m. and Sun from 1 to 5 p.m.; closed major holidays; admission is free. 500 College Ave.; (630) 752-5909; www.billy grahamcenter.com.

Wheaton honors its native sons and daughters at the **DuPage Heritage Gallery.** Here, displays and films tell their stories, describing how they con-tributed to the state and nation. The list includes football icon Red Grange, America's King of Salt Joy Morton, and author of *Anna and the King of Siam* Margaret M. Landon. The gallery is open Mon through Fri from 8 a.m. to 5 p.m.

Neighborhood Battle

Wheaton is the county seat of DuPage County, but that wasn't always so. Originally, Naperville owned the title, but a vote in 1867 overturned the decision to allow the county courthouse to remain there and designated Wheaton as the new county seat.

After Wheaton's rush to build a courthouse, the next hurdle was acquiring the court records, as Naperville officials refused to forfeit them. Animosity grew between the communities until finally, in a dramatic midnight raid by Wheaton operatives, the paperwork was lifted from the locked Naperville courthouse.

The hostile act spurred a lawsuit between the two towns. As the trial loomed, Naperville removed the remaining documents to Cook County for safekeeping. It was an unfortunate move because the paperwork burned along with most of Chicago in the 1871 Great Chicago Fire. Hence, in the heat of battle, it became definitive that Wheaton was final victor.

and Sat from 8 a.m. to noon; admission is free. The gallery is located in the atrium of the DuPage County Center at 421 N. County Farm Rd.

The **DuPage County Fair** features traditional farm and home-arts exhibits and concerts by big-name artists, and all of the events are eclipsed by the perennial favorite, the Demolition Derby. The fair is held the third week of July; admission is $6 for adults, $3 for seniors, and $1 for children ages three through eight. 2015 W. Manchester Rd.; (630) 668-6636; www.dupagecounty fair.org.

Also in Wheaton is **Cantigny,** the former estate of the late Colonel Robert R. McCormick, celebrated publisher of the *Chicago Tribune.* Tours of the restored mansion, known as the **McCormick Museum,** are free, but group sizes are limited so make your reservation as soon as you arrive. More than twenty of the thirty-five rooms are open for viewing. European and Chinese art, artifacts, and antiques are displayed beside the McCormick family's furniture and memorabilia. Colonel McCormick's private office features exotic wood paneling and a wet bar that can be raised from the floor behind a secret door, a requirement for entertaining during Prohibition. It's a real treat to stand on the veranda and view the unimpaired, impeccably manicured garden vista—and the rose garden is stunning during the summer months. The mansion is open Feb through Apr, Fri through Sun from 9 a.m. to sunset; May through Oct, Fri through Sun from 7 a.m. to sunset; and Nov through Dec, Fri through Sun from 9 a.m. to sunset; closed in Jan. Parking is $8, but admission to the grounds and house are free. 1 S. 151 Winfield Rd.; (630) 668-5161; www.cantigny.org.

The grounds are also home to the ***First Division Museum at Cantigny,*** Colonel McCormick's recognition of the military, particularly the "Big Red One," the First Infantry Division of the U.S. Army, in which he served during World War I. The 38,000-square-foot homage features life-size dioramas and interactive experiences such as the illusion of riding a transport onto the shores of France during the heat of battle. The opening hours and days mirror those of the mansion tour, but if you arrive early, take a stroll through the gardens, watch the fountains, and visit the white-marble tomb of the colonel and his beloved wife, Amy, and the grave of their German shepherd. A $5 parking fee is charged at the entrance gate, and admission to the museum is free. 1 South 151 Winfield Rd.; (630) 668-5161; www.firstdivisionmuseum.org.

The ***DuPage County Historical Museum*** acts as a repository for artifacts relating to the county's history. The museum building itself is a striking 1891 Romanesque limestone structure. Besides Victorian vignettes and various interactive galleries, there's an unexpected draw: model trains that fascinate and entertain audiences on the third and fifth Sat of each month from 1:30 to 3:30 p.m. The museum is open Mon through Fri from 9 a.m. to 4 p.m. and Sat from 10 a.m. to 4 p.m.; closed on Sun. 102 E. Wesley St.; (630) 682-7343; www.dupagehistory.org.

Some of the state's most picturesque suburban countryside can be found along the eastern side of ***Kane County,*** where the ***Fox River*** serves as a focal point for the towns and villages that abut it. Can you picture 600 Corvettes circling through these lush back roads? That's part of the entertainment during the ***Bloomington Gold Corvette Show.*** Home base for the show is the ***Pheasant Run Resort*** in St. Charles, where potential buyers and sellers gather to enjoy the classic American sports car. Cars are judged, accessories are sold, and the highlight is a memorable caravan spin in the country. The show is held the

Riverbank

Colonel George Fabyan and his wife, Nelle, named their Fabyan Forest Preserve homestead Riverbank due to its proximity to the Fox River. The colonel's wealth came from textiles, and when he retired here, his full interest turned to decoding. In fact, he assembled a group of ciphering scholars to assist him in cracking the codes used in the secret correspondence of U.S. enemies during both World Wars.

The Fabyans hired Frank Lloyd Wright to expand and modify their Riverbank home and added an eclectic assortment to the property including a zoo, an extensive artwork collection, Japanese relics, and even an Egyptian mummy that may or may not be a fake.

third week of June; admission is based on activities chosen. The Pheasant Run Resort is located at 4051 E. Main St., St. Charles. Contact the resort at (630) 584-6300 or by visiting www.pheasantrun.com. Or, contact Bloomington Gold Corvette at (309) 888-4477; www.bloomingtongold.com.

Further south is *Aurora,* the state's second-largest city with a population over 170,000. The Fox River runs through Aurora, making it a natural transportation hub for moving goods, a fact that was not lost on early settlers. Today Aurora is a blend of old and new with some of the best local shopping, entertainment, and educational activities around.

Start your tour at the *Aurora Regional Fire Museum,* which is located in the 1894 Old Central Fire Station. The building is completely renovated in true Victorian splendor; note the three grand bay windows along the second floor, and above that an onion-shaped dome. Visitors are treated to hands-on displays and ten vehicles dating from the 1850s to 1965. The museum is open Thurs, Fri and Sat from 1 to 4 p.m.; admission is $5 for adults and $3 for children. 53 N. Broadway St. (the corner of SR 25 and New York Street), with free parking behind the building (entering off LaSalle Street); (630) 892-1572; www.auroraregionalfiremuseum.org.

The *Paramount Theatre* is hard to miss with its 70-foot, flashing-light marquee. This 1931 grand dame of Art Deco decor has been an entertainment center and vaudeville palace. Designed by theater architects Rapp and Rapp,

brightidea

In 1908, Aurora's city fathers legally adopted the name "The City of Lights" to commemorate the fact that it was one of the first cities in the U.S. to adopt an electric lighting system for downtown streets back in 1881.

the theater features a classic split-foyer staircase, brilliant tapestries, and velvet draperies adorning the walls and stage. The ceiling sports a cobalt- and pastel-blue sunburst with *lots* of gold detailing, and a twinkling chandelier illuminates the seating below. The theater is located at 23 E. Galena Blvd.; for a show schedule and to purchase tickets, call (630) 896-6666; www.paramountarts.com.

For the mad scientist, amble over to the *SciTech Hands On Museum,* where over 200 science-related activities are ready to be twisted, turned, bent, tugged, and marveled over. There's also an outside science park for more lively fun, as long as the weather permits. The museum is open Wed through Fri from 10 a.m. to 3 p.m. and Sat from 10 a.m. to 5 p.m.; closed Sun through Tues; tickets are $8 for general admission, $7 for seniors, and free for children under age three; 18 W. Benton St.; (630) 859-3434; http://scitech.mus.il.us.

And now to a place that's decidedly for adults: *America's Historic Roundhouse Complex.* Constructed in 1856 by the Chicago Burlington and

Quincy Railroad as a locomotive repair and storage garage, this limestone roundhouse was the first built in America and is the oldest such structure remaining in the U.S. This place is 70,000 square feet of giant rooms; besides the America's Brewpub Restaurant, there are fourteen bars, a comedy club, piano bar, microbrewery, and outdoor courtyard. Dining hours are Mon through Thurs from 11 a.m. to 10 p.m., Fri and Sat from 11 a.m. to 11 p.m., and Sun from 9 a.m. to 9 p.m.; for reservations call (630) 892-0034; www.walter paytonsroundhouse.com.

North of Aurora on the outskirts Batavia is the ***Fermi National Accelerator Laboratory (Fermilab),*** the U.S. Department of Energy's laboratory for physics research and home to the world's most powerful particle accelerator, the ***Tevatron.*** Visitors must stop their vehicle at an entrance checkpoint, provide identification, and use the map provided to navigate the grounds. Note, heed the posted signs! This isn't a place to wander off, as security guards monitor the whereabouts of all cars.

Before you reach the official buildings, you'll pass through the ***Fermilab Natural Areas,*** consisting of restored prairie, marshlands, and wetlands that are home to birds, deer, butterflies, and a myriad of frogs, fish, and creepy crawlers. The lab is proud of its conservation, a legacy that began as early as 1969 when the lab's director made provisions to house a herd of wild American bison. Now numbering between forty and sixty, the bison still roam the grounds behind a securely fenced pasture. It's especially fun to watch them in spring when the new calves are testing their muscle among the big boys. The Fermilab grounds are open daily, mid-Oct to mid-Apr from 8 a.m. to 6 p.m. and the rest of the year from 8 a.m. to 8 p.m. ***Wilson Hall*** and the ***Lederman Science Center*** are open for self-guided tours. Hours are Mon through Fri from 8:30 a.m. to 4:30 p.m. and Sat from 9 a.m. to 3 p.m.; (630) 840-3000; www.fnal.gov.

Tucked in the woods, away from the traffic and buzz of SR 31, there's a unique place called ***Mooseheart Child City and School.*** The philanthropic arm of the Loyal Order of Moose opened the residential facility and school in 1913, and since then more than 11,000 youngsters have crossed the threshold into the caring arms of teachers and staff whose life mission is to make the road a little smoother for children in need. Tours are given Mon through Fri from 9 a.m. to 4 p.m. and Sat and Sun from noon to 4 p.m., but it's best to call ahead; admission is free; 155 S. International Dr., Batavia; (630) 906-3601; www.mooseheart.org.

Batavia is the oldest city in ***Kane County.*** During the 1850s, the once-small hamlet emerged as the world's windmill manufacturing leader, earning it the nickname "The Windmill City." Visitors to the ***Batavia Riverwalk Park***

can view seven faithfully restored examples of Batavia's windmills as produced from 1880–1942; enter the Riverwalk off the Huston Street plaza; and stroll along the **Depot Pond,** past the **Batavia Dam** and the **Riverwalk Flower Sanctuary.**

Down River Street, you're bound to notice the tall chimney with the word CHALLENGE running along the stack. The building was the former home of the **Challenge Windmill Factory** and now houses several shops. The factory is located at 515 N. River St. The city celebrates its heritage with a carnival, live music, plenty of arts and crafts booths, and lots of food during the **Windmill City Festival.** The event is held the second weekend of July; admission is free; located along downtown streets; (630) 879-5235; www.bataviaparks.org.

Batavia co-hosts another popular summer event called the **Fox River Mid-American Canoe and Kayak Race.** Amateur enthusiasts start the 6-mile water excursion at the Batavia VFW landing, or further north the 10-mile race begins at Mount Saint Mary Park in St. Charles; the finish line is in Aurora at McCullough Park. There are entry fees for participants, but watching the action is free, so pack a lunch and bring a chair. The event is held in early June, and the launches begin at 9 a.m. from St. Charles and at 10:30 a.m. from Batavia; the Batavia VFW is located at 645 S. River St.; the event hotline is (630) 859-8606; www.foxvalleyparkdistrict.org.

The **Depot Museum,** a formerly abandoned depot from the Chicago, Burlington and Quincy Railroad, is now the home of the **Batavia Historical Society.** The quaint terminal offers a permanent exhibit that gives a glimpse into one of Mary Todd Lincoln's most desperate times with a replica of her living space during her incarceration at **Batavia's Bellevue Place Sanitarium.** Both the dresser and the bed are the same that Mrs. Lincoln used during her stay. Mrs. Lincoln was eventually freed

littlehouseon theprairie

The former president of the Challenge Windmill Company, Frank Snow, was a client of Frank Lloyd Wright, who designed and built a classic Prairie-style home in Batavia for Snow in 1906. The private residence can be seen from the street at 637 N. Batavia Ave.

from the asylum and sent to live with her sister in Springfield, Illinois. The museum features an antique telegraph station, refurbished 1907 train caboose, life-size Native American sculpture, and charming Victorian-era gazebo. Take special note of the **Newton Wagon;** these wagons were used to transport "salesman sample" windmills. The museum is open Mar through Nov on Mon, Wed, Fri, Sat, and Sun from 2 to 4 p.m.; admission is free; 155 Houston St.; (630) 406-5274; www.bataviaparks.org/park27.htm.

While driving toward **Geneva,** keep your eyes open for the entrance to the **Fabyan East Forest Preserve.** Suddenly you might think you've made a wrong turn and ended up in Denmark because a classic five-story windmill stands majestically in the middle of the grassy park. The **Fabyan Windmill,** built between 1850 and 1860, is a national and state landmark, and in 1980 it graced a commemorative U.S. postage stamp. The structure was moved here in 1914 from its original site in Oak Brook by Colonel George Fabyan. Today it's fully operational, having been restored by a renowned Dutch craftsman to the tune of about one million dollars. It's said to be the most authentic Dutch windmill in the U.S. Tours run from May 15 to Oct 15 on Sat and Sun, from 1 to 4 p.m.; closed during winter; 1925 S. Batavia Ave.; (630) 232-5980.

crazyhouse

The former Batavia Bellevue Place Sanitarium where Mary Lincoln was incarcerated is now a condominium and rental development. If you'd like to drive by, the 1853 native limestone structure stands at 333 S. Jefferson St.

Within sight of the windmill on this lush, 600-acre estate is the **Fabyan West Forest Preserve** and the home and gardens of Colonel George Fabyan and his wife, Nelle. The **Japanese Gardens and Tea House** have been restored and attract amateur and professional photographers alike. The family home, the **Fabyan Villa Museum,** is open for tours May 15 to Oct 15 on Wed from 1 to 4 p.m. and Sat and Sun from 1 to 4:30 p.m.; admission is $2 for adults and $1 for children. (630) 377-6424; www.ppfv.org/fabyan.htm. The gardens are open only on Wed from 1 to 4 p.m. and Sun from 1 to 4:30 p.m., as the grounds are made available for weddings and other events requiring professional photographers; admission is $1; (630) 377-6424; www.ppfv.org/fabyan.htm.

As you continue north on SR 25, you'll notice obviously older stone houses along the way. These homes are typical of the early Scandinavian residents who lived a simple and practical lifestyle in the town of **Geneva.** The architecture here is so prized that more than two hundred buildings and residences have been recognized with landmark status by the National Register of Historic Places.

As the county seat of **Kane County,** Geneva's centerpiece is the **Kane County Courthouse,** built in 1892 and still in use today. Inside, the walls are richly decorated with mosaics and inlayed marble, and a series of antique wrought-iron railings accent each floor level, noticeable as the eye looks upward toward the classic ceiling dome. The courthouse is located at 100 S. Third St.; (630) 232-5950.

The **Geneva History Center** features exhibits, artifacts, and handiwork that tell the story of the people and events that shaped the county. The center is open Tues through Sat from 11 a.m. to 4 p.m., and from Apr through Dec on Sun also from noon to 4 p.m.; admission free; 113 S. Third St.; (630) 232-4951; www.genevahistorycenter.org.

Considering that the population barely grazes 20,000, this town is active, hosting numerous events throughout the year. As one of the longest-running events in the state (more than sixty years), Geneva's **Midsommar Festival Swedish Days** is also one of the most popular in the region. Originally organized to celebrate the town's heritage, the gala features Swedish arts and crafts, food, music, and customs common in the culture. Plan to linger at the demonstrations of quilting and hand-painted flowers called rosemaling, and don't forget to grab a *kanelbulle* (cinnamon roll), *vafflor* (waffle) or *ostkaka* (cheesecake) for the ride home. The festival runs six days at the end of June; admission is free; (630) 232-6060; www.genevachamber.com/swedishdays.html.

Repeatedly voted the "Best Craft or Art Show" in the suburbs and the state, the **Geneva Arts Fair** is a juried outdoor event that features more than 140 artists and craftspeople from around the nation showing their wares along

TOP ANNUAL EVENTS

YEAR-ROUND

Kane County Flea Market
St. Charles
first weekend of every month
(630) 377-2252

MAY

Lilac Festival
Lombard
(630) 620-5700

JUNE

Swedish Days Midsommar Festival
Geneva
(630) 232-6060

JULY

Alpine Fest
Lake Zurich
(847) 438-5572

DuPage County Fair
Wheaton
(630) 668-6636

AUGUST

Momence Gladiolus Festival
Momence
(815) 472-6353

OCTOBER

Apple Festival
Long Grove
(847) 634-0888

Garfield Farm Harvest Days
La Fox
(630) 584-8485

Geneva's most coveted business district of renovated Queen Anne and Victorian homes. There's pottery, fiber art, printmaking, glass, fine art, photography, and handmade jewelry from which to choose. The fair is held in late July on Sat and Sun from 10 a.m. to 5 p.m.; admission is free; located on South Third Street; (630) 232-6060; www.genevachamber.com/artfair.html.

Another event held with the backdrop of beautiful turn-of-the-century homes is the *Geneva Concours d'Elegance,* a show of prized antique and modern automobiles sure to please rabid car collectors, hobbyists, or those who just admire unique automobiles. Best of all, the entry fees paid by the car owners are donated to a worthy charity. The show is held the third weekend in Aug from 10 a.m. to 4 p.m.; admission is free; located along South Third Street; (630) 584-3107; http://genevaconcours.net.

The land along the *Fox River* is both wooded and rolling, and of all the communities nestled alongside her, *St. Charles* might be considered the most picturesque. The city has taken good advantage of the waterfront by creating parks and greenways for outdoor activities. For starters, the *Fox River Trail* makes St. Charles a perfect town for walking and bicycling as the paved path extends north to the city of Algonquin and as far south as Aurora. On the east side of the river is *Pottawatomie Park,* where the St. Charles Park District maintains the *River View Miniature Golf Complex,* canoes and two-person paddleboats, volleyball and tennis courts, a swimming pool, and picnic areas. Hours are subject to seasons and weather conditions, and the cost varies according to activity; there's a parking and usage fee for nonresidents. Pottawatomie Park is located at 8 North Ave.; (630) 584-1028; www.st-charlesparks.org.

If you want to get on the river, try the old-fashioned paddle wheelers reminiscent of the days of Robert Lewis Stevenson: the **St. Charles Belle** and the **Fox River Queen** will make you feel like singing tunes from *Showboat.* With a passenger capacity of one hundred, the boats ease up and down the lazy river and offer a refreshing perspective of the beautiful riverbanks. Hours of operation vary seasonally from June through Aug; the boats leave from Pottawatomie Park at 3:30 p.m. on weekdays, 2, 3, and 4 p.m. on Sat and Sun, and also at 5 p.m. on Sun. In May, Sept, and Oct, the boats operate on weekends only; tickets cost $7.50 for adults and $6.00 for children; (630) 584-2334; www.st-charlesparks.org.

If you see straw in the street, it's probably time for the *St. Charles Scarecrow Festival,* which draws more than a hundred entries sure to terrify even the most confident crow. There's music and lots of seasonal treats. The festival is held the second week of Oct, Fri and Sat from 9 a.m. to 10 p.m. and Sun from 9 a.m. to 6 p.m.; admission is free. The event takes place at *Lincoln*

Park, at Main and Fourth Streets on the west side of the Fox River; (630) 377-6161; www.scarecrowfest.com.

A coinciding event called *Autumn on the Fox Arts and Crafts Show* attracts more than 160 artisans from around the U.S. and features handmade home decor items, clothing, jewelry, and homemade food. The show is held the second week of Oct on Fri and Sat from 9 a.m. to 5 p.m. and on Sun from 9 a.m. to 4 p.m.; admission is free; 8 North Ave. in Pottawatomie Park on the east bank of the Fox River; (630) 377-6161; www.scarecrowfest.com.

One of the more unusual outdoor activities occurs in a graveyard. It's called the *Grave Reminders Cemetery Walk* and it's a unique way to get some fresh air and exercise, and learn about local history at the same time. Costumed docents from the *St. Charles Heritage Center Museum* will greet you at *North Cemetery* and portray long-gone residents such as Mary Todd Lincoln's psychic adviser, Caroline Howard. Tours are given in early Oct on Sat from 1 to 3 p.m.; admission is $3 for adults and $1 for children, and you must prepurchase tickets at the Heritage Center Museum, 215 E. Main St.; the cemetery is located on the west side of SR 25 at Fifth Avenue; (630) 584-6967; www.stcmuseum.org.

Visit the changing displays at the *St. Charles Heritage Center Museum,* which covers events, residents, and local businesses from 1833 to the present. The museum is open Tues through Sat from 10 a.m. to 4 p.m. and on Sun from noon to 4 p.m.; closed on Mon and holidays; admission is free; 215 E. Main St.; (630) 584-6967; www.stcmuseum.org.

Bargain hunters know where to shop, and that's why the *Kane County Flea Market* is still going strong. Since 1967 the event has grown to over 1,000 dealers selling their wares on the twenty-five-acre Kane County Fairgrounds. An estimated 25,000 shoppers eagerly scan the booths and tables during this two-day treasure-trove extravaganza, which is open rain or shine. The flea market is held the first weekend of each month on Sat from noon to 5 p.m. and Sun from 7 a.m. to 4 p.m.; admission is $5 for adults and free for children under age twelve; parking is free (and hopefully, if it's raining you won't get stuck in the mud—that comes from the voice of experience); 525 S. Randall Rd.; (630) 377-2252; www.kanecountyfair.com.

Before leaving St. Charles, stop by the restored *Hotel Baker,* a majestic carved-stone and brick landmark built in 1928 by St. Charles native Edward J. Baker. It was a diamond when it opened, and still maintains that resort ambience as it overlooks the *Fox River Dam* waterfall. Have a leisurely dinner at the *ROX City Grill* or linger at the *ROX Lounge;* during the summer make a reservation to sit on the veranda overlooking the river. Before you leave, ask to see the fabled *Rainbow Room,* an oval-shaped space beneath a high rotunda with a backlit glass floor. This room has hosted the likes of Louis Armstrong and the big bands of Tommy Dorsey and Guy Lombardo, and it continues to thrive as a dance venue with local live entertainment. The hotel is located at 100 W. Main St.; (630) 584-2100; www.hotelbaker.com.

Outside of St. Charles in the small town of *La Fox* is the *Garfield Farm and Inn Museum,* a circa 1840s living-history farm where visitors can experience the era through the preserved buildings and farmland. Archaeologists have cited this as a premier example of early pioneer farm life, and the National Register of Historic Places has recognized it as the largest historical farm in Illinois.

Nearby are the *20-Mill Creek Prairie* and the *Sedge Meadow.* Together the area covers over thirty acres, but it's the twenty acres of unplowed land that is of most interest to historians and agriculturists as it is the closest example of a true natural prairie that exists today. Here native grasses and plants thrive as they did in the mid-1840s.

The museum hosts several events every month, but two are especially noteworthy. During the *Heirloom Garden Show* in mid-August, you can view and purchase fruits and vegetables that are cultivated from rare or heirloom seeds. If you dare to cook like a pioneer, you can fill up your bag with some of the more unusual produce like black or purple tomatoes, or red, white, or blue potatoes. In early October join in the *Sunday Harvest Days,* an 1840s festival with demonstrations of blacksmithing, weaving, and good-ole farm cooking. The farm museum is open from June to Sept on Wed and Sun from 1 to 4 p.m. or by appointment; admission is $3 for adults and $2 for children; festival events cost about $6, with additional charges for seminars or classes; 3N016 Garfield Rd.; (630) 584-8485; www .garfieldfarm.org.

South Elgin is home to an unusual working museum filled with nostalgia for the older set and novelty for the younger: the *Fox River Trolley Museum* teaches by way of experience as visitors travel a 4-mile stretch of electrified track along the Fox River via an antique trolley car. There are also displays of various railway cars on-site. The museum is open May 15 to Nov 1 on Sun from 11 a.m. to 5 p.m., and add Sat from 11 a.m. to 5 p.m. from the end of June through Labor Day; admission is $3.50 for adults and $2.00 for seniors and children ages three through eleven; an all-day ticket is $7.00; 361 S. La Fox St.; (847) 697-4676; www.foxtrolley.org.

Although *Elgin* boasted a thriving business district in the 1800s with companies like the David C. Cook Publishing Company and Borden's Milk Company selecting it as their base of operations, people are more likely to associate the town with another product: the Elgin watch. While the nation was

What's the Time?

Today, just like the company which closed in the 1960s, the main factory building of the Elgin National Watch Company is gone. However, one major structure still remains. The Elgin National Watch Company Observatory was built in 1910 as a way for scientists to determine the exact time using stars and the meridian with pinpoint accuracy. The observatory was retired in 1959 and donated to the Elgin School District, which added a planetarium, the first school planetarium in the state. It's now called the Elgin U-46 Planetarium, and although it isn't open to the public, it's a vital part of the educational experience for Elgin's schoolchildren. To have a look at the exterior, drive by it at 312 Watch St.

rapt with the Civil War, *The Elgin National Watch Company* produced its first product, and over time grew to outproduce its competition, both domestic and international. The growth of the company caused a surge in the town's population, doubling it rapidly and requiring housing to support the workers and their families.

Elgin has been recognized for the significant maintenance and value of its many older neighborhoods, and visitors interested in architecture might want to make a trip through town as part of their Sunday drive or consider taking a *Historic Elgin House Tour* sponsored yearly by the *Gifford Park Association.* The walk has been popular for more than thirty years, as visitors are invited to inspect a variety of houses both inside and out, from Foursquare homes to Romanesque mansions. Docents, many dressed in period costumes, provide lively scripted presentations and answer questions. Held in early September, the event runs from 9 a.m. to 5:30 p.m., and different neighborhoods are featured each year; admission is about $16.50; (847) 742-4248; www .gifford-park-assoc.org.

There are four major historical districts in Elgin containing more than 650 homes listed under the protective umbrella of the National Register of Historic Places: *Elgin's First Local Historic District,* where workers and managers lived side by side in cottages standing next to mansions; the *Spring/ Douglas Historic District* in northeast Elgin, which was dubbed "Fashionable Avenue" in a newspaper in 1884; the *D.C. Cook/Lovell Area District,* which contains some of the most popular architectural styles, such as Queen Anne, Prairie, and Craftsman dating from 1862–1926, as well as the greenspace *Esmeralda Park;* and the *Elgin National Watch Historic District,* which features worker housing as well as various buildings constructed by the watch company.

Before the Secret Service

Allan Pinkerton worked as a cooper after he arrived in Dundee in 1842, but he had an interest in law enforcement and eventually became sheriff in both Kane and Cook Counties. He opened the nation's first private protection services agency and received widespread publicity when he uncovered an assassination attempt on President-elect Lincoln in 1861.

Pinkerton and his men conducted spy activities for the Union during the Civil War, but fell out of favor with the public when, years later, his agency took assignments from various businesses to interfere with trade unions during the labor unrest of the late 1800s. He is thought to have coined the phrase "private eye" because his logo was an open eye and his slogan was "We never sleep." His business was known as the Pinkerton National Detective Agency, but many shortened it to the Pinkerton Guards or the Pinkertons.

After all of this driving, head to **Walton Island,** a lovely four-plus-acre haven in the middle of the Fox River suited for walking and bicycling. Originally developed as a Works Progress Administration project during the Great Depression, today it's been improved with paved walkways, extensive landscaping, lighting, and a Prairie-style shelter. The island is located at the end of Symphony Way. For more information contact the Elgin Parks & Recreation Department, 100 Symphony Way; (847) 931-6123.

A bit north of Elgin is the town of **West Dundee,** whose most famous resident may have been Allan Pinkerton, a cooper turned secret agent and spy who contracted his services during the Civil War. Look for a state historical marker along Third Street that designates the site of his homestead.

While in **Dundee,** visit the **Haeger Factory Store,** where the phrase "Made in America" has been true since 1871, when founder David H. Haeger opened his brick manufacturing company, the Dundee Brickyard. It was a timely decision, as that same year the Great Chicago Fire torched the city, making Haeger's bricks a vital necessity. In the early 1900s the company took on a new phase of creating vessels for the floral industry before finally transitioning into fine pottery. The family-owned business sells its wares online and at the **Haeger Factory Store.** Haeger received a *Guinness Book of World Records* award in 1976 for its "World's Largest Hand-Thrown Vase," an 8-foot-tall, 650-pound showpiece that can be ogled at the on-site **Haeger Museum.** The store and museum are open Mon, Thurs, and Fri from 10 a.m. to 6 p.m. and Sat and Sun from 11 a.m. to 5 p.m.; admission is free; 7 Maiden Lane; (847) 783-5420; www.haegerpotteries.com.

South Suburban

Besides Chicago, there are several other Illinois cities that have gained noto-riety in the nation's lexicon due to their "starring" roles in movies and televi-sion. *The Blues Brothers* movies are linked to *Joliet,* but there's more to the *Will County* seat than the *Statesville Correctional Center,* Roman Catholic churches, and the penchant of some for wearing sunglasses.

The nation's first junior college was founded here in 1901 by William Rainey Harper and J. Stanley Brown. Six students became the inaugural class of *Joliet Junior College.* They matriculated in the stone building designed by Daniel Burnham and Frank Shaver Allen at 201 E. Jefferson St., which now houses *Joliet Central High School.* And over the years, hardworking families have spent their Sundays in the pews of the 150-plus houses of worship spread throughout the city.

Joliet has become one of the fastest-growing communities in the state, with more than 140,000 residents calling it home. Like many cities that spent generations thriving on industry for revenue, Joliet has accepted the challenge to convert from manufacturing to a service-based economy.

In 1990 the Illinois legislature approved gambling but with a twist: Gaming was not permitted on land. The stipulation provided for the birth of riverboat gambling. Cities blessed with a river became candidates for the new income generator, and Joliet won two of the original nine statewide enterprises. Float-ing southwest of downtown along the *Des Planes River* is *Argosy's Empress Casino Joliet* at 2300 Empress Dr. and *Harrah's Joliet Casino* at 151 N. Joliet St. Between the pair, patrons can test their luck on over 2,000 slot machines.

Another change is the thundering sounds of the area's two raceways: the revitalized *Route 66 Raceway,* which features dirt-oval stock, drag, and demolition events, and its sister facility and NASCAR sensation, the *Chica-goland Speedway.* For race information call (815) 727-7223 or check www .route66raceway.com or www.chicagolandspeedway.com.

To kick off the *Chicagoland Speedway NASCAR Nationwide Series,* attend the annual *Race Fan Rally,* where the public is invited to a meet-and-greet of NASCAR drivers and view race cars close-up. There's also a classic car show, live music, and plenty of munchies. Be prepared for lines, as this is a major event, sometimes attracting over 45,000 people. The rally is held Friday evening, the night before the big race on the second Saturday in July, from 4 to 11 p.m.; admission is free; located along Chicago Street in downtown Joliet; www.racefanrally.com.

If you're looking for something more sedate, tour the historic *Rialto Square Theatre,* long dubbed "The Jewel of Joliet." As another surviving

Start Your Engines

Old-time names like Richard Petty and Mario Andretti give true fans chills, but if you're not into watching a race, maybe you'd like to test your mettle at driving an Indy or NASCAR racer around the track. During the year, professional driving schools visit the Chicagoland Speedway and offer participants that opportunity of a lifetime. Only twenty tracks nationwide offer these programs. Prices, dates, and times vary so check the Web site for details at www.chicagolandspeedway.com and click "Driving Schools."

example of the work of theater designers Rapp and Rapp, the Rialto was commissioned by the Ruben brothers, who poured a staggering two million dollars into the 1926 project. The lobby is patterned after the Hall of Mirrors in France's Palace of Versailles. Eighteen Corinthian columns topped with golden scrollwork and detailed bas-relief images of mystical creatures encircle the grand rotunda. The dome is reminiscent of Rome's Pantheon, and the massive hand-cut crystal and bronze chandelier, nicknamed the "Duchess," hangs suspended from an elaborately decorated medallion. The *Barton Grande Theatre Pipe Organ* waits inside the richly outfitted auditorium, and there's not a bad seat in the place. Tours for individuals are scheduled each Tues at 1:30 p.m., but it's wise to confirm; tour admission is $5; 15 E. Van Buren St.; (815) 726-6600; www.rialtosquare.com.

The *Billie Limacher Will-Joliet Bicentennial Park* is a community complex situated beside the Des Plaines River and host to seasonal concerts by guest musicians at the outdoor amphitheater. Bring a blanket or chair, buy a hot dog, and prepare to tap your feet. Concerts run from June to Aug on Thurs at 6:30 p.m.; admission is free; 210 W. Jefferson St. at Bluff Street; (815) 740-2216; www.bicentennialpark.org.

In the 1830s Joliet was just one stop along the extensive canal system built to move goods from the Great Lakes to the Mississippi River and onward south to the Gulf of Mexico. Cities, towns, and hamlets in Will, Cook, La Salle, and Grundy Counties became stations for the *Illinois and Michigan Canal (I&M),* and populations, businesses, and settlements expanded along the waterway, bringing prosperity with it. From 1836 to 1848 men from every corner of the state signed on to excavate the 96-mile canal by hand. It was a grueling undertaking, and the great hopes and expectations that should have accompanied such a feat were cut short with the expansion of the railway system and the constant expense of silt removal from the canal system. In an attempt to preserve this vital story of

Illinois history, the National Park System created the *Illinois and Michigan Canal National Heritage Corridor.*

The present-day town of *Lockport* proudly celebrates this early heritage with many remarkable examples of canal-era buildings still standing. One example of local limestone architecture is the *Gaylord Building,* which is owned by the National Trust for Historic Preservation and superintended by the *Canal Corridor Association.* Built in 1838, the building features grand archways that were the entry point for wagons loading and unloading goods. Today the restored structure contains a frequently changing exhibit gallery, visitor center, and restaurant. The building is open Tues through Sat from 11 a.m. to 5 p.m. and Sun from noon to 5 p.m.; closed on Mon; admission is free; 200 W. Eighth St.; (815) 838-9400; www.gaylordbuilding.org.

The four-star *Public Landing Restaurant* sets a relaxed tone and offers fine dining, so don't expect cheeseburgers. But when it's in season, do ask for their fantastic peach cobbler. The restaurant is open Tues through Thurs from 11:30 a.m. to 9 p.m., Fri and Sat from 11:30 a.m. to 10 p.m., and Sun from 11:30 a.m. to 8 p.m.; closed on Mon; 200 W. Eighth St.; (815) 838-6500; www .publiclandingrestaurant.com.

The *Will County Historical Society* maintains an artifact-packed museum in the former *I&M Canal Commissioner's Headquarters,* built in 1837. You can just picture the commissioner sitting in his office and watching the canal traffic from this perch. Well-informed docents provide tours. The museum is open seasonally, Tues through Sun from noon to 4 p.m.; closed from late Nov until mid-Feb; admission is $3 for adults, $2 for seniors, students, and members of the military, $1 for children ages six through seventeen, and free for children under age five; 803 S. State St.; (815) 838-5080; www.willcountyhistory.org.

"Everything Illinois" would be a good way to describe the exhibits at the *Illinois State Museum Lockport Gallery.* Fine art, textiles, sculpture, and more, all produced by Illinoisans from past to present are showcased and frequently changed. The museum is housed in the historic *Norton Building.* Built in 1850 of limestone, it features those familiar large arch windows that canal buildings required for the delivery, storage, and processing of grain. The gallery is open Mon through Fri from 9 a.m. to 5 p.m. and Sun from noon to 5 p.m.; closed on Sat; admission is free; 201 W. Tenth St.; (815) 838-7400; www .museum.state.il.us/ismsites/lockport.

The *Old Congregational Church* is home to the *Gladys Fox Museum,* which is operated by the Lockport Township Park District and features photographs and area memorabilia about Dellwood Park and the canal system. The church, which was built in 1839, is the oldest masonry house of worship in the state. That in itself makes it worth a look. The museum is open Mon through Fri from 1 to 4 p.m.; admission is free; 231 E. Ninth St.; (815) 838-0803.

Perhaps the best way to feel the vitality of this old-time canal town is to attend the annual *Old Canal Days Festival* when all the museums are open and the entertainment is a blend of old-fashioned fun and modern convenience. Along the main thoroughfare, the town is abuzz with live music, food, and competitions such as the "Old Canal Days Race," "Battle of the Bands," and "Baby Contest." The festival is held the third week of June, with the parade starting on Fri at 6:30 p.m.; admission to the festival is free, but the contests require entry fees; (815) 838-4744; www.lockportcanaldays.com.

If you're ready for a gourmet meal served in a romantic setting, try *Tallgrass.* The redbrick Victorian building is over one hundred years old, and be forewarned that there are steps to navigate. Inside, the ambience is of another, more refined era, as the dining room mood is warmed by the flames of original gas chandeliers. Plan to linger here, as the menu and relaxed atmosphere are decidedly European. Recommendations include the soup trio, the veal, and if you want dessert, the chocolate-raspberry tower. Reservations are

Hidden in Plain Sight

Overlooking the banks of the Kankakee River are not one, but two remarkable Frank Lloyd Wright homes. They were the Kankakee residences of sisters, and both were designed by Wright in 1900 and built in 1901, making them the first examples of Wright's transitional Prairie School of design. Right now, these homes can only be admired from the street. The *Warren Hickox House* sits at 687 S. Harrison Ave. and is a private residence.

The companion home is known as the *B. Harley Bradley House,* and the exterior features Wright's low, long lines but also has a rather high hip roof. From the inside looking out, it's easy to see his vision of harmony between the land and his structure, as the river blends with the dark woodwork framing the windows, giving the appearance that the landscape beyond is a fine painting. As was typical, Wright drew the details of the furnishings, rugs, windows, and even the china. The stable is connected to the residence by a complementary veranda whose high-pitched roofline disguises the fact that it was intended as a storage barn for horses and carriages. Although this property is currently privately owned, a nonprofit organization is hoping to purchase it for a house museum.

In the meantime, the current owners have meticulously renovated the stable and opened a fine gift shop of collectibles and Wright-related items. The *Bradley House Stable Shop and Museum* is open only by appointment, so please call before visiting. The house is located at 701 S. Harrison Ave., Kankakee; (815)802-1421; www .wrightinkankakee.org.

recommended, as meals are served at seating times, typically 5:30 and 7:30 p.m. 1006 S. State St.; (815) 838-5566; www.tallgrassrestaurant.com.

Going south you'll come to a small town that has a unique feature: The **Kankakee River** runs through it—literally. But **Wilmington** has made the most of the breach by touting itself as the "Island City" and turning the land into two green spaces called the **North and South Island Parks.**

The Wilmington **Catfish Days Festival** has its roots underwater. When **Forked Creek** surged into the basements of homes in a section known as "Catfish Town," the association stuck; hence the name of festival. Enjoy the parade, contests, carnival, laser light show, and flea market, and you can bet there's catfish on the menu. The festival, held the last weekend of July, starts on Thurs at 5 p.m. and ends on Sun at 3 p.m.; admission is free. The event takes place along downtown streets—just follow the signs; (815) 476-7966.

If you're feeling a bit English, stop at the **Chester Manor Tea Room and Cafe** where you'll be treated to traditional homemade delicacies and, of course, perfectly brewed tea. The *Tea House Times* has cited the Chester Manor Tea Room as a "Reader's Top Choice." Chester Manor is open Wed through Sun from 11:30 a.m. to 5 p.m.; 116 S. Kankakee St.; reservations are requested and can be made by calling (815) 476-1055.

If you're in need of a burger, try the **Launching Pad Drive-In,** a retro luncheonette that's been around since 1960. The one-story brick building is rather modest, but never fear that you'll pass it by, as it's guarded by the **Gemini Giant!** In fact, the giant is probably more of a draw than the food, thanks to the dedicated travelers who frequent **Old Route 66.** It's common to see families posing in front of this 36-foot fiberglass astronaut. At least, with his space helmet (which is illuminated inside at night) and rocket in hand (it's been stolen at least twice over the years), one would guess that's what he's supposed to be. It's probable that he spent his younger years, say in the 1950s to early 1960s, as a Muffler Man before he was recruited into the space program at a time when America was anticipating the landing of a man on the moon. (Word is that he has a twin brother named **Tall Paul** living in Atlanta, Illinois, but that giant's peddling hot dogs.) So after you've taken your photographs and had a good laugh, do stop at the restaurant and order their famous chocolate malt to go. The restaurant is located at 810 E. Baltimore St.; (815) 476-6535.

Because of its location in the **Kankakee River Valley,** the 6,000 or so Wilmington residents are surrounded by rich opportunities when it comes to the great outdoors. Both the federal and state governments are involved in managing projects that affect the quality of life for all who visit this small town.

The federal government officially entered the prairie preservation movement by authorizing the conversion of the former U.S. Joliet Army Ammunition Plant into the *Midewin National Tallgrass Prairie.* The Illinois Land Conservation Act of 1995 authorized the transfer of nearly 20,000 acres of Illinois land from the U.S. Army to the U.S. Forest Service. Now, an ongoing and in-depth restoration project is eclipsing past attempts at re-creating the original prairie. This is the first federally designated tallgrass prairie in the nation, and 22 miles of trials are available for hiking, bicycling, or horseback riding.

Before you take to the winding nature paths, stop first at the *Midewin Welcome Center* to view the exhibits, schedule a tour, and find out the routes that are off-limits. Note that this area is used for hunting and scientific studies, so it's imperative that you get the latest updates and stay on the paths. The center is open Mon through Fri from 8:30 a.m. to 4:30 p.m., and seasonally on Sat at the same time; guided tours are seasonal in spring, summer, and fall, so call ahead to confirm times; 30239 S. Rte. 53; (815) 423-6370; www.fs.fed.us/mntp.

The *Des Plaines Fish and Wildlife Area* is an Illinois State Park with all the nature perks of hiking, camping, fishing, and picnicking, but this park also features a number of dog-training fields where trainers direct their canines through the mazes of marshes and brush. Special training events are held here. The park is located at 24621 N. River Rd.; (815) 423-5326.

If whipped cream is your idea of a taste of heaven, then *New Lenox* has the event for you. How about entering the pie-eating contest at the *Old Campground Festival?* For more than thirty years, the United Methodist Church of New Lenox has opened its grounds for a community get-together that features over one hundred arts and crafts booths, performances by local talent, and

Historic Homes

Downtown Wilmington is architecturally rich with vintage buildings and plenty of antiques shops along the main stretch, but there are two interesting structures to catch as you go through town. The first is the octagonal *Schutten-Aldrick House,* which was built by carpenter David Aldrick in 1856 and features a hollowed center from the roof to the basement. The records are not definitive, but it's thought that slaves were housed in this center alcove as part of the Underground Railroad. The building located at 600 S. Water St., is not open for tours.

A second interesting building is the *Stewart House,* the three-story 1836 hotel of Peter Stewart, an early Wilmington settler. This is another place that may have played a role in the Underground Railroad. This building, at Kankakee Street and Outer Drive, is also not open for tours but worth a drive by when you're in the area.

lots of food and fun. The festival, held the last Sat of June, opens at 9 a.m., and the pie-eating contest is at 12:30 p.m. prompt; admission is free, and free shuttles are available when parking spaces run out, so watch for the signs; 339 W. Haven Ave.; (815) 485-8271; www.umcnl.com.

As the county seat, *Morris* is the keeper of all historical items relating to *Grundy County.* The *Grundy County Historical Society* maintains the county museum, which includes artifacts from the Civil War and both World Wars, as well as a vintage train caboose from the EJ&E (Elgin, Joliet and Eastern) Railway. The museum is open Thurs through Sat from 10 a.m. to 3 p.m.; donations are requested; 510 W. Illinois Ave.; (815) 942-4880; www.grundy countyhs.org.

Everybody in the county gets corny at the *Grundy County Corn Festival,* where it's five full days of crazy corn fun at various sites in town. Of course, there are the traditional corn dogs, caramel corn, and sweet corn on the cob. Don't miss the Corn, Grain and Flower Show, or my personal favorite, the Crackerbox Derby. Hey, after you've seen this race, you'll start building your own entry for next year! There's a flea market, hobby and handicraft exhibits, and a parade that lasts two hours. Cap off the day with a leisurely boat ride on the Illinois River. The festival is held the third week of Sept; admission is free. The Corn Festival Office is located at 909 N. Liberty St.; (815) 942-2676; http://cornfestival.org.

Southeast of Morris, at the *Goose Lake Prairie State Natural Area* off Pine Bluff Road, an early log cabin stands as a tribute to the pioneer spirit. The *Cragg Cabin* was built by John and Agnes Cragg in the late 1830s and served as a place for respite along the *Teamster Trail,* which connected Chicago and Bloomington. When the Cragg family grew to six children, John Cragg added a second story to the log residence, turning it into Grundy County's first two-story home. Somewhere along the line, the fancy cabin (by pioneer standards) acquired a nickname: The Palace.

To celebrate the pioneer lifestyle, the nature preserve hosts the Annual *Cragg Cabin Festival.* Craftspeople dressed in period costumes reenact the activities required for survival on the prairie, such as blacksmithing, soap and candle making, bobbin arts, quilting, spinning, and wood carving. There are also demonstrations of Native American crafts and dances, and lessons in following animal tracks. The Goose Lake Prairie State Natural Area is located at 5010 N. Jugtown Rd., Morris; (815) 942-2899.

Have you ever tasted burdock root stew or hot compote of violet greens? This might be your big chance, as the *Incredible Edibles Festival,* which is held at the Goose Lake Prairie nature preserve at the same time, serves up settlers' favorites.

Back in Time

Southeast of Morris is the state's largest remaining natural prairie. Boasting more than 2,500 acres, the **Goose Lake Prairie State Natural Area** will take you back to Illinois in the early 1800s, with its long vistas of 12-foot tall cordgrass, big bluestem, and 2-foot-tall northern prairie dropseed swaying to and fro for as far as you can see. This was the vision seen by the earliest Illinois settlers, who called it a "sea of grass with pretty flowers." Put yourself in those times and imagine a herd of buffalo, a pack of wolves, or a rash of muskrat spreading the grasses as they run in the distance; listen for the prairie chickens and red-winged blackbirds; and watch for the red-tailed hawk circling above. At one time, more than 60 percent of Illinois was active prairie like this.

Considering the story behind the early settlement of this area, it's amazing that the Goose Lake Prairie remnant survived. At one time the land held the glittering 1,000-acre Goose Lake, but don't expect to see it now. The lake was drained over the course of time by pioneers eager to use the clay bed beneath for the manufacture of pottery, jugs, and bricks. In fact, this park is situated along Jugtown Road and "Jugtown" was the name of an informal settlement of potters who lived along Goose Lake's clay-rich banks and worked in what is thought to be Illinois' first pottery manufacturing enterprise.

In October 1855 a potter named William White joined with financier Charles Walker to form White and Company. At the peak of business, Walker had invested over $12,000 in the firm, a whopping sum in 1860. Unfortunately, money couldn't solve the challenges that beset them. Although Chicago provided an eager marketplace for drainage tiles, moving the heavy tiles across rutted roads to the canal for transport into the city proved impossible. The Panic of 1857, which bankrupted many businesses, didn't help, either. Faced with creditors' lawsuits, the partners ended their ten-year alliance, leaving a skilled worker population without a means of income and sealing the demise of the hamlet of Jugtown. The land was spent, the lake ruined, and the community just drifted away.

If you're an angler who prefers fishing from the shoreline or by small boat, move to the **Heidecke Lake Fish and Wildlife Area** of the park, where a perfect companion to the dry bed of Goose Lake is the man-made, 2,000-acre **Heidecke Lake.** The wildlife area is located at 5010 N. Jugtown Rd., Morris; (815) 942-6352.

Touted as one of the cleanest rivers in Illinois and listed on the Federal Clean Streams Register, the scenic **Kankakee River** might best be viewed by traveling down the waterway. The route is especially beautiful as you pass through the 11-mile stretch of the **Kankakee River State Park,** where the constant flow of the water has etched outcroppings and canyons into the natural limestone banks. This river was first explored in 1679 by Frenchman Robert de La Salle and his men, and it's easy to put yourself into their mindset as you glide past the thick brush and heavily wooded riverbank and wonder what's beyond the water's shoreline.

This river is rated as a Class 1 stream, which means it's gentle and suitable for travel by families and beginners. To rent a ride, try **Reed's Canoe Trips,** a longtime family operation that provides everything you need for an excursion that varies in miles and lasts anywhere from two to five hours. Reservations are recommended; bad weather can interfere with your plans, so be prepared. Reed's is open May 1 to Sept 30, with canoe launches daily from 8 a.m. to 5 p.m. 907 N. Indiana Ave., Kankakee; (815) 932-2663; www .reedscanoetrips.com.

Back on land, take particular note of the park's **Rock Creek Canyon,** where artistic-looking cedars appear to cling to the striking limestone canyon walls, and a waterfall rewards the hiker who makes it to the end of the sometimes difficult trail. The Kankakee River State Park entrance is located at 5314 W. Rte. 102, Bourbonnais; (815) 933-1383.

For more than twenty-five years, serious Midwest anglers have dedicated themselves to "catching the big one" at the **Kankakee River Valley Fishing Derby,** where the winnings are as big as the fish. Over $300,000 is paid out for the largest fish caught in various categories, and special prizes are awarded for those reeling in a tagged fish. Call or check the Web site for current rules. The derby is held at the end of June; admission is $20 per family for ten days of fishing; (800) 747-4837; www.kankakeefishingderby.com.

There's more fun on the Kankakee River during the **Power Boat Nationals on the Kankakee River,** an Outboard Performance Craft (OPC) National Championship race featuring 200 entries from all over the nation. The speedboats often reach 140 miles per hour, and races run every day. The riverfront is turned into party central with live music, eating contests, and a craft fair. But, hands down, the second most popular sport happens early Saturday evening during the "Cardboard Boat Races." Daredevil locals pay an entry fee to construct a river-worthy vessel out of cardboard and materials provided by the park district. When it's time to launch, everyone gets a good laugh. This is a "do not miss." The event is held over Labor Day weekend, Sat through Mon, with races beginning at 11:30 a.m.; admission varies per day and is charged by carload; located at River Road Park, Kankakee; (800) 747-4837; www.visit kankakeecounty.com.

Kankakee has the honor of being the only town in the state to have had three of her native sons elected to the office of Illinois governor: Lennington Small (1921–1929), Samuel Shapiro (1968–1969), and George Ryan (1999–2003). The **Kankakee County Museum** heralds this fact in its permanent exhibit titled "The Three Governor's Gallery." The museum is housed in the **Dr. A.L. Small House,** which was Lennington Small's birthplace and his family homestead. The first floor of the limestone home is open to the public and most of the decor is original to the Small family.

Also on the grounds of the **Governor Small Memorial Park** are the one-room **Taylor School House** and the **Column and Freedom Gardens,** where an array of interesting items, such as an antique column, school bells, and an 1887 iron fountain, are surrounded by lovely gardens. The **Kankakee County Historical Society** is the oldest in the state, and it maintains an active role in the museum and research library. The park is open Apr 1 to Oct 1, Tues through Fri from 10 a.m. to 4 p.m. and Sat and Sun from to 4 p.m.; call for winter hours; admission is free. It is located at 801 S. Eighth Ave.; (815) 932-5279; www.kankakeecountymuseum.com.

Momence is the oldest town in northeastern Illinois and is still often called by the name early settlers bestowed upon it: "Border Town." Fur traders traveling between Fort Dearborn in Chicago and Vincennes, Indiana, considered Momence the endpoint for their route because the untamed Wild West frontier lay just outside the city limits. The name *Momence* is attributed to the Pottawatomie Chief Momenza, whose tribe called this area home.

For generations the prime local industry revolved around the gladiolus, a flower that springs from a bulb and has a hearty constitution. To celebrate its biggest cash crop, the town throws the **Momence Gladiolus Festival,** a five-day affair with a different theme each year, although the blooming gladioli are undoubtedly stars of the show. If you love parades, this event is for you, as there are four on the schedule, plus a flea market, a garden show, street dance, and an official "Adult Bean Bag Tournament." The festival is held in late June or early Aug; call the hotline at (815) 472-6353 or check www.gladfest.com for current dates. Events run from Wed at 7 p.m. to Sun at 4 p.m.

As much as the other gathering is about flowers, the **Squawk and Oink Barbeque Festival** is about meat. The Momence Park District sponsors this event filled with barbecue contests, a grill raffle, live music, and samples of some fine eating at affordable prices. The festival is held on the Monday of Labor Day weekend from 10 a.m. to 3 p.m.; admission free; located at the Momence Island Park at 79 East Mill St.; (815) 472-2670; www.momencepark district.net.

Northwest Suburban

If you long for the old days when the Golden Arches meant 15-cent burgers, head to **Des Plaines,** where you can refresh your memories by driving through the

McDonald's #1 Store Museum. The yellow arches that beckon drivers onto the grounds are an original sign; even the "Speedy" mascot is present with his sign touting the low-priced hamburgers. This isn't an operating restaurant but a re-creation of the original store, and it was built from the first restaurant's blueprints to insure accuracy. Male mannequins "work" at the vintage fryers and grills, all dressed in authentic uniforms from about 1955. The museum is open from Memorial Day to Labor Day; admission is free. 400 N. Lee Street; (847) 297-5022. Oh, and if all this reminiscing makes you hungry, just dodge across the street, where a bright and shiny—and functioning—McDonald's awaits to take your orders.

If you wish to go further back into your childhood, check out the ***Choo Choo Restaurant*** down the street, where burgers and fries are delivered on the flatcars of a well-worn model train, to the delight of kids and adults alike. It's a tradition that's been ongoing since 1951, and because there are only twenty-seven seats along the delivery circuit, everyone is expected to "chew, chew, then move your caboose" within thirty minutes so others can enjoy the prime seats. Make sure you bring cash because, just like in the good old days, they don't take credit cards. The restaurant is open Sat through Wed from 10:30 a.m. to 3 p.m. and Thurs and Fri from 10:30 a.m. to 8 p.m. at 600 Lee St.; (847) 391-9815; www.thechoochoo.com.

Maybe all this classic food has given you the urge to shop for treasures, but if you're not keeping your eyes open, you're apt to miss what is touted as "Chicagoland's oldest and largest antique center" right here in ***Wheeling.*** Surrounded by four-lane roads and major malls and restaurants, the ***Sale Barn Square*** is a village enclave of nine shops tucked away from it all. The buildings are historical and include the one-room 1840 ***Tripp School,*** a renovated barn that's more than one hundred and fifty years old, and a century-old farmhouse. Buyers are temped by a wide array of antiques, estate-sale favorites, garden accessories, glassware, and clocks. There's also a bridal shop, a furniture restoration center, and ***Shirley's Dollhouse,*** which sells both antique and new dolls. The walkways are lined with gazebos, wishing wells, and flower-laden planters. If it weren't for the humming traffic noise, you might think you've escaped back in time. Hours vary for each store, but all are closed on Mon; 971 N. Milwaukee Ave.; (847) 537-9886; www.salebarnsquare.com.

Over in ***Buffalo Grove*** you'll find the ultimate pick-me-up: chocolate! At ***Long Grove Confectionery Company,*** you can watch as tempting treats are hand-dipped, rolled, and decorated underneath an antique stained-glass dome ceiling. You can start with a one-hour tour or dive right into the good stuff at the ***Long Grove Factory Store.*** Be forewarned that if it's hot outside, your purchases might melt, so unless you bring a cooler, you might just have to eat your stash all at once. Hour-long tours are given from 10 a.m. to noon, Tues through Thurs with reservations and on Sat without reservations; admission is $2; 333 Lexington Dr.; (888) 459-3100; www.longgrove.com.

If you feel guilty afterward, drive over to the store's namesake, the actual village of **Long Grove**, where you can walk off some of your indulgences as you check out the stores and sites along the rustic walkways. Despite boasting 120 businesses, Long Grove's downtown has maintained a rural feel and in 1960 was deemed the first Illinois Business Historic District, preserving the small town atmosphere for the enjoyment of future generations. To ensure you don't miss anything, begin your visit with a stop at the **Long Grove Visitor's Information Center**, where they will provide you with guidance and a map. They can also advise you on store hours, which vary with the seasons. The center is located at 307 Old McHenry Rd.; (847) 634-0888.

Some favorites include the village store of the company that started this trek in the first place, the **Long Grove Confectionery**, where sweet, hand-dipped, fresh strawberries and giant peanut butter cups await on racks behind glass displays. Ask about their myrtles! The shop is located at 220 Robert Parker Coffin Rd.; (847) 634-0080; www.longgrove.com.

The **Long Grove Soap and Candle Company** features the unusual, such as Beanpod Soy Candles, as well as traditional tapers and pillars. The pleasant fragrances of the candles and soap will also have you lingering here. The store is located at 128 Old McHenry Rd.; (847) 634-9322; www.longgrovesoapand candle.com.

At the **Long Grove Apple Haus**, they like to say, "Mom's apple pie was great—ours is better!" Well, when it comes to their specialty, Uncle Johnny's "Brown Bag" apple pie, it's almost hard to argue! A flaky crust, the perfect amount of spices, and the freshest apples make choosing tough, but don't tell Mom. Apple Haus is located at 230 Robert Parker Coffin Rd.; (847) 634-0730.

If you're looking for a meal with a view, consider the **Long Grove Café**, which overlooks the **Mill Pond** and fountain. Ask for a seat by the large windows, or sit on the outdoor patio for the best effect. Greek-American fare is served for lunch and dinner and ranges from steaks and salads to seafood and burgers; breakfast is served on weekends. The cafe is located at 235 Robert Parker Coffin Rd.; (837) 955-9600.

Another pick is a trendy, vintage-inspired apparel store called **Olivia's Past.** A lot of the clothing, shoes, and jewelry are displayed in armoires and drawers, making it feel as though you're rifling through your grandmother's dresser, but with her permission, of course. The store is located at 1440 Old McHenry Rd.; (847) 913-1988.

OTHER ATTRACTIONS WORTH SEEING IN NORTHEASTERN ILLINOIS

Argonne National Laboratory
Argonne

America's Roundhouse Complex
Aurora

Phillips Park
Aurora

Villa Olivia Ski Area
Bartlett

Brookfield Zoo
Brookfield

McDonald's Museum
Des Plaines

Wandschneider Park and Museum
Downers Grove

Lizzadro Museum of Lapidary Art
Elmhurst

Gross Point Light House and Lakefront
Evanston

Northwestern University Sculpture Garden and Galleries
Evanston

Chicago Botanic Garden
Glencoe

The Grove
Glenview

Marytown/St. Maximilian Kolbe Shrine
Libertyville

River Trail Nature Center
Northbrook

Ernest Hemingway Museum and Birthplace
Oak Park

Frank Lloyd Wright Home and Studio
Oak Park

Medieval Times Dinner Theater and Tournament
Schaumburg

Woodfield Shopping Center
Schaumburg

Westfield Old Orchard Center
Skokie

Beith House Museum
St. Charles

Hawthorne Race Course
Stickney

Nathan Manilow Sculpture Park
University Park

Cuneo Mansion and Gardens
Vernon Hills

Cosley Zoo
Wheaton

Baha'i House of Worship
Wilmette

Kohl Children's Museum
Wilmette

Kline Creek Farm
Winfield

Seven Bridges Ice Arena
Woodridge

Virtually every month provides the village with a reason to celebrate, but there are three festivals that require special mention. The **Long Grove Chocolate Fest** has become a rite of spring. The festival features three full days of demonstrations and workshops, and did I mention the amazing chocolate cake, chocolate-drizzled popcorn, chocolate donuts, and chocolate drinks? There's live music by the **Covered Bridge,** and food booths, too. The festival is held the first week of May every year.

Second on the list is the **Long Grove Strawberry Festival,** which features three full days of everything berry, from homemade strawberry ice creams, pies, and donuts to strawberry smoothies and baked goods. Three stages are lively with music and entertainment, and the shops are brimming with strawberry merchandise. This event is held the last week of June each year.

And for nearly twenty years, people have flocked to the **Long Grove Apple Festival,** where hot cider, gourmet caramel apples, and apple pies reign. It's another fun-filled three-day weekend of jazz, bluegrass, pony rides, and food booths, all set against the backdrop of colorful fall leaves. For more information on all of the festivals, contact the Visitor's Information Center at 307 Old McHenry Rd.; (847) 634-0888.

Back on Milwaukee Avenue continue north, where you'll discover one of **Lincolnshire's** most shocking sights: a massive pink castle. No, this isn't home to Barbie. It's the entrance to **Par King Miniature Golf,** another Chicagoland tradition that's been operating for more than fifty years. There are two eighteen-hole courses that feature favorite obstacles such as water traps, rotating figurines, a wooden carousel, and tricky roller coaster. An arcade, picnic area, and snacks round out the entertainment. The odds of winning a free game are one in thirty-two, so get putting! Regulations to play? Safety dictates you must be at least 48 inches tall. Par King is open daily in season; call to verify current hours based on weather conditions; admission is generally $7, but it goes to $8 after 6 p.m. on Fri, Sat, and Sun. 21711 Milwaukee Ave.; (847) 634-0333; www.par-king.com.

For a "nontraditional" mini-golfing experience, try the course in the basement community room of the **Ahlgrim Family Funeral Service.** Yes, it's really golfing in a funeral home. The course was first set up in the 1960s as a way to get people's minds off the reason for their visit, but it became such a novelty that the Ahlgrim's invite the public to try their skills. It's especially popular around Halloween. Call for availability, as the room is closed during funerals. The course is open 9 a.m. to 9 p.m.; admission is free; 201 N. Northwest Hwy., Palatine; (847) 358-7411; www.ahlgrimffs.com.

Over in **Vernon Hills,** waiting behind a mature, treed buffer, is the **Cuneo Mansion and Gardens,** a thirty-two-room Italianate house built in

1914 by the founder of the Commonwealth Edison Company, Samuel Insull. When Insull fell on hard times, John Cuneo Sr. purchased the property, and it remained in the family until the early 1990s, when it was opened to the public as a museum.

To call this 31,000-square-foot home grand is an understatement. Renowned mural artist John Mallin decorated various rooms with meticulous hand-panted artwork, including the Stations of the Cross along the walls of the chapel. Noted landscape genius Jens Jensen created the original gardens, and the Cuneo family expanded them to include a stage, manicured walkways, and foun-

athletesightings

If you're into Chicago sports but can't afford a game ticket, you might take to people-watching at the local stores in Vernon Hills. Sightings have been reported of Bulls, Bears, and Blackhawks players, but look, don't touch, because they're usually out with their families. Hey, they have to shop, too!

tains. A herd of white fallow ("nuclear") deer reside here, as well as strutting peacocks that might stroll the grounds with you. The museum is open Tues through Sun from 10 a.m. to 5 p.m. for self-guided tours with a guidebook, and Tues through Fri guided tours are at 11:30 a.m., 1 and 2:30 p.m., and last about seventy-five minutes. No tour tickets are sold after 4 p.m.; the museum is closed on Mon. Admission is $10 for adults, $9 for seniors, students, and children. If you just want to drive the grounds, admission is $7 per car. 1350 N. Milwaukee Ave.; (847) 362-3042; http://cuneomansion.org.

The museum and village coordinate to provide an annual drive-through event called *A Winter Wonderland Holiday Light Show.* From the warmth and convenience of your car, you can enjoy displays covered in thousands of lights. It's so exciting that even Santa breaks his routine to visit this show; call ahead to check his arrival time, though. The show, presented every evening from 6 to 10 p.m., begins the day after Thanksgiving and continues until the second day of January, with the exception of December 24 and 25, when the helper elves are getting ready for their own celebrations. Admission is $5 per car Mon through Thurs and $10 per car on Fri, Sat, and Sun; enter off Lakeview Parkway, not at the North Milwaukee Avenue entrance; (847) 367-3700; www .vernonhills.org.

Years ago, area residents were treated to a car dealer's jingle that called *Libertyville* "a beautiful place in the country." Well, the city has caught up to it a bit, but there are still pockets of that lost country lifestyle. If you're hankering to be around cows, chickens, and sheep, stop at *Lambs Farm,* a nonprofit organization dedicated to helping more than 250 adults with developmental disabilities transition into the workforce and live independently. An estimated 300,000 visitors enjoy the products and services offered from the quaint storefronts, which include a pet salon, thrift shop, country store, and a bakery where homemade treats are sold. For a hearty home-cooked meal (the corn bread gets rave reviews) try the **Lambs Farm Country Inn,** which serves breakfast on the weekends, lunch almost every day, and dinner on Fri and Sat nights. Reservations are recommended; (847) 362-5050.

Outside, there's a petting zoo, carousel, a miniature train, and mini-golf course sure to please the younger set. The farm is open Apr to Oct daily from 10 a.m. to 5 p.m., and Mar and Nov for weekend hours only; admission for all activities is $6 for adults and $12 for children ages two through twelve, and attraction tickets can be purchased individually for reduced fees. 14245 W. Rockland Rd.; (847) 362 5050 www.lambsfarm.org.

Consider visiting the home of noted Chicago architect David Adler, who was known for designing remarkable mansions such as a fifty-nine-room residence in Ipswich, Massachusetts, built in 1927. Adler's personal residence features many furnishings from the 1920s, and extensive landscape design. The property also houses the **David Adler Music and Arts Center,** where **Lake County** residents of all ages study music, art, and drama. The house is open year-round, with tours Mon through Fri from 9 a.m. to 9 p.m. and Sat from 9 a.m. to 4 p.m.; admission is free; 1700 N. Milwaukee Ave.; (847) 367-0707; www.adlercenter.org.

While cruising north on I-294 to **Gurnee,** it's hard to miss the massive wooden and steel railways rising from behind the fence beside you. These are the signature screaming roller coasters of **Six Flags Great America.** Guests who'd rather keep both feet on the ground can spend the day visiting the park's themed villages, musical shows, glow-in-the-park parade, or the latest attraction, **Hurricane Harbor,** a water park with slides and rafting that is included with the theme park admission. Special events such as **Fright Fest** are held on weekends in Oct. The park is open daily from May through Aug, starting at 10 a.m. and closing at varying times; it's open weekends only from Sept through Oct. Admission is $54.99 for guests 54 inches and taller, $34.99 for those under 54 inches, and free for children age two and under. Parking costs $15; located in Gurnee on Grand Avenue (SR 132), 1 mile east of I-94; (847) 249-4636; www.sixflags.com.

Across the street is a shoppers dream: **Gurnee Mills Outlet Mall.** There are some surprises here, so prepare for the unexpected. And wear your comfy shoes.

Or better yet, bring your skates! **Rink Side Sports** is an NHL-size ice-skating arena; check out "Cosmic Skating" on Saturday night, the restaurant, and the video arcade, too. Hours vary with the seasons; skate rental is $4 per pair; admission is $6 for adults, $5 for children ages four through twelve, and free for children age 3 and under. Enter the Gurnee Mills Outlet Mall at the TJ Maxx and JCPenney stores; (847) 856-1064; www.rink-side.com.

And there's another unexpected venue at this mall: Check out the cold-blooded inhabitants of **Serpent Safari,** a combination reptile zoo and pet shop. Have your photo taken with one of the slithery residents or just take the guided tour. Admission is $6.95 for adults and $4.95 for children ages three to twelve; enter the mall at entry "C" and then turn left; (847) 855-8800.

If you're so inspired to continue exploring the exotic, stop for lunch at the **Rainforest Cafe,** where you can visit with macaws and toucans and then eat underneath the branches of a talking banyan tree. Enter at mall at entry "D" and turn right; (847) 855-7800. The Gurnee Mills Outlet Mall's general hours are Mon through Fri from 10 a.m. to 9 p.m., Sat from 10 a.m. to 9:30 p.m., and Sun from 10 a.m. to 9 p.m.; 6170 W. Grand Ave.; (847) 263 7500; gurneemillsmall.com.

The Gurnee Park District sponsors **Gurnee Days,** an annual get-together with a theme that changes every year, adding to the fun. You can count on a parade, amusement rides, concerts, fireworks, and great food. The event is held the second weekend of Aug; admission is free; located at the Village Center in **Viking Park,** Gurnee; (847) 249-9613.

One of the more amazing educational facilities in the state, and possibly the nation, is the 6,000-acre **Tempel Farms** in the hamlet of Old Mill Creek, where the **Tempel Lipizzan** stallions breed, train, and perform in the tradition of Vienna's Spanish Riding School. This is the largest herd of Lipizzan stallions in the world, and the farm has hosted Olympians and hopefuls alike

Checking for Cheops

A slam-on-your-brakes moment comes along Dilleys Road between Milwaukee Avenue and Wadsworth Road (in south Wadsworth, just northwest of Gurnee) as you pass a 200-ton towering rendition of Ramses II, and then realize that the statue is guarding the **Golden Pyramid House.**

This replica of Egypt's Great Pyramid of Cheops stands 64 feet high, is awash in twenty-four-carat gold plate, and surrounded by a moat. Contractor James Onan built this unusual family home in 1977. The house is located at 37921 Dilleys Rd.

It's important to remember that this is a *private residence* and is a "drive-by" attraction. Suppress the temptation to park at the gate or enter the fenced-in yard…yes, there is a gift shop sign, and no, it's not actually open to the public.

in national and junior national championship dressage events. For a special treat, catch a ninety-minute performance of these highly trained horses and then stay to tour the historic stables. Hours of performances vary and are held from June to Sept, with special fall and winter dates from Oct to May, so call or check the Web site for details. Admission is $18 for adults, $15 for seniors, $10 for children ages four through fourteen, and free for children under four; 17000 Wadsworth Rd.; (847) 623-7272; www.tempelfarms.com.

The town of *Waukegan* offers something for everyone with its dynamic harbor for outdoor activities, museums, historic districts, and entertainment venues such as the *Genesee Theatre.* Opened in 1927, the building fast became the premier area attraction at the time, but like many enterprises, it suffered a downturn in use and closed in 1989. The city then revitalized the structure to the tune of $23 million and reopened it in 2001. Today, the 2,300-seat structure is outfitted with replicas of the drapes, wall coverings, and light fixtures found in the original design, and an antique Baccarat crystal chandelier greets theatergoers in the grand lobby. Plays, comedians, concerts, and movies are on the calendar, but whether you have tickets or not, this place is worth a peek inside. The theater is located at 203 N. Genesee St.; (847) 782-2366; www.geneseetheatre.com.

For history buffs, stop at the *Waukegan Historical Society's* complex, where the *Haines House Museum* provides a slice of life from the 1870s and the *John L. Raymond Research Library* maintains thousands of documents and photographs for serious study. Every year on the fourth Sunday of June, the society sponsors the *Tour of Homes,* which opens four selected historic Waukegan residences for a public house walk. For additional information or to purchase tickets, contact the society at (847) 336-1859 or info@waukegan historical.org. The museum is open Tues, Thurs, and Sat from 10 a.m. to 4 p.m.; admission is free; (847) 336-1859. Library hours are Wed through Fri from 10 a.m. to 2:30 p.m.; (847) 360-4772. The museum and library are located at Bowen Park, 1917 N. Sheridan Rd.; www.waukeganhistorical.org.

And then there's the water! *Waukegan Harbor* is the perfect location to watch sailboats skirt the waves, walk the wooden promenade, or play on the nearby beach. The harbor is open from Apr 1 to Nov 1. If you're a sport fisherman without a ride of your own, book an excursion through the *Waukegan Charter Boat Association,* a consortium of experienced professional captains who will guide you to the best places for angling success with lake, brown or rainbow trout, or coho or chinook salmon. Call (847) 244- 3474; www.wcba.info.

As you near the Illinois-Wisconsin border on I-294 North, look to the west and you might find yourself asking if that's a U.S. military storage depot. Yes, there are planes, including at least one F-15 Eagle, and camouflage-covered helicopters, plus more transport vehicles and tanks than you can imagine. These are the acquisitions of Mr. Russell, whose hobby is just a little bigger and takes up a bit more space than typical collections. The artifacts are sort of rusty at the 15-acre outdoor **Russell Military Museum,** but they still raise a spirit of pride when you consider where they've been and how they've aided our servicemen and women. The museum is open daily from 10 a.m. to 5 p.m.; admission is $7.50 for adults and $5.00 for children. Watch the Web site for special-event Sherman tank rides and helicopter flights ranging from $10 to $35. 43363 Old Highway 41, Zion; (847) 395-7020; www.russellmilitary museum.com.

There are several Illinois towns that were founded by men of religion. **Zion** is one such place. Founded in 1900 by preacher and healer John A. Dowie, Zion City, as it was originally called, was the home base for Dowie's Christian Catholic Church. At the time, the utopian village revolved around the prime business, which was a lace mill that Dowie imported to ensure the citizenry had employment. But the town survived in this form only for about seven years, as he died in 1907, leaving the financially strapped community to fend for itself. The **Zion Historical Society** has turned his restored, twenty-five room mansion into the **Historic Shiloh House Museum.** The house is open June through Aug on Sun from 2 to 5 p.m. and in Dec for the Christmas holiday season; admission is $5; 1300 Shiloh Blvd.; (847) 746-2427; www.zion hs.com.

Today, downtown Zion is a bustling place with shops and eateries. Consider parking your car and taking the **Zion Beeline Trolley** around town. Or pick up a picnic lunch here and take the trolley to the nearby **Illinois Beach Resort** or the **North Point Marina,** where you can eat by the water and watch the boats.

The 6½ miles of **Illinois Beach State Park** are a diverse mix of sandy beach, marshland, natural dunes, and wet prairies suitable for hiking, camping, swimming, fishing, and boating. Be forewarned that your peaceful exploration might be interrupted by black flies and mosquitoes, so slather on that bug spray and dress accordingly to protect yourself. Reservations for camping are highly recommended and sometimes mandatory, depending on the type of campsite you need, whether for an RV or tent. Reservations can be made only by snail mail! No e-mail or phone reservations are accepted, but to ask questions call (847) 662-4811. If you're not into roughing it, try the accommodations at the **Illinois Beach Resort and Conference Center,** and see if you can get a room overlooking the scenic beachscape. The resort is located at One Lake Front Drive; (847) 625-7300; www.ilresorts.com.

The ***North Point Marina*** is the largest marina on the Great Lakes, with 1,500 slips built on a state-of-the-art floating dock and configured to provide protection from Lake Michigan's notoriously choppy waters. The marina is located at 701 N. Point Dr., Winthrop Harbor; (847) 746-2845.

The northern part of Illinois is graced with eleven natural lakes of varying sizes, seven of which are linked by the Fox River. The perimeter of the ***Chain O'Lakes State Park*** encircles four of the larger bodies of water: ***Grass Lake, Marie Lake, Turner Lake,*** and ***Nippersink Lake.*** This area is a haven for water sports, hiking, camping, and picnicking. The park is open every day except Christmas and for registered hunters during hunting season only, from Nov 1 to Dec 15. Hours vary according to the seasons: Apr 1 through Oct 31, 6 a.m. to 9 p.m., and winter hours are from 8 a.m. to dusk; 8916 Wilmont Rd., Spring Grove; (847) 587-5512.

While in ***Spring Grove,*** stop at ***Richardson Farm,*** where corn mazes rule. For more than a decade, the farm has constructed what might very well be the largest corn mazes in the world. Some have covered twenty-eight acres, which translates to more than 11 miles of trails cut into the fields. Half of the fun is the yearly theme. Don't worry about getting lost, though; the trails are broken into segments so you can escape if you need a break. The farm is open from Aug 1 to Nov 1 on Wed and Thurs from 3 to 10 p.m., Fri from 3 to 11 p.m., Sat from 10 a.m. to 11 p.m., and Sun from noon to 10 p.m.; closed Mon and Tues unless it's Labor or Columbus Day, and all days depend on weather permitting; admission is $11.50 for adults, $10.00 for students, $8.50 for children and seniors, and free for kids under age four; additional fees are charged for extra activities; 9407 Richardson Rd.; (815) 675-9729; www.richard sonfarm.com.

In the village of ***Volo,*** there are more cars on display at the thirty-acre ***Volo Auto Museum*** than there are residents (about two hundred) calling that far western corner of ***Lake County*** home. Over three hundred classic vehicles are displayed in four buildings of a complex that includes antiques, a food court, a grassy park, and artisan and mercantile mall. Hollywood favorites stand among the beauties, but why just look? If you can afford the rental fee, you can drive the 1966 Batmobile, the 1973 Ferrari Daytona featured in *Miami Vice,* or even the 1966 Lincoln Continental "Deathmobile" from the movie *Animal House.* The museum is open daily from 10 a.m. to 5 p.m.; admission is $9 for adults, $7 for seniors, $5 for children ages five through twelve, and free for children under five. (815) 385-3644; www.volocars.com.

The ***Lake County Discovery Museum*** in ***Wauconda*** gets high marks for its versatility in teaching history in a way that appeals to most everyone. Hands-on displays encourage participation. A popular feature is the "vortex roller coaster" theater, which "transports" visitors into prehistoric Illinois. Rotating displays of the museum's 1.5 million-piece American postcard collection, circa 1878–1975, give a unique perspective of history through this ever-popular form of communication. The museum is open Mon through Sat from 11 a.m. to 4:30 p.m. and Sun from 1 to 4:30 p.m.; admission is $6.00 for adults and $2.50 for children ages four through seventeen; on Discount Tuesdays adults pay $3.00 and children are admitted for free; 27277 N. Forest Preserve Rd.; (847) 968-3400; www.lcfpd.org/discovery_museum.

Visitors are invited to celebrate living off the land at the museum's **Farm Heritage Festival.** Antique tractors, machinery, and farming tools are on display, and demonstrations of sheep herding, live music, and wagon and train rides are part of the fun. The festival is held in late-Sept; admission is $8 for adults, $4 for children ages four through seventeen and seniors, and free for children ages three and under; (847) 968-3400.

They call it the "Village of Yesteryear," and that's a good description for the hamlet of **Richmond,** where the dedicated citizens have maintained and renovated nearly forty homes and downtown buildings, many that were originally built in the 1850s. Walk or drive the town with the help of an official **Richmond Tour** booklet or CD, which are available for purchase at City Hall and downtown stores. Don't miss the **Wooden Railroad Trestle Bridge,** more than a century old, just outside of town.

ringsofthepast

As you tread the streets of Richmond, the "Village of Yesteryear," look down to see the hitching rings embedded in the sidewalk; in bygone days this is where horsemen tethered their steeds.

There are plenty of antiques shops tucked between the specialty stores, but note that most are closed on Monday. A favorite is **Anderson's Candy Shop,** which has been producing hand-dipped chocolates since 1919. Their meltaway fudge and English toffee have earned them the title "Best in the State." The shop is open Tues through Sat from 9 a.m. to 5 p.m. and Sun from noon to 5 p.m.; 10301 Main St.; (815) 678-6000; www.andersonscandyshop.com.

For a tasty Irish-American meal, visit **Doyle's Pub,** which is housed in a section of an old mill. The inviting wraparound porch is cozy, and weekday specials include a prime-rib dinner and traditional Friday fish fry. The pub is located at 5604 Mill St.; (815) 678-3623; www.doylespubrocks.com.

The end of summer ritual here is called the **Round-Up Days Festival.** Take in the music, food, and special exhibits of quilts, local crafts, and arts. The festival is held the last weekend of Aug; admission is free; located along city streets; (815) 678-4040; www.richmond-il.com.

Possibly **McHenry County's** most recognizable town is its county seat of **Woodstock.** Chances are that when you see the town square with its unusual gazebo, you'll have a sense of déjà vu. Movie fans might recognize this location from the 1993 film *Groundhog Day* starring Bill Murray.

The novelty of posing as Punxsutawney, Pennsylvania, continues today with Woodstock's own **Groundhog Days Celebration.** The festivities include a parade, a walking tour of movie sites including the bed-and-breakfast featured in the film, a free screening of the movie, and the weather prognostication of local groundhog celebrity Woodstock Willie. There's food and music, too. The celebration is held the weekend around the national holiday of Feb 2; admission is free. Located downtown; contact City Hall, (815) 338-4301 or McHenry County Convention and Visitors Bureau, (815) 363-6177; www.woodstockil.gov.

Listed in the National Register of Historic Places, the **Woodstock Opera House** is the year-round home of the Woodstock Musical Theatre Company and former stage for many notable alumni, including Bill Murray, Buddy Rich,

groundhog lighting

There's one event Punxsutawney, Pennsylvania, doesn't have at its official Groundhog Day celebration that Woodstock does: the official "lighting of the groundhog statue," which is stationed on top of the ornate Woodstock Opera House. Much like the illumination of a community Christmas tree, a crowd gathers to *ooh* and *aah* when the light switch is flipped.

Geraldine Page, Glenn Miller, Dizzy Gillespie, and John Ashton. Built in 1889, the theater has been lovingly preserved and updated to provide audiences with a state-of-the-art experience. Hours and admission vary per production. 121 W. Van Buren St.; (815) 338-4212; www .woodstockoperahouse.com.

If you're looking for a nice place to spend the night, this area is flush with great bed-and-breakfast establishments. Two are worth mentioning here. **The Bundling Board Inn Bed and Breakfast** is a 1910 Queen Anne with classic Victorian interior located about 3 blocks from downtown. Their chocolate cherry pecan cookies, baked from a private recipe, will transport you out of this world. If you have a group that books three or more rooms, they'll host a Death by Chocolate Slumber Party for you. The B&B is located at 220 E. South St.; (815) 338-7054; www.bundlingboard.com. Another recommendation is the **Alexandria House Bed and Breakfast,** an 1865 home that blends antiques and collectibles with more modern carpeting and wall colors, and satisfies completely with comfortable parlor and bed chambers. Awaken to a gourmet candlelight breakfast served on fine china. If you care to bring your friends, they offer a Murder Mystery night, complete with vintage costumes provided for role-playing. Six participants are required to solve the "Whodunit?" The Alexandria House is located at 315 Dean St.; (815) 206-5000; www.alexandria bnb.com.

The quaint town of *Union* is steeped in history, starting with the *McHenry County Historical Museum*, which sits right in the middle of town. The complex includes a research library, the 1847 *Gannon Log Cabin*, which was the home of one of the town's founders, and the 1895 one-room *Harmony School*, which is staffed with costumed interpreters. The main museum houses exhibits relating to the Civil War, women's fashion, and prairie needlework, including a fine quilt collection. The museum is open May to Oct, Tue through Fri from 1 to 4 p.m. and Sun from 1 to 4 p.m.; admission is $5 for adults and $3 for seniors and children; the family rate (two adults and two or more children is $12; 6422 Main St.; (815) 923-2267; www.mchsonline.org.

The society also sponsors special events on the museum grounds, with the annual *Cider Festival* being one of the largest. There's live music, harvest demonstrations, farming displays, a white elephant sale, ample baked goods, and of course, fresh apple cider. The festival is held the first weekend of Oct, beginning at 11 a.m., with an antique tractor parade at 1 p.m.; admission is free; 6422 Main St.; (815) 923-2267; www.mchsonline.org.

If you suddenly think you're feeling a rumbling beneath your feet, it's probably coming from just outside of town at the *Illinois Railway Museum.* Home to the nation's largest collection of railway equipment, the fifty-six acre campus holds more than 400 pieces of historic railway objects, including diesel and steam engines, interurbans, elevated cars from Chicago's famous "L," streetcars, and a classic silver Burlington Zephyr streamliner. This isn't just a walk-through museum. Every day they offer rides so that guests will experience the excitement of the roaring thunder and whistles produced by these grand machines. And one of the most amazing things about this museum is that it's completely manned by volunteers.

The museum hosts a number of special events during the summer months, with the most popular being the Fourth of July *Trolley Pageant* and the mid-August *Day Out with Thomas the Train.* Trains operate daily June through Aug, but only on weekends in Apr, May, Sept, and Oct. On weekends the grounds are open 9 a.m. to 6 p.m., but park operations don't begin until 10:30 a.m. and end at 5 p.m. On weekdays the grounds open at 10 a.m. and close at 5 p.m., and park operations begin at 10 a.m. and end at 4 p.m. Admission includes unlimited rides; prices depend on the season, ranging from $8 to $12 for adults and $4 to $8 for children; a one-price pass option helps with the cost for larger families. Call for special-events pricing. 7000 Olson Rd.; (815) 923-4000; www.irm.org.

Now it's time to dust off your cowboy boots and head south of Union to a different kind of settlement: *Donley's Wild West Town.* Stroll the "Street of Yesteryear" and check out the old-time saloon, blacksmith shop, and nickelodeon. Take lessons in cow roping or practice your skills in archery, tomahawk toss, or Huck Finn's favorite, the slingshot. There are OK Corral pony rides, a little kids' canoe water ride, and a petting zoo, too. Have a cowboy's favorite meal at the *Old West Steakhouse;* then, with your belly full, gather round to watch a Wild West gunfight reenacted by professional stuntmen who shoot it out from rooftops and dramatically fall from porches. You'll have to remind the kids not to try this at home! If you're feeling pretty, stop by the photography studio for a sepia-toned image of yourself dressed in provided vintage attire. And if you're lookin' to get rich, head over to the *Sweet Phyllis Mine* to pan for gold (pyrite); they'll even provide you with a souvenir bag to carry your riches. Donley's Wild West Town is open daily from Memorial Day through Labor Day and weekends only in Sept and Oct. Hours are from 10 a.m. to 6 p.m., with gunfight shows at noon and 2 and 4:30 p.m.; admission is $15 for everyone over two years old and free for those under two. 8512 S. Union Rd.; (815) 923-9000; www.wildwesttown.com.

Places to Stay in Northeastern Illinois

ELMHURST

Holiday Inn
624 N. York Rd.
(630) 279-1100
www.hielmhurst.com

GENEVA

The Herrington
15 S. River Lane
(630) 208-7433
www.herringtoninn.com

LAKE FOREST

Deer Path Inn
255 E. Illinois Rd.
(847) 234-2280
www.dpihotel.com

LINCOLNSHIRE

Marriott Lincolnshire Resort
10 Marriott Dr.
(847) 634-0100
www.marriott.com

LISLE

Hilton Lisle/Naperville
3003 Corporate West Dr.
(630) 505-0900
www1.hilton.com

Hyatt Lisle
1400 Corporetum Dr.
(630) 852-1234
http://lisle.hyatt.com

LOMBARD

Embassy Suites
707 E. Butterfield Rd.
(630) 969-7500
http://embassysuites1
.hilton.com

MUNDELEIN

Round-Robin Bed and Breakfast Inn
231 E. Maple Ave.
(SR 176)
(847) 566-7664
www.roundrobininn.com

SELECTED VISITORS BUREAUS AND CHAMBERS OF COMMERCE

Illinois Bureau of Tourism—Travel Information
(800) 2-CONNECT (226-6328)

DuPage Area Convention and Visitors Bureau
915 Harger Rd., Suite 240
Oak Brook, 60523
(630) 575-8070

Elgin Area Convention and Visitors Bureau
77 Riverside Dr.
Elgin, 60120
(847) 695-7540

Heritage Corridor Convention and Visitors Bureau
339 W. Jefferson St.
Joliet, 60435
(800) 926-2262

Lake County Convention and Visitors Bureau
5465 W. Grand Ave., Suite 100
Gurnee, 60031
(847) 662-2700

Oak Park Visitors Bureau
1118 Westgate St.
Oak Park, 60301
(708) 524-7800

St. Charles Convention and Visitors Bureau
311 N. Second St., Suite 101
St. Charles, 60174
(630) 377-6161

Illinois Bureau of Tourism
www.enjoyillinois.com

NAPERVILLE

Fairfield Inn by Marriott
1820 Abriter Court
(630) 577-1820
www.marriott.com

Hampton Inn
1087 E. Diehl Rd.
(630) 505-1400
www.chicagonaperville
.hamptoninn.com

Holiday Inn Select
1801 N. Naper Blvd.
(630) 505-4900
www.hiselect.com

OAK PARK

Under the Ginkgo Tree Bed and Breakfast
300 N. Kenilworth Ave.
(708) 524-2327
www.undertheginkgotree
bb.com

The Write Inn
211 N. Oak Park Ave.
(708) 383-4800
www.writeinn.com

SCHAUMBURG

Hotel Indigo Chicago—Schaumburg North
920 E. Northwest Hwy.
(847) 359-6900
www.hotelschaumburg
.com

ST. CHARLES

Hotel Baker
100 W. Main St.
(630) 584-2100
www.hotelbaker.com

WAUKEGAN

Ramada Inn
200 N. Green Bay Rd.
(847) 244-2400
www.ramada.com

ZION

Illinois Beach Resort and Conference Center
1 Lake Front Dr.
(847) 625-7300
www.ilresorts.com

Places to Eat in Northeastern Illinois

EVANSTON

Blind Faith Café
525 Dempster St.
(847) 328-6875
www.blindfaithcafe.com

Oceanique
505 Main St.
(847) 864-3435
www.oceanique.com

Pete Miller's Steakhouse
1557 Sherman Ave.
(847) 328-0399
www.petemillers.com

GENEVA

Mill Race Inn
4 East State St.
(630) 232-2030
www.themillraceinn.com

LAKE FOREST

Deer Path Inn
255 E. Illinois Rd.
(847) 234-2280
www.dpihotel.com

Egg Harbor Cafe
512 N. Western Ave.
(847) 295-3449
www.eggharborcafe.com

Organic Wellness Cafe
950 N. Western Ave.,
Unit B
(847) 535-9920
www.organicwellness
cafe.com

LIBERTYVILLE

The Country Inn Restaurant of Lambs Farm
I-94 and SR 176
(847) 362-5050
www.lambsfarm.org/
business/restaurant.html

Wildberry Pancakes and Cafe
1783 N. Milwaukee Ave.
(847) 247-7777
http://wildberrycafe.com

MCHENRY

Le Vichyssois
220 Rand Rd. (West Route 120), Lakemoor
(815) 385-8221
www.levichyssois.com

NAPERVILLE

BD's Mongolian Barbeque
221 S. Washington St.
(630) 428-0300
www.gomongo.com

Meson Sabika Tapas
1025 Aurora Ave.
(630) 983-3000
www.mesonsabika.com

Sullivan's Steakhouse
244 S. Main St.
(630) 305-0230
www.sullivanssteak
house.com

Traverso's Restaurant
2523 Naperville-
Plainfield Rd.
(630) 305-7747
www.traversosrestaurant
.com

ROMEOVILLE

White Fence Farm
1376 Joliet Rd.
(630) 739-1720
www.whitefencefarm.com

ST. CHARLES

Francesca's by the River
200 S. Second St.
(630) 587-8221
http://miafrancesca.com

VERNON HILLS

Tsukasa of Tokyo
561 N. Milwaukee Ave.
(847) 816-8770
www.tsukasaoftotkyo.com

WHEATON

Suzette's Creperie
211 W. Front St.
(630) 462-0898
www.suzettescreperie.com

WHEELING

Bob Chinn's Crab House
393 S. Milwaukee Ave.
(847) 520-3633
www.bobchinns.com

Don Roth's Blackhawk
61 N. Milwaukee Ave.
(847) 537-5800
www.theblackhawk.com

WILMETTE

Walker Bros. Original Pancake House
153 Green Bay Rd.
(847) 251-6000
www.walkerbros.net

NORTHWESTERN ILLINOIS

Lead Rush

The northwestern part of Illinois owes its legacy to lead. Most of us know the story of the California Gold Rush. Well, much like the craze that spurred the rapid settlement of the far western U.S., the discovery of lead in the mines surrounding *Galena* brought scores of workers eager to purchase land and dig their claim. The interesting thing about it is that this "lead rush" took place a good twenty years before the gold rush, yet most history books omit this American story. The first flatboat of locally mined ore was sent down the Mississippi River in 1816, and by the 1830s about 85 percent of the nation's lead was mined from the Galena area. Even the choice of the name *Galena* is tied to the earth, as it is Latin for the phrase "lead sulfide."

The early settlers to this neck of the woods were a rough and ready crowd, driven to exhaustion and often using primitive tools to extract their quarry in hopes of making quick cash. Even with the fees charged for leases and royalties by the Federal Lead Mine District, wealth grew, as did the population. Mansions dotted the hillsides surrounding the downtown

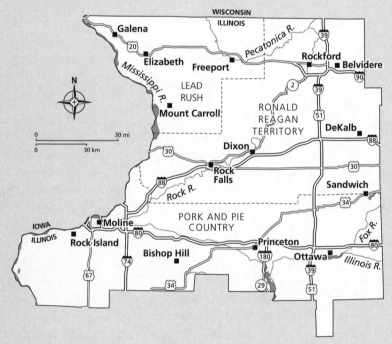

WISCONSIN

ILLINOIS

Galena

Pecatonica R.

39

20

Elizabeth

Freeport

Rockford

Belvidere

Mississippi R.

2

39

90

N

LEAD
RUSH

RONALD
REAGAN
TERRITORY

51

Mount Carroll

DeKalb

0   30 mi

0   30 km

30

Dixon

88

Rock
Falls

30

Rock R.

Sandwich

88

34

PORK AND PIE
COUNTRY

IOWA

Moline

80

ILLINOIS

Fox R.

80

Rock Island

Princeton

Ottawa

Illinois R.

74

Bishop Hill

180

39

67

34

29

51

business district, and Galena became a vital business center and county seat of *Jo Daviess County.* Today, over a million visitors stop in Galena.

The obvious starting point is about 8 miles outside of town at the *Vinegar Hill Historic Lead Mine & Museum,* the only historic mine in the area with clearance for public tours. First worked in 1822, the land and mine have remained in the Furlong family for more than three generations. The tour guide takes visitors more than 200 feet into the tunnel, and at the deepest point it's over 50 feet below ground. The museum displays various tools, the windless shaft where the ore was lifted from beneath the ground, ore samples, and family photos that make this museum more intimate than most. The museum is open from 9 a.m. to 5 p.m., daily from June through Aug and only on Sat and Sun in May, Sept, and Oct; admission is $5.00 for adults, $2.50 for students, and free for children under age five; 8885 N. Three Pines Rd.; (815) 777-0855.

Before exploring downtown Galena's many antique shops and pleasant restaurants, stop first at the *Galena History Museum,* which is housed in the redbrick 1858 Italianate *Daniel Barrows Mansion.* View exhibits about

AUTHOR'S TOP TEN PICKS

Galena
Illinois
(877) GO-GALENA (464-2536)
www.galena.org

Starved Rock State Park
Utica
(815) 667-4726
www.starvedrockstatepark.org

Bishop Hill State Historic Site
Bishop Hill
(309) 927-3345
www.bishophill.com

John Deere Historic Site
Grand Detour
(815) 652-4551
www.deere.com/en_US/attractions/historicsite

Oregon
Illinois
(815) 732-2100
www.oregonil.com

White Pines Forest State Park
Mt. Morris
(815) 946-3717
http://dnr.state.il.us

Tinker Swiss Cottage Museum
Rockford
(815) 964-2424
www.tinkercottage.com

Sandwich Antiques Market
Sandwich
(815) 786-3337

Magic Waters Water Park
Cherry Valley
(815) 966-2442
www.magicwaterswaterpark.com

Apple River Fort State Historic Site
Elizabeth
(815) 858-2028
www.appleriverfort.org

the town's early history and register for a one-hour walking tour that runs on Sat at 10 a.m. from May to Oct or by appointment; the cost is $5 per person. The museum is open daily except for major holidays from 9 a.m. to 4:30 p.m.; admission is $4.50 for adults and $3.50 for children ages ten through eighteen. 211 S. Bench St.; (815) 777-9129; www.galenahistorymuseum.org.

Sitting high on the hill overlooking downtown Galena is the modest, but stately, Federal–style **Ulysses S. Grant Home.** After the Civil War, Grant returned to a hero's welcome in Galena. This private residence was purchased for the Grants by a group of prominent Galena citizens and given to them as part of the general's homecoming celebration. The Grant children bequeathed the property to the city of Galena in 1904, with instructions that the home be maintained as a memorial to their father, but the financial burden of maintaining the estate forced the city to deed the property to the state. Many of the items inside belonged to the Grant family. The house is open Apr to Oct, Wed through Sun from 9 a.m. to 4:45 p.m., and Nov through Mar, Wed through Sun from 9 a.m. to 4 p.m.; donations are requested; 500 Bouthillier St.; (815) 777-3310; www.granthome.com.

Many of the homes built during the lead boom are still standing in Galena, a fact that makes this area a hot tourist attraction. The **Belvedere Mansion** is just one of the notable Galena properties that have been lovingly restored. While the decor is a bit eclectic, visitors are transported to a bygone era as soon as the door opens. Tours run daily from late May to Oct, 11 a.m. to 4 p.m.; admission is $10; 1008 Park Ave.; (815) 777-0747.

Another remarkable example of a period home is the **John Dowling Stone House** built in 1826 and recognized as the oldest residence in Galena. Pioneer John Dowling used it as a home for his family and a trading post. The house is open daily for tours from 11 a.m. to 4 p.m.; donations are requested; 200 Diagonal St.; (815) 777-1250.

Repeat Resident

After a fifteen-year military stint and six subsequent miserable years as a business-man, Ulysses S. Grant arrived at Galena in 1860 with his wife and young family. They rented a small house, and Grant joined his brothers to work in their father's leather shop. In June 1861 he received the call to serve as a colonel for the 21st Illinois Volunteer Infantry Regiment at Cairo. Leaving his family in Galena, Grant heeded the request, and by war's end he was the Union general who'd accepted Confederate general Lee's final surrender. When he returned to Galena, his family accepted the town's thank-you gift of a brick home on the hill overlooking the downtown.

The **Old Market House** is a handsome Greek Revival–style, two-story brick building with single-story wings on either side—a favorite architectural style in late-1700s America, although this building was built in 1845. The house was the town's popular meeting spot, much like today's malls, where vendors sold their wares to the citizenry indoors. The building also served as city offices and jail. Stop at the **Galena Welcome Center** information desk here to ask general questions about Galena and view the exhibits by the **Galena-Jo Daviess County Historical Society.**

presidential estate

Ulysses S. Grant visited his Galena home only twice after becoming president. Caretakers maintained the property in anticipation of his eventual return.

Old Market House is open daily from 9 a.m. to 5 p.m.; donations are requested; 123 N. Commerce St.; (815) 777-3310; (the same as Grant's home), www.grant home.com.

Downtown you'll easily spend hours browsing in antiques and gift stores, and unique shops that specialize in European chocolates, rare books, teddy bears, yarn and needlework, toys, candles, beads, and handmade crafts. If you're not into shopping, walk along the river, rent a kayak, or take a paddle-boat ride. When it's time to eat, don't be surprised that most of the restaurants feature late-afternoon opening times: plan to grab nibbles along the way, like fresh-baked bread, cookies, cheese, granola, or other goodies sold in town, and save room for a great evening dinner.

Try **Fried Green Tomatoes** for Italian fare. Housed in the same building where Ulysses S. Grant worked in his father's leather business, the exposed brick and original stenciling on the walls maintain the historical relevance of this building. When you're at Fried Green Tomatoes, you should order the fried green tomatoes! They're lightly breaded and smothered in mozzarella cheese and marinara. Then move to the second course; the lasagna is a house favorite, and the veal *piccata* is melt-in-your-mouth good. Reservations are recommended. The restaurant is open Mon through Thurs from 5 p.m. to closing time and Fri through Sun from 3 p.m. to closing time; 213 N. Main St.; (815) 777-3938; www.friedgreen.com.

For something light and fun, seek out the woman with the pink hair! She's the owner of **Miss Kitty's Grape Escape,** a little hideout that bills itself as a "wine and martini lounge." This place does open earlier, but it's not exactly a family-friendly menu; for instance, there's the Build Your Own Bloody Mary Buffet every Sat from 11 a.m. to 3 p.m. for those who want to start early. Finish with a piece of homemade pie from the local **Huron Farms** that's served here as an exclusive. There's live music every Sat and Sun at 9 p.m. and no cover charge, so consider tipping the band. Miss Kitty's is open Mon through Fri from 5 p.m. to 1 a.m. and Sat and Sun from 11 a.m. to 1 a.m. 233 S. Main St.; (815) 776-9463; www.grapeescapegalena.com.

Grape growers have discovered that this area of the state provides excellent conditions for bountiful crops, and several wineries have taken root here. The vintners of the Lawlor family are in their third generation as owners of two popular wineries. The **Galena Cellars Winery** inhabits an 1840s granary that is easy to find as it's the first building inside the city's protective floodgates. Pause in the tasting room to test the local products. The family-owned business produces 60,000 gallons a year and grows over twenty types of grapes in its vineyard. The winery is open Jan through May, Mon through Thurs and on Sun from 9 a.m. to 6 p.m., and Fri and Sat from 9 a.m. to 8 p.m.; 515 S. Main St.; (815) 777-3330.

After browsing the store, head to the **Galena Cellars Vineyard,** about 6 miles outside of town, for a vineyard tour. They also have a cozy guesthouse or bedroom suite if you'd like to spend the night among the purple. The vineyard is open Mon through Thurs from noon to 6 p.m. and Fri through Sun from 11 a.m. to 8 p.m.; call for tour times and reservations; tours cost $5 and include wine tasting; 4826 N. Ford Rd.; (815) 777-3235; www.galenacellars.net.

Galena boasts more than thirty bed-and-breakfast inns, making it a premier "getaway" destination. Take your pick from a log cabin, a B&B overlooking the river, or one up on the hill for a grand view of downtown; there's lodging for every whim and taste. Because of all the competition, innkeepers work very hard to ensure that their patrons are happy. Listings can be obtained at the Information Center at the **Old Train Depot** (101 Bouthillier St.; 877-444-5805; www.galena.org) or the Galena Welcome Center at the Old Market House (123 N. Commerce St.; 815-777-3310; www.visitgalena.org or www .galenachamber.com).

Here are two recommendations from personal experience: If you ever wanted to sleep in a turret room, ask for the Anna Suite at the stunning 1893 **Queen Anne on Park Avenue.** The beds are sweet-dreams comfortable, the antique decor is interesting and fun (check out the antique purse collection and the 225-piece Dickens Village), and the breakfast will wow you. Don't forget to leave time to relax on the wraparound screened porch and stroll through the lovely Victorian garden with a gazebo and fountain. The B&B is located at 208 Park Ave.; (815) 777-1078; www.galenaparkavenue.com.

Another great pick is the **Steamboat House Bed and Breakfast,** a Gothic Revival mansion built in 1855—talk about spacious! There are nine bedrooms, with seven baths and fireplaces, spread over three floors with over

7,000 square feet of living space. This was the former home of steamboat captain Daniel Smith Harris and his wife, Sarah. The Steamboat House is located at 605 S. Prospect St.; (815) 777-2317; www.thesteamboathouse.com.

One of the more unusual and often overlooked sites in town is **The Old Stockade.** This was once a refuge for settlers hoping to escape an impending attack during the Black Hawk War of 1832. The owner of the property serves as the tour guide and is extremely knowledgeable about 1800s Galena, as well as the home and history of the stockade. The site is open Sat from 1 to 4 p.m.; donations are requested; 208 Perry St.; (815) 777-1222; www.cjart.net/stockade.htm.

Following Route 20 south of Galena, you'll see a 100-foot-high observation post called the **Long Hollow Tower.** Built by the Illinois Department of Transportation in 1984, this timber platform, with its 180 round-trip of stairs, is well worth the climb: The view is an unspoiled 360 degrees of rolling Jo Daviess County. Pause to take photos here, and then share a picnic at one of the nearby tables at the park below.

harrisfamily

Steamboat captain Daniel Smith Harris married a talented, complex woman—Sarah Harris. She became a physician at age fifty, specializing in the era's taboo subject of women's ailments, and she opened her house to the Underground Railroad. In her spare time, she concentrated on her hobby of studying and cultivating roses.

Now that you've practically seen it by air, it's time to drive the rest of the way to the farming town of **Elizabeth,** a small community of about 600 people. During the 1832 Black Hawk War, this rural hamlet was considered vulnerable, so the citizenry constructed the **Apple River Fort.** It was a smart move, as Black Hawk himself led a raid on the town with over one hundred of his men, forcing the townsfolk to take refuge inside the walls of the small timber fort. Legend has it that a woman named Elizabeth coordinated the return fire that repelled the attack, and thereafter the village became known as Elizabeth in her honor. Today, the **Apple River Fort State Historic Site** stands on the footprint of that original fort, and visitors can learn the story of the incursion at the reception center, then walk the short distance to tour the fort. The historic site is open Wed through Sun from 9 to 5 p.m., but call before visiting as hours can vary; donations are requested; (815) 858-2028.

Nearby is the **Chicago Great Western Railroad Depot,** an 1888 building on the National Register of Historic Places. This depot served as the center of commerce and transportation for the area, and today visitors can see the restored waiting room and view exhibits chronicling the story of the railway nicknamed the "Maple Leaf Route" because of the pattern outlined by the rails overland. The depot is open Sat and Sun from 11 a.m. to 5 p.m., but it's wise to call ahead; donations are requested. South Myrtle Street; (815) 858-2343.

Another history-related site is the **Elizabeth History Museum,** which contains a personal set of exhibits covering village history, lead mining, and the family stories of local settlers. The museum is open weekends, May through Oct, 11 a.m. to 3 p.m.; 231 N. Main St.; (815) 858-3355.

Downtown Elizabeth features little shops, a grocery store, and a historic church used as a wedding chapel. There's also an unexpected artistic community here, almost hidden unless you know to look for it: This area is home to a number of nationally known artists and artisans who specialize in painting, drawing, bronze work, carving, and pottery.

Meet Paul Eshelman of **Eshelman Pottery.** From his studio in an 80-plus-year-old brick building, Paul has been creating pottery for more than twenty years. His work is both functional and artful, with diverse inspiration drawn from various cultures, including American Shaker and Chinese. When you visit, take special note of his unique red-stone pottery. The studio is open 9 a.m. to 5 p.m.; 238 N. Main St.; call ahead at (815) 858-2327; www.eshelmanpottery.com.

At **Studiowork** you'll find Adrienne Seagraves creating her pottery; her shop features paintings and other artwork by local artists. The shop is open daily, but hours may vary so call ahead. 130 N. Main St.; (815) 858-3588.

After a long day of golfing, sightseeing, or shopping, wouldn't it be nice to relax and have a nice homemade dinner? For a twist on the typical bed-and-breakfast, try the **Dinner and Dreams Guesthouse and Antiques,** where you can shop in their fine first-floor antiques store before your hosts treat you to a specially prepared evening meal. The attic of this hundred-plus-year-old home has a great family room, and the wraparound porch is a nice place to enjoy your coffee. Oh, and they serve a continental breakfast, too. The B&B is located at 120 W. Main St.; (815) 858-2357; www.dinneranddreamsinc.com.

In the rolling hills outside of downtown Elizabeth, you'll find another popular vineyard called **Massbach Ridge Winery.** In the grand scheme of grape growing, this business is relatively new, but they've already garnered gold metals and recognition for their wines. The eighteen-acre vineyard and mountain and valley views from their front porch are well worth the drive, but don't forget to sample their Traumen, a multiple gold–winning sweet red; and just ask and they'll give you a tour. The winery is open Mon through Sat from 11 a.m. to 5 p.m. and Sun from noon to 5 p.m.; the tasting fee is $3; 8837 S. Massbach Rd., Elizabeth; (815) 291-6700; www.massbachridge.com.

Now on to the Mallard Capital of the World: **Hanover** is home to the **Whistling Wings Duck Hatchery,** said to be the largest duck hatchery in the world. Hundreds of thousands of mallards are raised here yearly and sold, typically for release into the wild. The hatchery isn't open to the public, but a gift store sells wildlife souvenirs and items that celebrate the mallard. The hatchery is located at 113 Washington St.; (815) 591-3512.

In early fall Hanover celebrates **Mallardfest,** a community party that includes a picnic, parade, live music, and fireworks along the banks of the Apple River. The height of the event is the duck-calling contest, so start practicing! The event is held on Fri and Sat in mid-Sept, 9 a.m. to dusk; located at White Park on the south side of the Apple River; contact Village Hall at 207 Jefferson St.; (815) 591-3800; www.hanover-il.com.

Before you leave town, make certain to stop at the **Crescent Falls Dam** and pause to listen to the calming roar of the water.

Mount Carroll, the county seat of **Carroll County,** received its name from Charles Carroll, who signed the Declaration of Independence while a representative of Maryland. The town is a snapshot of late 1800s architecture, and the **Mount Carroll Historic District,** with its **Mesker Brothers** nineteenth-century facades, is listed in the National Register of Historic Places and thought to be among the finest preserved districts in the U.S. The **Mount Carroll Chamber of Commerce** provides self-guided walking-tour maps. 18939 Timber Lake Rd.; (815) 244-2255; www.mtcarrollil.org.

The **Owen P. Miles Museum** is a grand 1873 Italianate mansion that is also home to the **Carroll County Historical Society.** The museum features county-related exhibits, and daily house tours are available. The museum is open Mon, Tues, Thurs, and Fri and every other weekend from 10 a.m. to 2 p.m.; donations are requested; 107 W. Broadway; (815) 244-3474.

Mount Carroll's annual **Mayfest** celebration is filled with live music, art, food, and sports activities at the Campbell Center. The event is held Memorial Day weekend; 600 S. College St.; (815) 244-2411; www.mount-carroll.il.us.

Enter the **Mount Carroll City Hall** to see the **USS Hissem brass bell.** Native son ensign Joseph Metcalf Hissem received the Navy Cross and the Purple Heart for his actions during the Battle of Midway in 1942. A Navy

Annex Addition

The centerpiece of the Mount Carroll city square is the **Civil War Memorial,** which has been recognized as the only known military monument that includes an annex. Apparently, a design oversight caused the original structure to be too small to accommodate the 1,284 names of local soldiers, so an addition was required. The uniqueness of the annex caused this tribute to be recognized by *Ripley's Believe It or Not.* It's thought that Illinois artist Lorado Taft sculpted the statue on top of the monolith.

destroyer escort ship (DE-400) was christened the USS *Hissem* in his honor and sailed the world's waters for more than thirty years before being decommissioned. At that time, the U.S. Navy presented the ship's bell to the city of Mount Carroll. City Hall is open Mon through Fri from 8:30 a.m. to 4:30 p.m.; 302 N. Main St.; (815) 244-4424.

Allow yourself time to enjoy a picnic lunch at *Point Rock Park;* then play a round of Frisbee golf along the banks of the Wakarusa River. And while you take a leisurely hike, you might see kayakers lazily floating down the river or fishermen catching smallmouth bass.

Is it real or is it fake? That's what you'll be asking as you approach the wild-looking house called *The Raven's Grin Inn.* Yes, there's a car on the roof, and a giant skeleton head with working jaw sitting next to the front door. Owner Jim Warfield's house tour has become a local legend. From the outside to the inside, it's a combination of performance art, mind games, and haunting; you decide if the haunting is real! Warfield himself acts as the guide for this sensory-packed extravaganza. Tour times are daily from 7 p.m. to midnight, plus matinees on Sat and Sun from 2 to 5 p.m.; all performances require reservations; admission is $12; 411 N. Carroll St.; (815) 244-4746; www .hauntedravensgrin.com.

Museum and archivist professionals arrive at the *Campbell Center for Historic Preservation Studies* from all over the world to learn how to restore, protect, and maintain their collections. This unusual educational facility is housed in what was formerly Shimer College, founded in 1853. If you have the time and patience to learn the delicate arts of protecting leather and cleaning dust from oil paintings, this might be the school for you. The center is located at 203 E. Seminary Dr.; (815) 244-1173; www.campbell center.org.

Sharing the campus is another unique venture called the *Learn Great Foods Culinary Adventure;* it's a foodies nirvana and eco-friendly, too. Sign up for a week retreat, a culinary day tour, or just a few hours of tasting; a tour might include visiting organic gardens or a buffalo farm, meeting the farmers and walking the farm, then returning to the school to cook a healthy meal at the elbow of a professional chef, using fresh ingredients from the gardens. There's also a chocolate adventure with classes taught by professional candy makers. Healthy never tasted so good! Learn Great Foods is located at 203 E. Seminary Dr.; (866) 240-1650; www.learngreatfoods.com.

If you need some drama in your life, the *Timber Lake Playhouse* will fit the playbill. The semiprofessional summer theater performs multiple productions during the summer months for adults, with special presentations directed toward children. The comfortable theater seats 375, and you can choose from matinee or evening shows. It's best to purchase tickets in advance. The season runs from June 1 to late Aug; 8215 Black Oak Rd.; (815) 244-2035; www .timberlakeplayhouse.org.

The *Timber Lake Resort* (not affiliated with the playhouse but essentially next door) is a modern camping facility with space for RV and camper-type camping and cute one- and two-bedroom Lincoln log–style cabins with all the comforts of home except the pots and pans and the stove (cooking is outside only). There are 200 wooded acres to roam, an eleven-acre lake suitable for canoeing and paddleboats, a general store, swimming pool, and planned activities every weekend such as an annual lighted boat parade, Christmas in July, and Mardi Gras. The resort is located at 8216 Black Oak Rd.; (815) 244-1600; www.timberlakeresort.com.

Traveling east of Mount Carroll, you'll find *Lanark,* another small town where time seems to have stopped. Though the town was founded in 1861, many of the downtown buildings are older, but they're well maintained and interesting examples of early architecture. Lanark might seem like the last place to find descendents of the Pilgrim Miles Standish, but the owners of the *Standish House Bed and Breakfast* are just that. The home is a 1882 Queen Anne–style building, but the tales from the hosts are rooted more in the 1620s. Guests will enjoy the English and American antiques and the Irish details throughout the home, and the breakfasts are highly enjoyed, too. The Standish House is located at 540 W. Carroll St.; (815) 493-2307.

The bed-and-breakfast also hosts the official croquet tournament during Lanark's summer festival called *Old Settlers Days.* Other events over the three-day celebration are held throughout the town and city park, and include a kiddie tractor pull, books and crafts sale, live music, an old-fashioned cake-walk, outdoor movie, and pork chop dinner. The event is held the last week of June; 108 W. Carroll St.; (815) 493-2431; www.lanarkil.com.

Southeast of Lanark is *Roger's Creek Grist Mill* in Milledgeville. This is a green operation—the owners have repurposed a 1922 mill that they moved to their property. They then collected the necessary working parts and equipment from throughout the Midwest to get the mill up and producing stone-ground whole flours and grains. Mixes for muffins and pancakes as well as freshly ground flour are available for sale in the tiny shop. Note: The mill is modest and located in a residential area, but the products are fun and first-rate. The mill is open only on Sat, and it's wise to call ahead to verify hours; 217 E. Fifth St.; (815) 225-7236; www.rogerscreekgristmill.com.

The *Mississippi River* hasn't always been a good neighbor to the cities that hug its banks; spring is often an anxious time for the town of *Savanna,* especially when the *Plum River* starts flooding, too. But it's a trade-off for the people living in this "sportsman's paradise."

Sitting just to the south of the **Mississippi Palisades State Park,** the area enjoys easy access to the 2,500-acre preserve and all of the activities it offers, from fishing, hunting, and hiking to cross-country skiing and sledding. The park is open from dawn to dusk; 16327A Rte. 84, Savanna; (815) 273-2731. Fishing is viable year-round, and the **Savanna Marina** downtown provides launch ramps at reasonable rates so boaters can take full advantage of the river. Those less into sports can take a leisurely walk in **Marquette Park** and watch the **Delta Queen** *riverboat* arrive from Dubuque, Iowa, and deliver passengers for shopping downtown.

Savanna has dozens of nooks and stores, and a few are worth a mention. Don't miss the **321 Art Gallery,** owned by a consortium of professional artists who work in a variety of mediums and share space in a historic building. Although it's not artistic in the strict sense, **The Plum-Patch** is located in the basement of this building and it's a source for exceptional handmade soaps, lotions, and lip balms, all natural and created without dyes or fragrances added (although some products with scents are available). The gallery is open Wed through Sat from 10 a.m. to 4 p.m. and Sun from 1 to 4 p.m.; 321 Main St.; (815) 273-2781; http://321artgallery.com.

The **Pulford Opera House Antiques Mall** is fun because it's located in a classic vaudeville palace; over 150 dealers sell their wares in the theater's balcony, stage, hallways, and orchestra pit. The mall is open Mon through Thurs from 9:30 a.m. to 5:30 p.m., Fri and Sat from 9:30 a.m. to 8 p.m., and Sun 11 a.m. to 6 p.m.; 324 Main St.; (815) 273-2661.

If you're too tired to drive home, stay at the **Blue Bed and Breakfast,** which sits in the heart of the action; the Mississippi River is visible from the back decks, and the antiques stores and shopping are downstairs and across the street. The B&B is located at 321 Main St.; (815) 541-8684; www.blue bedandbreakfast.com.

Quiet little **Cedarville** is home to one of our nation's most influential activists, although social reformer Jane Addams created change in a manner that was almost as quiet as the town from which she hailed. The 1889 **Cedarville School Museum** houses a permanent exhibit about Jane and hosts numerous changing exhibits that bring fresh insight into her humanitarian work. The museum, staffed by the **Cedarville Area Historical Society,** is open from May to Oct on Sat and Sun from 1 to 4 p.m. and by appointment; admission is free; 450 W. Second St.; (815) 563-4485.

Jane Addams was born in 1860 and lived in a house that still stands in town, but it's a private residence and visitors are not welcome. She founded the Settlement House Movement in the U.S. with the opening of Hull House in Chicago. The work garnered her the 1931 Nobel Peace Prize, but by the time she received word of the honor, she was already suffering from cancer. She died in 1935, and after a funeral on the grounds of Hull House her body was transported to Freeport, then interred in her family's plot near the grave of her beloved father.

To visit Jane's grave, follow Red Oak Road out of town ¼ mile west, past her favorite childhood place, *Cedar Creek,* to the entrance of the *Cedarville Cemetery.* Heed the small signs to the granite obelisk that bears the name Addams, on the right side of the road. Jane's grave lies next to the monument, beneath a stone that modestly describes her in her own words: JANE ADDAMS OF HULL HOUSE AND THE WOMEN'S INTERNATIONAL LEAGUE FOR PEACE AND FREEDOM.

There's a legend that says the town of *Freeport* received its name from the wife of early settler William Baker, who accused her husband of operating a free port for everyone who came into town because he refused to charge riders on his ferry across the *Pecatonica River.* By 1827, most settlers were arriving in Freeport from Pennsylvania and bringing their German tastes with them. A demand for pretzels was filled by the Billerbeck Bakery, which opened in 1869 to produce the favorite treat. As a result, Freeport became known as *"Pretzel City, USA."*

The *Pretzel City Festival* celebrates this tradition with two days of fun, including a pretzel recipe contest, crowning of the Pretzel Prince and Princess, a 5K race, and the Cardboard Boat Regatta, which floats down *Yellow Creek.* The festival is held the last weekend in June; admission is free; located at Krape Park, 1799 S. Park Blvd.; (815) 232-2121 ext. 245; http://pretzelcityusa.org.

And speaking of *Krape Park,* this is a terrific public gathering place where you're greeted by a waterfall churning over a limestone cliff surrounded by densely wooded acreage and peaceful gardens. There's a fishing pier and paddleboat rentals along Yellow Creek, the

thefreeport pretzels

The sports teams at Freeport High School are called the Pretzels, and their mascot, the pretzel, earned them a spot on ESPN's "Most Unusual School Mascot" list.

Yellow Creek Adventure Golf Course, open to all ages for a nominal fee, the *Koenig Amphitheater,* which hosts summer concerts, and the *Krape Park Carousel,* which has provided over two million rides during its fifty-plus-year history; at 25 cents a ride, it's a bargain, too. The park is open during daylight, and the attractions run from early May to late Sept, from noon to dusk; admission is free; 1799 S. Park Blvd.; (815) 235-6114; www.freeportparkdistrict.org.

Play Ball

If you ever dreamed of playing professional baseball, but discovered you just didn't have the arm to make it in the majors, then **Little Cubs Field** is the place for you. Built as an exact replica of the Cubs' Wrigley Field, only smaller, it's accurate down to the color of the brick, the ivy (which was started from ivy cuttings at Wrigley), and the magical marquee. This field, though, was built by volunteers who donated their time, expertise, and materials.

There are thirty features replicated in this mini version, so if you've ever been to the real field, you're bound to see the similarity and feel like this is that hallowed ground. As long as a prearranged game isn't taking place, you're welcome to play, no matter your age. So go ahead—bring your bat and ball (no hard balls though) or stop at the third-base dugout, where balls and bats are available for free use as long as you remember to put them back. Take the mound, start the windup (but hold the spitting), and send that fastball right across the strike zone; then listen to the applause. This is one place where you can still dream! The field is open from Apr to Oct 31; admission is free; 24 W. Stephenson St., Freeport; (815) 233-1350; www.littlecubs field.com.

It was in downtown Freeport during the campaign for the U.S. Senate that Abraham Lincoln met his oppoonent, Stephen A. Douglas, and conveyed a strong opinion regarding slavery. The second Lincoln-Douglas debate took place in Freeport in what is now called **Lincoln-Douglas Debate Square.** That meeting is immortalized today in a life-size bronze sculpture, created by artist Lily Tolpo. It depicts Lincoln sitting and Douglas standing and commemorates the Aug 27, 1858, discussion that put forth Lincoln's *Freeport Doctrine* on slavery. The sculpture is located at the corner of East Douglas Street and North State Avenue.

As the county seat, Freeport hosts the **Stephenson County Courthouse.** A remnant of the former historic building that was replaced by today's modern version is the **Civil War Soldiers Monument,** a stone obelisk that was dedicated in 1871 and features life-size bronze figures of the four branches of the military dressed in Civil War garb. The statue, which is listed on the National Register of Historic Places, is located at 15 N. Galena Ave.; (815) 235-8266.

The **Stephenson County Historical Museum** is home to the Stephenson County Historical Society and contains many artifacts of local interest, but there are two unexpected exhibits worth a look here. The museum owns the largest collection of **Arcade cast-iron toys** in the world. The Arcade Manufacturing Company operated in Freeport from 1885 to 1953 and produced many familiar favorites, such as the 1915 Yellow Cab, the toy Fordson tractor, ladder fire trucks, banks, and horses. Deciding they should expand their line for girls, in 1922 they manufactured miniature kitchen items that copied those that were used by mothers in kitchens all over America: There was the toy food chopper, then the Arcade stove, and finally a cardboard dollhouse outfitted with surprisingly delicate and detailed cast-iron furniture.

The second display that will cause you to linger is of that of the **Dirksen Silver Filigree Company,** which was opened in 1896 on South State Street by a German silversmith named Gerrit Dirksen. After settling in Freeport, he first opened a grocery, but in the back room of his store he practiced his art, creating flatware with open handles that held finely scrolled flowers, leaves, and vines. The museum is open Wed through Sun, from noon to 4 p.m.; admission is $3 for adults and $1 for children ages six through twelve; 1440 S. Carroll Ave.; (815) 232-8419; www.stephcohs.org.

The next place will take some arranging to visit, but it's well worth the effort. The **Critter Camp Exotic Pet Sanctuary** is the only nonprofit licensed animal sanctuary of its kind in the U.S. and home to more than thirty species, and over two hundred abandoned exotic pets. Tours include educational information and touching and holding some of the animals: Meet a fennec fox, African pygmy hedgehog, bearded dragon, or Quaker parrot. The sanctuary is open daily year-round, but appointments are mandatory for the safety of the animals. Admission is $10 per person (tax deductible), but there's also a "work for tour" program in which visitors can earn their entry fee by volunteering for three hours to clean cages; 824 Church St., German Valley; (815) 266-1342; www.crittercamp.biz.

Standing atop a bluff overlooking the Yellow Creek Valley is the **Black Hawk War Monument** that commemorates the 1832 **Battle of Kellogg's Grove,** the last battle Chief Black Hawk fought on Illinois soil. Then-militiaman Abraham Lincoln was summoned to help bury the dead. Some fifty years later, the soldier's graves were moved here and a 34-foot-tall stone tower was built and dedicated in 1886 as a proper memorial. Today, the park is open for picnics, and a log cabin has also been relocated nearby. The site is open dawn to dusk; admission is free; located near the township of **Kent** at **Black Hawk Battlefield Park,** on North Monument Road south of US 20; (815) 233-1357.

Twenty-six miles south of Freeport and 12 miles north of Dixon is the town of **Polo,** which served as a stop along the **Galena Trail** between the cities of Galena and Peoria. Today's population is under 3,000, yet there is a very active core of citizens who maintain the **Polo Historical Society.** The group has acquired a number of properties that serve as preserved historical landmarks, with several standing along North Franklin Avenue. The 1853 **Aplington House** is the former home of town founder Zenas Aplington and current location of the *Polo History Museum.* As you tour the house, think about the fact that Abraham Lincoln slept here for two nights in 1856. The home is open for tours "by chance" unless you schedule an appointment, so call ahead; donations are requested; 123 N. Franklin Ave.; (815) 946- 4142; www.polohistoricalsociety.org.

The group also owns the first brick house in Polo, the 1854 *Burns House,* which is the current location of the *Blackhawk Waterways Convention and Visitors Bureau.* Dr. W. W. Burns served as the town's first doctor and later became mayor. This is a good place to get information about the area if the history museum is closed. The visitor center is open Mon through Fri from 8 a.m. to 4:30 p.m.; admission is free; 201 N. Franklin Ave.; (815) 946-2108; www .bwcvb.com.

Next is the *Campbell House,* which was built in 1875 of local blue lime-stone and was Judge Campbell's home and law office. Today it's still occupied by a law firm and not open to the public unless a reservation for a tour is prearranged with the history museum. The house is located at 111 N. Franklin Ave.; (815) 946- 4142.

Just outside of Polo along the Galena Trail is the 1878 *Henry School,* which contains exhibits about early *Ogle County* education and the Black-hawk War. The school is open Apr through Oct on Wed from 1 to 3 p.m., or by appointment through the Aplington House; located south of Polo on SR 26; (815) 946-4142.

The most intriguing and easily accessible of the sites is the *Buffalo Grove Lime Kiln,* which operated from 1850 to 1875. This structure is built of large fieldstone and wood and stands in a field among boulders and rocks. Pioneers burned rock in this furnace from a nearby quarry to create a lime mortar that was used to chink and daub the timbers and stonework of local build-ings. Lime mortar was a key requirement for construction until the advent of cement. It's possible to view inside the kiln door and see the grates where the rock was fired. This structure was restored thanks to the members of the Polo Historical Society, and in 2002 it was named to the National Register of Historic Places. The kiln is open daily; admission is free; located next to a working quarry, on Eagle Point Road just west of Polo; (815) 946-4142.

If you happen to be in the area in June, attend *Polo Town and Country Days.* It's a four-day small-town extravaganza of food, games, tournaments, pig scramble, a parade, and fireworks. The event is held the third week of June from Thurs at 5 p.m. to Sun at 3:30 p.m.; around Polo City Hall, (815) 946-3514; www.polodays.org.

Ronald Reagan Territory

Even though it is the county seat of **Lee County,** the town of **Dixon** might have remained a sleepy hamlet had it not been for the rare success of one of its former residents. Although Ronald Wilson Reagan was born in an apartment building in Tampico, it was in nearby Dixon where he spent his youth. Life in 1920s Dixon was a slice of Americana; Reagan was an avid library patron, and he mastered swimming at the YMCA and became a local hero as a lifeguard. He played football and dreamed of becoming a big-time sportscaster. Reagan managed to live a life that movie directors would have rejected as too far-fetched; that of an Illinois kid from a small river town who would be elected the fortieth president of the United States. Dixon has embraced its Reagan legacy by honoring the man in several ways.

lifeguardlegend

It's reported that Ronald Reagan saved seventy-seven lives over the course of his summers on lifeguard duty, and the Loveland Community House Museum purports to have the proof in the form of a log that he notched every time he saved a soul from drowning.

Start at the **Heritage Crossing Riverfront Plaza** to see a handsome bronze statue overlooking the **Rock River,** depicting Reagan atop his favorite palomino. This is the work of Illinois artist Don Reed and it is aptly titled **Begins the Trail.**

Although the Reagan family lived in several Dixon residences, the home that Reagan mentioned in his autobiography was a white, two-story, simple house built in 1891, where the family lived when he was between the ages of nine and twelve. Today, the **Ronald Reagan Boyhood Home** has been restored and faithfully decorated in furniture from the era when the Reagan family resided here. The home is listed on the National Register of Historic Places, and volunteers conduct tours. The house is open Apr through Oct, Mon through Sat from 10 a.m. to 4 p.m., Sun from 1 to 4 p.m.; and in Mar on Sat from 10 a.m. to 4 p.m., Sun from 1 to 4 p.m.; closed Nov through Feb. Admission is $5 for those age thirteen and up and free for children age twelve and under. 816 S. Hennepin Ave.; (815) 288-5176. www.ronaldreaganhome.com.

Out front, take a minute to pause by the life-size **Ronald Reagan Memorial Statue** standing in **Reagan Memorial Park.** The president stands with his arms extended forward, with kernels of corn cradled in his hands; the image commemorates the state's contribution to farming and to feeding the world.

The community conducts a unique seven-day celebration during the **Reagan Trail Days Festival.** For those expecting a presidential experience,

Community Tribute

Shortly after Ronald Reagan accepted the nomination as the Republican candidate for U.S. president, a Dixon mailman walking his normal route realized that the Reagan homestead was for sale. In the interest of preserving local history, he began a campaign of his own to purchase the property. Within that year the home was purchased for $31,500, the mortgage was retired as paid in full, and the restoration was started on both the residence and the barn.

By the time President and Mrs. Reagan visited his home during the town's birthday celebration for him on February 6, 1984, the property had been decorated and restored to reflect the years in the 1920s when the Reagan family lived there. Reagan was so touched by the generosity of the townspeople that he thanked the enthusiastic crowd by saying, "If anyone wants to know about community and what community is all about, come and see Lee County and Dixon, Illinois."

there's a gala with cocktails, dinner, and dancing, and a golf tournament, as well as a wine tasting. For a more traditional hometown event, try the historical downtown walk, the Dixon picnic at Lowell Park (where they have pontoon boat rides too), an ice-cream social, municipal band concert, and fireworks. In honor of Reagan's favorite treat, there's also a Jelly Belly tasting contest. Held the first week of Aug; daily times vary, as does the cost of certain events, but many events are free; located at various places around Dixon; (815) 288-2308; www.reagantraildays.net.

By the way, *Lowell Park,* located about 3 miles north of Dixon, is the place where Reagan was employed as a lifeguard from 1926 to 1932. The 200-acre park on the Rock River was established in 1907 and is on the National Register of Historic Places. There's a nature center, picnic shelters, hiking, fishing, and boating along the river. The park is open dawn to dusk; admission is free; 2114 Lowell Park Rd.; (815) 284-3306; www.dixonil.com.

The *Loveland Community House Museum* features Reagan and Civil War memorabilia, plus exhibits on town founder John Dixon. The museum is open on Wed from 1 to 4 p.m., Fri and Sat from 9 a.m. to noon, and the first Sat of each month from 9 a.m. to 3 p.m.; 513 W. Second St.; (815) 284-2741.

The people of Dixon are full of volunteer spirit, and perhaps the best example of that began in the late 1950s when the Dixon Men's Garden Club planted several flower beds of pink petunias throughout town. Today pink petunias line miles of Dixon's roads, thanks to hundreds of local residents who work with the garden club to plant the posies each spring. The spectacle has garnered both state and national recognition, and to celebrate its favorite flower, Dixon holds an annual *Petunia Festival* in which the theme is "The

Pink, The Proud, The Petunias." The party includes a Ribfest, bingo, midway, movie night, raffles for big prizes (how about a new Harley?), parade, and fireworks. And don't miss the food booths along the "Taste Trail." The festival is held for five days over the Fourth of July weekend along downtown streets, at Page Park, and the Rock River; admission is free. (815) 284-3361; www .petuniafestival.org.

You'll see other monuments along the Rock River. On the north bank you'll find the **Lincoln Statue** at the site of the Fort Dixon fortification, which was built to protect the militia during the 1832 Black Hawk War. That area along *Lincoln Statue Drive* also contains a granite and bronze marker that recounts Lincoln's military service, and a second stone tribute that depicts the life of John Dixon.

Prairie, wetland, and woodland: It's that mixture that makes the *Nachusa Grasslands Preserve* a successful remnant prairie. Because the terrain was too difficult to farm, it remained fallow and was allowed to germinate and thrive without interference other than occasional grazing. There are over 2,800 acres to explore here, and special things to see such as the federally threatened species of prairie bush clover, flame flower, and forked aster; look for the gorgone checkerspot butterfly and Blandings turtles, and watch out for badgers. Begin your visit at the entrance off Lowden Road and read the instructions posted on a kiosk before entering the prairie; wear long-sleeve shirts and long pants, hard shoes, and sunscreen or a hat, and bring water. This site has no bathrooms, so plan ahead. The Nature Conservancy manages the preserve, which is open daily from dawn to dusk; admission is free. 8772 S. Lowden Rd., Franklin Grove; (815) 456-2340.

A prime example of Victorian architecture, the *Amboy Depot Museum* features a classic brick and cut limestone exterior, eight decorative chimney caps, 11-foot-high interior ceilings, and a grand curved staircase. This stately building was once home to the Illinois Central Railroad's depot and division headquarters; hence the nineteen rooms. The 1876 structure fell into disrepair until *Amboy* residents fought to restore it as part of a three-building museum complex that includes the one-room *Palmer School* and the 1924 Illinois Central *Amboy Freight House.* A handsome steam locomotive and

plaquemarks thespot

Near the Amboy Depot Museum are two plaques: One marks the site of the first Carson, Pirie, Scott and Company store, while the other stands as tribute to the early believers of the Reorganized Church of Jesus Christ of Latter-Day Saints, who settled here and are now known as the Community of Christ.

1920s Norfolk and Western caboose sit outside. The museum is open Wed, Thurs, and Sun from 1 to 4 p.m. and Fri and Sat from 10 a.m. to 4 p.m.; donations are requested; 50 Southeast Ave.; (815) 857-4700; www.amboydepot museum.org.

The *John Deere Historic Site* is located in the town of *Grand Detour.* As a blacksmith with a reputation for meticulous workmanship, Deere arrived here in 1836, following acquaintances from his Vermont hometown to settle in this promising place. He soon heard complaints about the tenacious black Illinois soil that stuck to farmer's plow blades like glue. Deere experimented until he invented the world's first "self-scouring" plow. Today Deere's original homestead and blacksmith shop are open for tours; examples of his early scouring plows stand in front. The site is open May through Oct, Wed through Sun from 9 a.m. to 5 p.m.; admission is $5 for those age twelve and older; 8334 S. Clinton St., Grand Detour; (815) 652-4551; www.deere.com/en_US/attractions/historicsite/index.html.

Oregon is truly a small town with a lot going on; there are three state parks, one state forest, ten city parks, and as county seat of *Ogle County,* it hosts the *Ogle County Courthouse.* Built in 1891, the redbrick and limestone structure is picture-postcard perfect, with a high and striking cupola as its focal point. It is listed in the National Register of Historic Places, and no longer assumes the burden of holding daily court, but serves as office space for county agencies. The courtyard is also notable, with a Lorado Taft sculpture titled **The Soldiers' Monument,** a cast-iron 1896 fountain nicknamed *Iron Mike,* a war memorial, and cannons sharing the grounds. The monument is located at 400 S. Washington Ave.

Adjacent to the courthouse is the *Oregon Commercial Historic District,* which starts along the 300 block of South Washington Avenue and is made up of forty-four buildings and additional structures representing numerous architectural styles, including Romanesque Revival, Queen Anne, Italianate, and Art Deco. This is a town to walk and browse.

By the *Oregon Dam* is another popular shopping place to visit, one especially for those interested in watching artisans at work. About twenty companies sell their wares under the historic roof of *Conover Square,* the former Schiller Piano Factory, which was one of the prime employers in the area in the 1890s. The dam served as a power source for the factory and the city. You can purchase baskets or make an appointment to create one of your own at *Basket Beginnings* (815-732-7181; www.basketbeginning.com). Or stop at *Slip and Slurry Pottery,* where the resident potter might be busy at the potter's wheel and welcomes you to watch (815-732-3367). There's also a jewelry shop that sells supplies or finished works, a cheese store, gourmet coffee and chocolate shop, and businesses that specialize in antiques, aromatherapy, and collectibles. There are two attractions here also: The **Black Hawk Model Railroad Club** maintains a display that runs on the weekends and during special events, and the **Billy Barnhart Museum** features antique toys, sleighs, and other novelties. Both exhibits have free admission. The stores of Conover Square are independently owned and have varying hours of operation, so it's best to check the Web site or call ahead; 201 N. Third St.; (815) 732-3950; www.conoversquare.com.

There are numerous museums in Oregon, but due to a variety of reasons—from funding, to all-volunteer staffs, to the unpredictable weather, especially in winter—many of these small operations are open by chance or appointment. With that in mind, military history buffs will appreciate the modest **Stuka Military Museum,** where displays contain an array of items ranging from the Civil War to Operation Desert Storm. The museum is located at 3178 S. Daysville Rd.; (815) 732-2091.

The **Chana School Museum** is a two-room schoolhouse that was used from 1883 to 1953. Don't be mistaken by the exterior; you're liable to miss it because the building looks more like a church with a steeple than a school with a bell tower. It is listed on the National Register of Historic Places and is open and run by volunteers. Your best chance for a tour is on Saturday or during local celebrations or events. If it's not open when you arrive, feel free to peek in the windows; you can also take an enjoyable hike in the surrounding park. The museum is located in Oregon Park East at 201 N. River Rd.

largerthanlife

Although Lorado Taft's Native American statue overlooking the Rock River in Oregon was the first concrete monolithic statue, another one currently holds the record as the largest: It's the statue of Christ, titled *Cristo Redentor,* in Rio De Janeiro, Brazil.

It's reported that renowned sculptor Lorado Taft stood on the bluff overlooking Oregon and contemplated the rushing Rock River below. He glanced toward his colleagues and noticed that most were standing with their arms folded across their chests. The thought crossed his mind that the Indians who'd called this land home must have struck a similar pose as they watched the churning water. The inspiration spurred his design of a statue titled **The Eternal Indian.** It's the world's first concrete monolithic statue, and it was completed on Dec 20, 1910. The figure, which many affectionately refer to as Chief Black Hawk, is 50 feet tall and weighs an estimated 100 tons despite being hollow. The surface is a combination of cement and pink granite chips, and the interior is reinforced with iron rods. Standing more than 100 feet above the Rock River, it is visible across the river as travelers pass over the *River Bridge.* To stand next to the monument, visit *Lowden State Park.* The monument is open year-round dawn to dusk; free; 1411 N. River Rd.; (815) 732-6828.

To see additional works by the 1898 *Eagle's Nest Art Colony* artists, who worked side by side with Taft during summers near Lowden State Park, stop by the second floor of the *Oregon Public Library Gallery,* where their artwork is displayed. The gallery is open Mon through Thurs from 9 a.m. to 8 p.m. and Fri and Sat from 9 a.m. to 8 p.m.; 300 Jefferson St.; (815) 732-2724; http://oregon.lib.il.us.

Oregon is the type of town where it's fun to forgo chain hotels and stay at a B&B. Consider the *Pinehill Inn Bed and Breakfast,* an establishment highly rated by state and national newspapers and magazines. The 1874 Italianate brick mansion is listed on the National Register of Historic Places and inside there's so much architectural detail to enjoy: seven marble-surround fireplaces, an original rose-glass window, a French silk mural, and 12-foot ceilings graced by elaborate medallions. And if you've ever considered opening a bed-and-breakfast, Pinehill hosts the *Bed and Breakfast College,* a two-day, power-packed course that will put you on track to owning your own inn. Pinehill Inn is located at 400 Mix St.; (815) 732-2067; www.pinehillbb.com.

Over at the *Patchwork Inn Bed and Breakfast,* you might have the opportunity to sleep in the same room Lincoln did when he dined and lodged here in the 1850s. The inn is located at 122 N. Third St.; (815) 732-4113; www .patchworkinn.com.

One of the best ways to enjoy the unspoiled natural beauty of the Rock River's sandstone cliffside embankments and unspoiled ancient trees is by traveling on the river's smooth surface. You can lease a small boat at *TJ's Bait and Canoe Rentals* and select from a two-hour, four-hour, or overnight adventure; they'll provide lifejackets, paddles and pickup van. Make a reservation to ensure that your canoe or kayak is waiting. TJ's is located at 305 S. First St.; (815) 732-4516; http://tjscanoerental.com.

Another excursion is offered on the **Pride of Oregon,** a reproduction of the 102-foot riverboat *Rosie O'Shea.* Choose between a lunch or dinner cruise, or just take a 15-mile lazy river ride on this eco-friendly waterwheel; bring your camera because you might see bald eagles in the trees, depending on the time of year. Sightseeing cruises run Apr 15 through Nov 15; tickets cost $12 for adults and $7 for children under age ten. Located at the dock alongside Maxson Riverside Restaurant, 1469 N. Illinois Rte. 2; (815) 732-4540; www .maxsonrestaurant.com.

By the way, if you're just looking for dinner by the water, *Maxson Riverside Restaurant* offers a lovely view from its deck overlooking the river. Call ahead to make sure they reserve a waterside table for you. The restaurant is located at 1469 N. Illinois Rte. 2; (800) 468-4222; www.maxsonrestaurant.com.

There are some nice choices for restaurants out in this "parks and picnics" haven, such as *La Vigna Restaurant,* where the decor is old-fashioned but the service and food are top-notch. Finish your meal with one of their home-made sorbets. The restaurant is located at 2190 S. Daysville Rd.; (815) 732-4413.

One of the more amazing sites in the area, available for viewing just a handful of days, is man-made, thanks to the *Fields Project and Arts Festival.* Hundreds of high school students and volunteers create sculptures in local fields; these are giant works of art that cover about fifteen acres and are best seen from the air—so that's what happens! *Ogle County Airport* pilots supply airplane rides to anyone desiring to view the art from the sky. If you're not into flying, there's still plenty to enjoy at *Mix Park,* including live music, food, and arts and crafts sales and exhibits. The festival is held on the fourth Sat and Sun of June, from 10 a.m. to 4 p.m. Begin at the *Arts in the Park* site at Mix Park, 701 S. Fourth St., Oregon; then head to the airport at 3019 W. Rte. 64, Mount Morris; (815) 298-0457; www.oglecountyairport.com.

While in *Mount Morris* visit the *Official Illinois Freedom Bell,* an 1860s replica of the Liberty Bell in Philadelphia. Ronald Reagan participated in the dedication of the bell in 1963, and the town rings it thirteen times every year on the Fourth of July at 1 p.m. to commemorate the tradition followed in colonial America. An extension of the tolling of the bell is the *Let Freedom Ring Festival,* which is all Americana, with a hot dog supper, ice-cream social, community band concert, parade, and fireworks. Abe Lincoln and Stephen Douglas might be socializing with the crowd, so keep your eyes open. The festival is held five days around the Fourth of July; admission is free; located downtown along Main Street, Mount Morris; (815) 734-6425; www.letfreedom ringfestival.com.

The town of *Fulton* is serious about its Dutch heritage—so much so that the townsfolk banded together to import a special monument, the *De Immigrant Windmill,* a fully operational mill that was built by master craftsmen in the Netherlands, then shipped to Fulton, where Dutch workman reassembled it using the Old World technique of wooden peg construction. It stands as a tribute to the immigrants who settled the town. Take a moment to watch the mesmerizing motion of the great wooden blades rotating slowly against the bright blue sky. The vision whisks you to another place and time, away from traffic jams, the Internet, and business deadlines. There's a practical side to the landmark: Ground buckwheat, corn, rye, and wheat flour can be purchased at the gift shop. The mill is open from May to Oct; hours vary seasonally, so you might want to call ahead, but they are usually between 10 a.m. and 5 p.m. on weekdays and 1 and 5 p.m. on Sun; located at Tenth Avenue and First Street; (815) 589-4545.

At the beginning of May, the town is abloom with thousands of tulips and the mood is one of celebration at the ***Dutch Days Festival.*** Visitors can tour the windmill, enjoy the arts and crafts and quilt shows, observe stippling and fine needlework demonstrations, and learn how to dance in wooden shoes. And, of course, there's lots of food—from cheese and pastries to potatoes and cabbage. The Saturday parade is more of a Broadway production, with costumed dancers demonstrating Dutch traditions. The festival is held on Fri and Sat from 9 a.m. to 4 p.m.; located along downtown streets; (815) 589-4545 or (815) 589-2616; www.cityoffulton.us.

The ***Martin House Museum*** is managed by the ***Fulton Historical Society*** and contains an unexpected collection of artifacts including the military uniform of Ronald Reagan. In the Dutch Treasures room you'll see traditional costumes and a display of Dutch dolls. The museum is open daily from 2 to 4 p.m. or by appointment; admission is free; 707 Tenth Ave.; (815) 589-3809.

If you're in the mood for a peaceful stroll, visit ***Heritage Canyon,*** a self-guided nature walk along old-fashioned brick pathways spread throughout a twelve-acre nature preserve. Yellow arrows will direct you, and quaint reconstructed buildings along the route are reminiscent of life in the mid-1800s. The nature walk is open daily from 9 a.m. to 5 p.m.; donations are requested, and during special events there's a $2 fee for adults and children over age fourteen; 515 N. Fourth St.; (815) 589-4545.

headsortails?

The town of Sterling won its name by virtue of a coin toss.

Sterling's proximity to the Rock River gave it a serious economic advantage; waterpower attracted major manufacturing companies, and the town became known as the "Hardware Capital of the World." Paul W. Dillon was the founder of Northwestern Steel and Wire, and upon his death in 1980 his fourteen-room, Italian Renaissance–style mansion was bequeathed to the ***Sterling Park District.*** Today the ***Dillon Home Museum*** stands exactly as he left it, full of antiques, collectibles, and priceless artifacts. Built in 1857, the home was added to the National Register of Historic Places shortly after becoming a public museum. The last steam-powered locomotive to operate in the U.S. sits on the south lawn of the five-plus-acre grounds, having been "saved" by Dillon, who kept the old ***No. 73 steam locomotive*** to switch train cars long after it was economically feasible, perhaps because he realized it was the end of the era. The museum is open Tues, Thurs, and Sat from 10 a.m. to noon and from 1 to 4 p.m., and on Sun from 1 to 5 p.m.; 1005 E. Third St.; (815) 662-6202.

The restored Dillon brick barn and carriage house are now home to the **Sterling-Rock Falls Historical Society.** The society maintains the **Sterling-Rock Falls Historical Society Museum,** where displays cover the history and growth of Sterling and the nearby town of **Rock Falls,** from prehistoric times to the industrial revolution. The museum is open Tues, Thurs, and Sat from 10 a.m. to noon and from 1 to 4 p.m., and on Sun from 1 to 5 p.m.; 1005 E. Third St.; (815) 662-6215.

As you pass through downtown, look for the eighteen **Sterling Murals** painted on city buildings along First through Sixth Streets. Many honor local groups or citizens such as founder Hezekiah Brink. The project is managed by the **Sterling Mural Society.** Maps are available by calling the Century 21 real estate office at (815) 626-5421.

Don't miss the two **Lincoln Historical Markers;** one is located at 607 E. Third St. and a second at the corner of Sixth Avenue and Sixth Street.

The **Sterling Public Library** and Woodlawn Arts Academy host the annual **Storytelling and Arts Festival,** where professionals spin their tales to the delight of audiences. The topics vary, as do the content and judging, so the event is broken into two segments: Adults Only and Family Day. The festival is held the first weekend of Sept; Adults Only is on Fri, with juried performances from 6 to 8 p.m. and mature-audience performances from 8 to 10 p.m.; Family Day is Sat from noon to 5 p.m., and spooky stories run from 7 to 10 p.m.; admission is $7 on Fri; a free-will donation is requested on Sat; the festival is held at Woodland Arts Academy, 3807 Woodlawn Rd.; (815) 625-1370; Sterling Library is located at 102 W. Third St.; (815) 625-1370.

The **Sterling Municipal Band** has a long and storied history, having once performed for an 1856 Republican rally where Abraham Lincoln spoke. This is a top-notch group of community musicians that plays symphonic and popular tunes throughout the summer, so bring your folding chairs to the **Grandon Civic Center** band shell. Concerts are presented June to Aug on Wed at 7:30 p.m.; admission is free; East Fourth Street, Route 2, Sterling; (815) 625-7973; www.sterlingmunicipalband.com.

For country fun, visit the **Whiteside County Fair.** These people know what they're doing; the fair is over 140 years old and still going strong because

fireescape

Tragedy was averted in 1912 while the residents of Sterling enjoyed a rousing performance by the renowned Ringling Brothers Circus. Unbeknownst to the crowd, fire had engulfed a nearby barn, and the wind tossed burning debris onto the circus tent, igniting the fabric and burning it to the ground. Miraculously, no one, human or beast, was hurt in the fire.

Foot Folk Art

When you arrive at Rockford's *Midway Village,* Soxanne the sock monkey will greet you at the entrance. Of all the exhibits at the complex, this one has caught the imagination of people familiar with the city's legacy of knitting factories. Rockford is home to the "sock monkey," a stuffed character created from a brown- and white-flecked sock that was originally produced by one of the city's largest manufacturing enterprises, the Nelson Kitting Company of Rockford. The red-heel work socks were manufactured for sixty years from 1932 to 1992, but they became a toy during the Great Depression when thrifty mothers recycled worn-out socks to make dolls. The concept grew in popularity for decades, to the point that in the 1950s the company included patterns for monkey dolls inside sock packages.

it gives people what they want: a draft horse show, tractor pull, demo derby, harness racing, exhibits, and fair food galore. The fair is held in mid-Aug; 201 W. Winfield St., Morrison; (815) 772-7329; www.whitesidecountyfair.org.

The city of *Rockford* was originally named Midway because of it's location between Chicago and Galena. The name was changed when settlers realized that at the point of the settlement, the Rock River contained ample stones that allowed an easy fording of the water.

Today the *Rock River* is the centerpiece of activity for the *On the Waterfront Festival,* thought to be the state's largest music event. Proceeds benefit local nonprofit organizations. This is three and a half days of nonstop tunes presented on five rocking stages by both area and nationally known artists. At the same time, there's the *Taste of the Waterfront,* with mouthwatering samples or regular portions sure to please every taste. Other activities include a 5K race along the Rock River, a carnival, a hot-air balloon flyover, and fireworks nightly at 9 p.m. The festival is held the last week of July, and music runs from 11:30 a.m. to 10:30 p.m. Admission is $18 for advance pass holders and covers entry for all three days; passes must be purchased before the event, online or at various local businesses. Admission at the gate is $15, and that's for entry on that day only, so it really pays to buy ahead. Shuttle service costs $1 per ride. Located downtown along East State Street; (815) 964-4388; www.onthewaterfront.com.

Long dubbed the "Forest City," Rockford is expanding into a place of gardens with trials, pathways, and botanical gardens; an arboretum and nature center now thrive among the city's parks and byways.

The nonprofit *Anderson Japanese Gardens* are more than just gardens; here you'll find a spiritual place of inspiration and renewal. The twelve acres were developed beginning in 1978 as the vision of Rockford residents Linda and John Anderson, and feature two separate areas: the Formal Garden and the Garden of Reflection. There are bridges, a granite pagoda, a traditional teahouse, ponds, and two waterfalls. The West Waterfall is quite a man-made feat; it took three years to construct. The five-story structure circulates 1,600 gallons of water per minute, and the rushing sound is as authentic and mesmerizing as a natural waterfall. The gardens are open May 1 to Oct 31, Mon through Thurs from 9 a.m. to 5 p.m., Fri from 9 a.m. to 15 minutes before sunset, Sat from 9 a.m. to 4 p.m., and Sun from 10 a.m. to 4 p.m.; admission is $7 for adults, $6 for seniors, $5 for children over age four, and free for children four and under; during the off-season, admission is free to all, but dependent on suitable weather conditions, so call ahead; (815) 229-9390; www .andersongardens.org.

Like so many other towns in this region of the state, waterpower and the railroad attracted businesses. Immigrants moved here for work, and at one point more Rockford residents spoke Swedish than English. The 1871 **Erlander Home Museum** is operated by the **Swedish Historical Society** and contains artifacts of the Swedish families who toiled in local mills as laborers, plus Swedish-made furniture and a doll collection. The museum is open Tues though Fri from 1 to 4 p.m. and on Sunday from 2 to 4 p.m.; admission is $5 for adults, $4 for seniors, and $3 for children ages three through seventeen; 404 S. Third St.; (815) 963-5559; www.swedishhistorical.org.

Although the **Tinker Swiss Cottage Museum** looks as though it should be sitting in the shadow of the Alps, it isn't a tribute to Swiss immigrants to the area, but instead the fantasy home of Robert Hall Tinker, who built the Swiss chalet in 1865 after touring Europe and becoming enamored with that country's architecture. Today it's listed on the National Register of Historic Places and is managed by the **Rockford Park District.** The home is filled with antiques, rare paintings, and keepsakes from the 1860s to the turn of the century. Extraordinary care has been taken to restore the multiple ceiling murals to the brilliance of their original appearance in the 1870s. The museum is open from Mar through Dec, Tues through Sun, with tours at 1, 2, and 3 p.m.; admission for is $6 for adults, $5 for seniors, and $3 for children ages five through seventeen; 411 Kent St.; (815) 964-2424; www.tinkercottage.com.

The **Midway Village Museum** is a turn-of-the-century Victorian village nestled on 137 acres where costumed docents provide tours of the twenty-four buildings along cobblestone streets. This is the place to learn about the women's baseball league and Rockford's own girls' team, the Rockford Peaches. Then tour the world through the international doll collection housed at the **Old Dolls' House Museum.** The museum is open year-round, but hours vary depending on the exhibit; admission is $6 for adults and $4 for children ages three through seventeen; 6799 Guilford Rd.; (815) 397-9112; www.midway village.com.

A resurgence of sock monkey folk toys has lead to the annual **Sock Monkey Madness Festival,** which features exhibits on Rockford's knitting industry, two-hour classes for all ages in the construction and decoration of sock monkeys and sock elephants, as well as the crowning of Mr. and Ms. Sockford. A tongue-in-cheek event of the weekend is the viewing of amateur filmmaker's entries in the **International Sock Monkey Film Festival.** The Sock Monkey Madness Festival is held the first week of Mar on Sat and Sun from 11a.m. to 5 p.m.; admission for is $8 adults, $4 for children ages three through seventeen, and free for children age two and under; 6799 Guilford Rd.; (815) 397-9112; www.midwayvillage.com.

It's quite easy to visit Rockford's biggest museums because they're connected to each other through the **Riverfront Museum Park,** which eases parking and congestion and makes it possible for guests to tour multiple sites during one visit. The park is located at 711 N. Main St.; (815) 962-0105; www .riverfrontmuseumpark.org.

The **Burpee Museum of Natural History** is housed in a beautifully modern facility where visitors learn about the Rock River Valley's history through the observation of specimens that inhabited this area of the state. Displays include the 21-foot skeleton of a very well-preserved dinosaur named "Jane." The museum is open Mon through Fri from 10 a.m. to 4 p.m., Sat from 10 a.m. to 5 p.m., and Sun from noon to 5 p.m.; admission is $7 for adults and $5 for children; 737 Main St.; (815) 965-3433; www.burpee.org.

Across the street is the **Rockford Art Museum,** which exhibits fine art of American masters and contemporary artists as well as glass and photography from local and international artists. Note: No book bags or totes are allowed inside. The museum is open Mon through Sat from 10 a.m. to 5 p.m. and on Sun from noon to 5 p.m.; admission is $6 for adults, $3 for seniors and students, and free for children under age 12; Tues is donation day; 711 N. Main St.; (815) 968-2787; www.rockfordartmuseum.org.

Next door is another contemporary building that houses the **Discovery Center Museum,** a two-story learning center of more than 250 interactive science and art exhibits. Outside, explore the **Rock River Discovery Park,** a multilevel space that encourages hands-on outdoor science play. The museum is open Mon through Sat from 10 a.m. to 5 p.m. and on Sun from noon to 5 p.m.; in summer the museum is open to 7 p.m. on Thurs; admission is $5 for adults, $4 for children under age 18, and free for children under age two; 711 N. Main St.; (815) 963-6769; www.discoverycenter museum.org.

If you're ready to take a break from the summer heat, then catch a wave or play in the sand at *Magic Waters Waterpark*, where the tunnel slide, with its heart-stopping 30-foot drop, will take your breath away, and a float along the lazy river will calm you back down. There's a nice picnic area, a concessions stand, and plenty of free parking. The park is open late May to Labor Day; admission is $22.95 for adults, $16.95 for seniors and children, $4.00 for tots age two and under, and free for those under age one; there are discounts for entrance after 3 p.m.; check the Web site for discounts and consider "Family Splash Pack" pricing; 7820 Cherryvale North Blvd., Cherry Valley; pay attention to road signs, as there's constant road construction around here; (815) 966-2442; www.magicwaterswaterpark.com.

Pioneer legend Daniel Boone didn't hail from Illinois, but his ability to master the pathways of the wilderness is probably one of the strongest reasons why in 1837 the fathers of *Boone County* named it in his honor. This county is a trailblazer's dream, with miles of paths connecting its towns and cities and extending into Wisconsin. A series of these routes is known as the *Boone County Historical Trail*. Each of its four main tracts was initially designed so that they could be navigated by wagon or horseback during the course of one day; in other words, the paths ran approximately 30 miles in length. They were originally identified as the South Pacific Route, the Piscasaw Route, the Blaine/State Line Route, and the Belvidere/Caledonia Route. Today these road-ways may be traversed by foot, bicycle, or car. To obtain a detailed map and notifications of trail conditions, call the *Boone County Conservation District* at (815) 547-7935 or visit www.boonecountyconservationdistrict.org.

The town of *Belvidere* is the county seat, and the original *Boone County Courthouse* stands in the center of town, surrounded by a more modern court and county office complex. The name *Belvidere* means "beautiful to view," and you'll agree that's an apt description as you look out over the banks of the *Kishwaukee River*, which flows through the center of town.

There are many municipal green spaces here, but one of particular note is *Belvidere Park*, where the 1845 *Baltic Mill* stands in the midst of a 105-acre, well-groomed esplanade along the Kishwaukee River. The building has been restored, is reached via a suspended footbridge, and is home to the *Boone County Arts Council* as well as a "Summer Concerts in the Park" series. Exhibits are open to the public. The *Baltic Mill Fine Art Fair* is held the third week of Aug and is free. The grounds are open from 6 a.m. to dusk and the mill from 9 a.m. to 5 p.m.; 1006 W. Lincoln Ave.; (815) 547-5711; www .belviderepark.org.

Most people would pass by an old cemetery for other sightseeing adventures, but the *Belvidere Cemetery* holds a remarkable jewel within its grounds.

As you drive the cemetery's winding route, you'll see a white, low, T-shaped building enhanced with blue-striped accents along the bottom and middle, under the roofline, and along the chimney. This is the ***Pettit Memorial Chapel,*** and if it looks strikingly familiar to you, then you know the work of Frank Lloyd Wright. It is the only memorial chapel designed by him, and it was constructed in 1907 at the behest of the widow of Dr. William Pettit, a Belvidere native and well-respected physician who practiced in the neighboring state of Iowa. The building is typical of Wright's Prairie–style architecture, although an early example, and has been added to the National Register of Historic Places. It was used for funerals until the 1920s, and today it is open for tours by appointment. The cemetery is located at 1121 N. Main St.; (815) 547-7642.

To learn specifics about the county, visit the ***Boone County Historical Museum,*** where full-size vignettes of antiques and artifacts display the lifestyle of early settlers and later residents. You'll see the interior of a church, a log cabin, a post office, and barber shop, plus antique automobiles. The museum is open Mon through Fri from 9 a.m. to 4 p.m. and on Sat from 10 a.m. to 3 p.m.; admission is free; 311 Whitney Blvd.; (815) 544-8391; www.boonecounty historicalmuseum.org.

The ***Boone County Conservation District*** holds several events during the year, but the most well attended is the ***Autumn Pioneer Festival,*** where costumed volunteers demonstrate the pioneer way of life through crafts, cooking, and construction. The festival is held the fourth weekend of Sept, on Sat from 9 a.m. to 5 p.m. and Sun from 10 a.m. to 4 p.m.; admission is free; 603 N. Appleton Rd.; (815) 547-7935; www.boonecountyconservationdistrict.org.

To add to the local flavor, there's a population of cougars, zebras, reindeer, and wallabies residing just outside of town at ***Summerfield Farm Zoo.*** Although it's only open one weekend a month, when it is open there's plenty to do: Take a hayride, watch the black swans swim in the lake, or stop by the petting zoo and gift shop. Because it's a small venue, visitors enjoy a personal experience with the wide range of critters living at this licensed, not-for-profit zoo. Summerfield is open monthly, May to Nov, on Sat and Sun from 10 a.m. to 4 p.m.; admission is $5 per person, with all proceeds paying for the care of the animals; 3088 Flora Rd.; Belvidere; (815) 547-4852; www.summerfield farminc.com. There's an old saying that eastern farmers used fences to keep their livestock in, while western farmers used fences to keep others out. Fencing the prairie was a major problem. The scarcity of trees meant lumber was used for building houses, not fences, and in areas where suitable rocks needed for stone walls and hedges were scarce, it became necessary to create a fence system to secure grazing livestock.

The first "thorny fence" was devised by a New York inventor in 1868, but proved too expensive and difficult to manufacture. Years later, DeKalb farmer Henry M. Rose unveiled his new fence design at the 1873 DeKalb County Fair. His display of a 16-foot wood rail with sharp brads exposed in a random pattern caught the attention of three DeKalb men: a farmer named Joseph F. Glidden; a hardware storeowner, Isaac L. Ellwood; and lumberman Jacob Haish. By the time they'd finished with their experimentation and fierce competitiveness, their hometown of **DeKalb** had become known as the "Barbed Wire Capital of the World."

When the dust settled, it was Glidden who successfully patented his version of barbed wire in 1874. He barbed his competition with the name "The Winner," and it became just that—the world's first commercially successful barbed-wire design. Glidden earned the title the "Father of Barbed Wire." Today visitors can learn of the acrimonious battle between Glidden and Ellwood by touring their properties.

Dedicated volunteers have banded to restore the **Joseph F. Glidden Homestead and Historical Center,** returning the redbrick Greek Revival structure to its original handsome appearance. There are numerous special events here, along with permanent displays, and the historic barn where Glidden perfected his invention is open for a peek. The center is open May through Nov on the first and third Sun each month, from noon to 4 p.m.; donations are requested; 921 W. Lincoln Hwy.; (815) 756-7904; www.glidden homestead.org.

The Ellwood House and Museum, a stately 1879 mansion renovated by different owners, displays Victorian, Colonial Revival, and Arts and Crafts features. At "the house that barbed wire built," as it was once known, visitors are treated to four floors of resplendent decor and opulence commonly seen during the Gilded Age. Besides this

goinggreen

In 1833, Illinois College professor Jonathan B. Turner devised a greener way to fence the prairie grasslands around his home by using a species of hedge called osage orange. Turner is considered the first person to use this fencing method. Interestingly, before Jacob Haish became entwined in a competition to develop barbed wire in the 1870s, he grew osage orange hedges as a sideline to his carpentry business.

sharpblend

In 1874 Joseph Glidden also patented the Glidden and Vaughn Manufacturing Machine for making barbed wire, which was based on his wife's modified coffee grinder. It's assumed that Mrs. Glidden's husband used part of his invention earnings to replace her coffee grinder, which he'd used to make his first prototypes.

remarkable home, the grounds contain the *Ellwood House Visitor Center* and the *Little House,* which is an 1891 mini-mansion suitable for use as a playhouse for children or as a large-scale dollhouse. Even Barbie would be jealous of this place! Guided tours run from Mar through Nov, Tues through Fri at 1 and 3 p.m. and Sat and Sun at 1, 2, and 3 p.m., and also in Dec for the holidays; admission is $8 for adults and $3 for children ages six through seventeen; visitor center exhibits are free; 509 N. First St.; (815) 756-4609; www .ellwoodhouse.org.

In 1922 the world was mesmerized by the discovery of the tomb of Egypt's King Tutankhamun. Still, it's hard to imagine that a rural Illinois farm town like DeKalb would score a theater inspired by that event. The 1929 *Egyptian Theater* was constructed to give theatergoers a sense of entering the doorway of an ancient tomb: Two pharaohs guard the front, and a stained-glass image of the sun god Ra greets visitors; the entrance is narrow, then widens to give the impression of moving from room to room until reaching the nearly 1,500-seat concert hall, instead of the grand burial chamber. Tours are given by appointment; 135 N. Second St., DeKalb; (815) 758-1215; www.egyptiantheatre.org.

DeKalb is the home of *Northern Illinois University,* so there are bound to be plenty of places to get good grub. But if you asked a student on the street, they'd probably point you to the nondescript, one-story building along the Lincoln Highway that's home to *Pizza Villa.* Talk about a hometown joint—this place has been serving its thin-crust pizza here for over fifty years. On Saturday night you'll find a line out the door, but don't despair—a carry-out window near the front makes pickup easy. Try their famous Beer Nuggets, tasty bites of fried beer dough topped with Parmesan cheese. Pizza Villa is located at 824 W. Lincoln Hwy.; (815) 758-8116; www.pizzavilla.com.

As corn country, the city sponsors *Corn Fest,* a celebration that's gotten so large they've had to relocate it to the airport. More than 120,000 attend this event and enjoy the concerts, helicopter rides, craft show, and lots of corn on the cob. The festival is held the third week of Aug, starting on Fri at 3 p.m. and ending on Sun at 6 p.m.; admission is free; located at the DeKalb Taylor Municipal Airport, 3232 Pleasant St.; (815) 748-CORN (2676); www.cornfest .com.

Sycamore remains the county seat of *DeKalb County,* despite challenges from its neighboring city DeKalb. The county courthouse is a wonderful structure built in 1905 of limestone; it has four front columns and carved pediments, plus a rear stone porte cochere. It is the anchor of the *Sycamore Historic District,* which was recognized by the National Register of Historic Places in 1978.

The annual *Sycamore Pumpkin Festival* is both a fun time for the community and an opportunity for local not-for-profit groups to raise awareness and funds. The festival opens on the courthouse lawn with the cutting of a giant cake; then it's on to two full days of carnival, races, a craft show, food, carved pumpkins, and finally a grand two-hour parade. The festival is held the last full weekend of Oct; 133 W. State St.; (815) 895-3456; www.sycamore pumpkinfestival.com.

You'll soon realize you're in the middle of serious farm country if you attend the *Sycamore Steam Show and Threshing Bee.* Sponsored by die-hard members of the *Northern Illinois Steam Power Club,* this is the opportunity to see the workhorses of farming equipment: steam powered machines demonstrating wheat grinding, a sawmill, a baling operation, a shingle mill, and field plowing. There's an antique steam-engine parade, a barrel-train ride, ladies' hobby tent, and flea market, as well as some down-home barbecue. The event is held the second week of Aug, starting bright and early on Thurs at 7 a.m. and continuing until 6 p.m. each day through Sun; admission is $6 for adults and free for children under age twelve; on opening day only, seniors pay $3; located at the Taylor Marshall Farm, 27707 Lukens Rd.; www.threshingbee.org.

Heading to the south of the county, you'll find the town of *Sandwich,* where antiques and festivals are the draw. The *Sandwich Fair* is more than one hundred years old and jam-packed with activities for all ages. Catch the western horse show, sheep dog demonstration, harness racing, and even a fiddle contest that draws a foot-stomping crowd. Events begin on Labor Day and continue all week, with gates opening at 8 a.m. and buildings at 9 a.m.; admission is $8 for adults, $4 for children ages six through twelve, and free for children under five; inquire about a season pass that covers admission through the entire event; located off Fairwinds Boulevard; (815) 786-2159; www.sandwichfair.com.

The *Sandwich Antiques Market* is two events in one: The *West Field Market* features a flea market, business booths, and crafts fair; the *East Field Market* hosts the traditional antiques and collectibles sale. The market is held Apr through Oct on the third weekend of the month, from 8 a.m. to 4 p.m.; admission is $5; 1401 Suydam Rd.; (815) 786- 3337; www.antiquemarkets.com.

When you visit *Ottawa,* you need to plan on leaving enough time to see everything. If the town needed a nickname, it might be "Tour City," as there's an *Ottawa Auto Tour,* the *Cell Phone Mural Tour,* the *Ottawa Lincoln Knew Tour,* and more. Your best bet is to start at the *Ottawa Visitors Center,* where they will help you plan your route. The center is open Mon through Fri from 9 a.m. to 5 p.m., Sat from 9 a.m. to 4 p.m., and Sun from 10 a.m. to 2 p.m.; 100 W. Lafayette St.; (888) 688-2924; www.experienceottawa.com.

The big summer event here is the *Ottawa Riverfest,* which is held in

Scout's Honor

The Silver Buffalo award is the highest honor presented to adults who have provided outstanding support or service to the Boy Scouts. The founder of scouting, Lord Baden-Powell, received the first; the "Unknown Scout" received the second; and the father of American scouting, William D. Boyce, received the third. In 1941 a statue of the Unknown Scout was placed near Boyce's Ottawa grave site to mark the thirtieth anniversary of the founding of the Boy Scouts of America.

conjunction with the *Taste of Ottawa.* It's a weekend of great music and wonderful food set against the backdrop of the spectacular Illinois River. The event is held the last weekend of July; admission is free for the music, but food cost $10 for nine tickets; located along the riverfront at Woodward Memorial Drive; (815) 433-0161, ext. 31; www.ottawariverfest.com.

Ottawa is the home of the "Father of American Boy Scouting," William Dickson Boyce. The *Ottawa Scouting Museum* relates the history of American Boy Scouting with exhibits and activities for scouts and visitors. The museum is open Thurs through Mon from 10 a.m. to 4 p.m.; admission is $3 for adults and $2 for children under age eighteen; 1100 Canal St.; (815) 431-9353; www.ottawascoutingmuseum.org.

Boyce died in 1929 and rests at the *Ottawa Avenue Cemetery* beside the Illinois River. Within site of his grave is a life-size statue of a 1920s-era Boy Scout titled **The Unknown Scout** that gazes ahead as if looking toward the future. The cemetery is open from dawn to dusk; 1601 Ottawa Ave.

While at the cemetery, look for the obelisk marking the grave of Ottawa philanthropist William Reddick, who began his earning life as a glassblower, then moved into politics, serving six terms as an Illinois state senator. In town, his impressive, twenty-two room Italianate-style home still stands. The 1856 *Reddick Mansion* was built at an estimated cost of $25,000. The exterior is 50 feet tall and the interior is decorated with flourishes of molded-plaster medallions, marble fireplaces, and detailed carving. The house is open Wed, Thurs, Fri, and Sun from 11:30 a.m. to 2:30 p.m. and Sat from noon to 2:30 p.m.; admission is free; 100 W. Lafayette St.; (815) 433-6100; reddickmansion.com.

The *Buffalo Rock State Park* sits about 3 miles west of Ottawa along a sandstone bluff that was a former strip mine. Here, two bison graze in an enclosure near the park's baseball diamond, and the tall oaks and pine trees overlooking the glittering Illinois River make a perfect backdrop for hiking and picnics. The most unusual aspect of this 298-acre natural haven is something that is man-made: the **Effigy Tumuli.** Designed and created by land artist Michael Heizer, the earthwork was completed in 1985 and echoes the work of Native American mound builders. This land art portrays abstract images of indigenous Illinois creatures: a turtle, frog, snake, catfish, and water strider. Free tours can be arranged through the office at Buffalo Rock State Park; 1300 N. Twenty-seventh Road, Ottawa; (815) 433-2224.

It might sound weird, but when visiting *Starved Rock State Park* you'll find a dramatic natural forest and all the conveniences of home, making this park attractive to almost any visitor. You can spend your day roughing it along the 13 miles of hiking trails and enjoying the breathtaking canyon and waterfall views, then spend the evening lounging with a good book by the crackling flames of the lodge's giant two-sided Joliet limestone fireplace. The *Great Hall* of the *Starved Rock Lodge and Conference Center* is decked out in original 1930s decor, complete with chunky wooden furniture and well-worn round tables; it's not tacky, but solid. The dining room serves tasty meals and buffets, or you can buy a sandwich and head to the woods for a picnic overlooking the Illinois River. If you'd like to stay overnight, book a room in the newer hotel wing or ask about the availability of a rustic nearby cabin. Starved Rock Lodge and Conference Center is located at SR 178 and SR 71, Utica, or for GPS input, 2668 875th Rd., Oglesby; beware that there have been complaints that this address sometimes takes people to a cornfield, so watch for signs; (815)

Good Deed

There's a popular legend about a Boy Scout helping an old lady cross the street—it's an image rooted in the scouting motto: "Do a good turn every day." Actually, it's also a parallel of the incident that Chicago businessman and publisher William D. Boyce experienced while walking to a meeting in London, England. Boyce became disoriented and unable to navigate through the dense fog, and as he struggled to get his bearings, a young British Boy Scout holding a bright lantern approached him. The unknown scout led Boyce to the address in question, then declined a tip from the wealthy man, explaining that he was just doing a "good turn."

Impressed by the young scout, Boyce stopped at the London scouting office to gather information about the organization founded by Englishman Robert Stephenson Smyth Baden-Powell. As an employer of hundreds of paperboys in Chicago, Boyce believed the youngsters back home would benefit from the lessons of scouting. Apparently, Boyce was unaware that many independent scouting groups were already active in the U.S., as part of the YMCA. On February 8, 1910, Boyce filed incorporation documents in Washington, D.C., to establish the first official scouting organization of the Boy Scouts of America.

667-4211; www.starvedrockstatepark.org.

In the early winter months, bird lovers flock to Starved Rock during **Bald Eagle Migration,** when eagles populate the bare tree branches, looking from a distance like leaves. For easy transportation, try the **Bald Eagle Trolley Tours,** which are arranged through the lodge. Don't forget your camera and binoculars, and wear your under-armor, wooly hats, and mittens because it's going to be cold. The event is held in Jan and Feb on Mon, Wed, Sat, and Sun; tour fees vary; transportation between the visitor centers costs $1; the full tour, with a hot lunch included, costs $24 to $29 for adults, depending on the meal or buffet, and $5 for children age ten and under; (815) 220-7386; www .starvedrockstatepark.org.

For additional information and trail brochures, stop at the **Starved Rock State Park Visitors Center.** Here you'll find interactive displays, short videos about the sites and area history, a concession stand, and best of all if you've been on the trails for a long time, bathroom facilities. The center is open daily from 9 a.m. to 4 p.m., except for Thanksgiving, Christmas, and New Year's Day, when the park is closed; located at 2668 East 875th Rd, Oglesby; (815) 667-4726.

If you have kids in tow and they've had enough of traipsing along hiking trails, try out **Grizzly Jack's Grand Bear Resort** just across the street from Starved Rock. This is a combination amusement and water park that's a change of pace from all that nature, and it's indoors, so lousy weather can't interrupt the fun. The grounds include several housing options, too: select from ninety-two lodge rooms, a two-story villa, or a three-story, 2,800-square-foot cabin in the woods that sleeps eighteen. This resort would be perfect for a family reunion or get-together. Note: There are some restrictions for the safety of very small children but plenty of other activities to replace the rides loved by bigger kids. Located at 2643 N. Illinois Rte. 178, Utica; (866) 399-3866; www .grizzlyjacksresort.com.

It's rare to see barges and towboats up close, but that's exactly what you'll find at **Starved Rock Lock and Dam,** a small operation that allows for lingering and asking questions. At the **Illinois Waterway Visitor Center,** representatives of the U.S. Army Corps of Engineers provide the opportunity for visitors to witness the day-to-day operations of a lock, depending on the weather. The lock is open daily (except for Thanksgiving Day, Christmas, and New Year's Day) from 9 a.m. to 5 p.m.; located at 950 N. Twenty-seventh Rd. (CR 34), Ottawa; (815) 667-4054.

Just around the corner from the lock on the far perimeter of the town of **Utica** is the **LaSalle County Historical Society and Museum.** Archaeological artifacts from the Grand Village of the Kaskaskia Indians are on display

OTHER ATTRACTIONS WORTH SEEING IN NORTHWESTERN ILLINOIS

Fiorello's Pumpkin Patch
Caledonia

Pecatonica Prairie Path
Freeport

Silver Creek and Stephenson Railroad
Freeport

Chana School Museum
Oregon

Hauberg Indian Museum and Chief Black Hawk State Historic Site
Quad Cities

Klehm Arboretum and Botanic Gardens
Rockford

***Channel Cat* Water Taxi**
Rock Island

Savanna Train Car Museum
Savanna

Warren Cheese Plant
Warren

here, as well the carriage used to transport Abraham Lincoln to his first debate with Stephen Douglas. Check the museum's calendar for special events such as trolley tours, dinner with Lincoln, and quilt shows. The museum is open Wed through Fri from 10 a.m. to 4 p.m. and Sat and Sun from noon to 4 p.m.; 101 E. Canal St., Utica; (815) 667-4861; www.lasallecountymuseum.org.

The LaSalle Rotary Club deserves kudos for its work to preserve local history by dredging a stretch of the original *I&M Canal* and organizing one of the most popular *LaSalle County* attractions: The **LaSalle Canal Boat** is an accurate replica of an 1848 packet boat. Enjoy a leisurely boat ride as costumed interpreters transport you back in time with information about 1800s transportation along the canal route. Stop at the ***Lock 16 Visitor Center*** to arrange your trip. The center is housed in a restored brick building that was home to a carriage maker around 1910. Reservations are recommended as maintenance schedules sometimes require closures; one-hour tours run Apr to Oct, Mon through Sat at 10 and 11 a.m. and 1, 2:15, and 3:30 p.m.; and Sun at 11:15 a.m. and 1 and 2:15 p.m.; admission is $12 for adults, $10 for seniors, $6 for children ages three through sixteen, and free for those under age three; 754 First St., LaSalle; (815) 220-1848; www.lasalleboat.org.

A short walk away is the glorious 1876 *Hegeler Carus Mansion.* Outside you're greeted by a grand entry with a split-staircase that curls round to the front door; inside the wall and ceiling murals are richly detailed works of art. An especially unique feature is the turnhall, a home gymnasium that may be one of the few of that era still remaining. The brick parabolic archway that supports the gym's soaring open ceiling will give you pause. This was once the residence of zinc entrepreneur Edward Hegeler. Later, when Hegeler's son-in-law, Dr. Paul Carus, took ownership, the home became a centerpiece for cultural, scientific, and religious dialogue. The home was designed by architect William Boyington, whose credits include the imposing Joliet State Penitentiary. The mansion is open year-round Wed through Sun, with tours on the hour at 1, 2, and 3 p.m.; admission is $7 for adults, $6 for seniors, and $5 for children in kindergarten through twelfth grade; 1307 Seventh St.; (815) 224-5892; www.hegelercarus.org.

Across the street is the *Julius W. Hegeler I Home,* which was a gift from Edward to his son. The 1902 redbrick residence is being prepared for renovation, but visitors are invited to walk through. Tours are by appointment only on Saturday afternoons; admission is $15; 1306 Seventh St.; (815) 224-5892.

Traveling northeast on SR 71 you'll come across the town of *Norway,* where in the early 1840s Norwegian pioneer Cleng Peerson set down roots for himself and other Norwegian families looking for religious and political freedom. Norway became the Midwest's first permanent Norwegian settlement, and Peerson is still affectionately nicknamed the "Norwegian Daniel Boone" for his determination to forge a new life in the Illinois wilderness. Watch for the *Cleng Peerson Memorial Cemetery,* where the *Norwegian Settler's State Monument* stone stands along with four other markers commemorating the community. Then stop at the *Norsk Museum,* which is housed in an old Lutheran Church, to see artifacts of early Norwegian settlers and many fine examples of rosemaling painting. The museum is open June through Sept, Sat and Sun from 1 to 5 p.m.; admission is free; located off SR 71 on CR 2631; the museum is run by volunteers, so contact the Norwegian National League with questions; www.nnleague.org.

Next, be prepared for one of those eye-blinking moments; yes, there's a propeller plane jammed nose first into the ground, but no, it's not an actual plane crash. It's the *Agricultural Crash Monument,* which is "Dedicated to all farmers and Ag related business folks that have lived through the Agricultural Crash of the 1980s." In other words, it's a powerful visual statement, purposefully placed at the edge of a farmer's field to highlight the struggles of the U.S. farm industry. The plane has received a fresh coat of silver paint as of late, seemingly confirming that it will remain in place as a "shock and awe" monument. Visit in daylight; admission is free; located southwest of Norway on SR 71.

On I-80 at exit 56 and the junction with SR 26 you'll see four 30-by-60-foot American flags; these lighted, 110-pound flags sit on the four corners of this intersection on the north side of Princeton. This is the *Flags of Freedom*

Memorial and the first segment of a long-term project by the Bureau County Veteran's Memorial committee to honor Bureau County servicemen and women.

Princeton boasts of its friendliness, and residents here will look you in the eye and say "hello" as you pass. The Main Street business area is a combination of historical and recent construction, and shopping opportunities are varied; visit the quilt and antique stores or one of the fun and quirky retailers along the way. Nestled in the middle of *Bureau County* as the county seat, Princeton is steeped in history, so expect to spend some time visiting the historic sites here.

Begin at the town square on South Main Street, where you'll find a remarkable statue that is thought to be one of the largest winged monuments in the nation. The 1913 *Bureau County Soldiers and Sailors Winged Victory Monument* sits across from the entry of the *Bureau County Courthouse,* and it contains eight bronze tablets engraved with the names of county volunteers who served in the armed forces. Standing 50 feet high, the granite and bronze statue was erected in 1913 and cost the amazing sum of $25,000 at the time of its dedication.

The *Bureau County Historical Society Museum* maintains two buildings that stand side by side, and both are open for tours. The Prairie Square–style mansion called the *Clark-Norris Home,* built in 1899–1900, features four floors of period artifacts. Next door is the *Newell-Bryant House,* which was built in 1853 and offers a glimpse of life before the Civil War as well as displays of costumes and photography. The historical society's extensive research library is also contained here. The museum is open from Marc to Nov, Wed through Sat from 1 to 5 p.m.; admission is $3 for adults and $1 for children age twelve and under; start your tour at 109 Park Ave. West; (815) 875-2184; www.bureaucountymuseum.com.

Early Princeton citizens and brothers Cyrus and John Bryant were well-known locals who participated in the antislavery movement, but there's another Princeton abolitionist who made it into the history books: Preacher Owen Lovejoy served five terms in the U.S. House of Representatives and is said to have been an acquaintance of Abraham Lincoln, but it was his work with the Underground Railroad that garnered him real national attention. With that in mind, it's interesting to tour the *Owen Lovejoy Homestead Museum* and wonder what those walls would say if they could talk. Listed on the National Register of Historic Places, the restored, fifteen-room home has been verified as a former station of the Underground Railroad. Both this home and the redbrick, one-room 1850 *Colton Schoolhouse,* which is also located on the grounds, are managed by the city, but questions are fielded by the

Princeton Chamber of Commerce. The museum is open May through Sept, on Fri, Sat, and Sun from 1 to 4 p.m.; donations are requested; located at East Peru Street (US 6, 1 mile from downtown Princeton) and the nearby intersection of SR 26; (815) 875-2616; www.lovejoyhomestead.com.

In celebration of their great community, Princeton residents host the annual **Homestead Festival,** a four-day extravaganza with a two-hour parade, dancing in the streets, class reunions, a princess pageant, pancakes, ice cream, art, a flea market, antique car show, pioneer crafts, horse-drawn wagons, and even helicopter rides. The festival is held the second week of Sept on Thurs through Sun; admission is free; located downtown on Main Street, although some events are at various locations, so check the schedule; (815) 875-2616 (Princeton Chamber of Commerce); www.homesteadfestival.com.

There are two covered bridges in the area; one is historic and the other is a replica, but both will require your camera. Start at the real thing: the 1863 **Bureau County Red Covered Bridge** is one of only five historic covered bridges remaining in the state, and spans more than 147 feet over **Big Bureau Creek.** Unfortunately, the creek sometimes transforms into a raging river, and over the years it has flooded and damaged this treasure. It's possible that you'll be able to drive through it, but don't be surprised if it's been closed for maintenance. No troll lives here, but you should honor the stern admonition that's posted above the entry: FIVE DOLLARS FINE FOR DRIVING MORE THAN TWELVE HORSES, MULES OR CATTLE AT ONE TIME OR FOR LEADING ANY BEAST FASTER THAN A WALK ON OR ACROSS THIS BRIDGE. The bridge is located 2½ miles north of Princeton on SR 26; watch for the colorful directional sign advising you to head west; (815) 875-2616.

The second specimen also crosses Big Bureau Creek and is called the **Captain Swift Covered Bridge.** It was built in 2006 and is the only two-lane covered bridge in the state. It's so tough that it even accommodates modern traffic, including semi-trucks. Staying true to the image of an old-fashioned covered bridge, it's completely constructed of lumber using the Burr truss method, which was designed by Theodore Burr in 1804. The outside planks are rough, weathered Douglas fir; the choice gives it a more aged appearance. The bridge is located west of Princeton at 1600 Avenue North, just south of Epperson Road; (815) 875-2616.

Keep your bulls away from this china shop: **Hoffman's Patterns of the Past** is a china, crystal, and flatware replacement service that carries more than 100,000 hard-to-find patterns in its 8,000-square-foot store. Yes, you read right—8,000 square feet. The place is so large that they've nicknamed themselves the "Sea of China." Hoffman's is open Mon through Sat from 9 a.m. to 5 p.m.; 513 S. Main St., Princeton; (815) 875-1944; www.patternsofthepast.com.

There's a "bridge to nowhere" at the **Hennepin Canal Parkway State**

Park. The *Old Hennepin Canal Bridge* is just one of the remaining structures along the former canal site; also look for the *Hennepin Canal Lift Bridge* along the way. The *Hennepin Canal* was completed in 1907 as a true experiment in engineering—the first American canal constructed of concrete rather than stone. In some ways it was practice for the construction methods used in the Panama Canal. When the canal era ended, a movement began to maintain it as a vital remnant of history; recreation was the most obvious use for the waterway and the pathways alongside it. This state park is one of the most hiking and cycling friendly, as the pathways are generally well maintained and the terrain is essentially flat, making navigation easy for most all age groups and skill levels. There's fishing, canoeing, and boating on the canal; bring your snowshoes, cross-country skis, and snowmobile here in the winter. Stop at the *Hennepin Visitors Center* for a map and information on restrictions. The park is generally open Mon through Fri from 8 a.m. to 4 p.m., but hours vary with weather so it's best to call ahead, especially in winter; 16006 875 East St., Sheffield, 1 mile south of I-80, exit 45, south on SR 40; (815) 454-2328.

A utopia on the prairie: That was the dream of Swedish spiritual leader Erik Jansson and his group of immigrant followers known as the Janssonists. In 1846 they traveled to the untamed wilds of Illinois expecting to form a communal settlement based on religious and economic freedom. They named it *Bishop Hill,* but despite their determination, they were no match for the unexpected bitter winters, rampant disease, and financial instability that befell the community. Disillusioned and broken, the survivors abandoned the movement in 1861. More than thirty years later in 1896, the Old Settlers' Association was formed with the goal of preserving the physical remnants of this unique village.

That early mission to save Bishop Hill has culminated with the settlement being recognized as a National Landmark Village, as well as being listed on the National Register of Historic Places. It is also an Illinois State Historical Site. Thus, several entities own and maintain portions of the settlement, so there's some independence in the hours of operation.

The Illinois Historic Preservation Agency manages several as state historic sites: the *Bishop Hill Museum,* the *Bishop Hill Colony Hotel,* and the *Bishop Hill Colony Church.* It's best to begin your self-guided tour of these three buildings at the museum, where an orientation video is shown and brochures are available. Be sure to see the ninety-six paintings of renowned Swedish artist Olof Kranz. The museum is open Nov 1 to Feb 31, Wed through Sun from 9 a.m. to 4 p.m., and Mar 1 to Oct 31, Wed through Sun from 9 a.m. to 5 p.m.; admission is $4 for adults and $2 for children age seventeen and under; the family rate is $10; located in the Bishop Hill Historic District; start at 304 S. Bishop Hill Rd.; (309) 927-3345; www.illinoishistory.gov/hs/bishop_hill.htm.

There are two annual events sponsored by the Illinois Historic Preservation Agency that hark back to nineteenth-century Swedish culture. First is the *Jordbruksdagarna,* a harvest festival with demonstrations of gathering and processing crops. The festival is held the last weekend of Sept on Sat and Sun from 10 a.m. to 5 p.m. And at Christmas the colony celebrates *Julotta,* which is a traditional morning service at the *Bishop Hill Colony Church* (nondenominational). The liturgy is conducted in both English and Swedish, beginning at 6 a.m.; (309) 927-3345; www.bishophill.com.

The *Colony Steeple Building* is maintained by the Bishop Hill Heritage Association, and the staff will register you for an hour-and-a-half walking or riding tour; reservations are advised. The building is open May 1 to Oct 31, Wed though Sun from 9 a.m. to 4 p.m.; donations are requested; 103 N. Bishop Hill St.; (309) 927-3899; www.bishophill.com.

See exhibits of home and farm life on the Illinois prairie at the *Henry County Historical Museum.* Special seasonal events include quilt displays or photographic histories. The museum is open May 1 to Oct 31, Tues through Sun from 10 a.m. to 4 p.m.; admission is $4 for adults and children $2 for children age seventeen and under; the family rate is $10. 202 S. Park St.; (309) 927-3528; www.bishophill.com.

Additionally, fifteen of the twenty-one original buildings are open as antique, quilt, and furniture shops or restaurants, and about 125 residents, including skilled artisans, currently call Bishop Hill home. There's a full calendar of annual events sponsored by the community. Consider attending the *Midsommer Music Festival,* where live music fills the air, traditional food is served, and you can participate in activities such as *midsommarstång* (maypole decorating). The festival is held the last Sun of June from 11 a.m. to 4 p.m.; (309) 927-3345.

Chocolate lovers won't want to miss the *Chocolate Walk,* a festival of heavenly chocolate confections presented by professional chocolatiers. The event is held the first Sat and Sun of Dec from 10 a.m. to 5 p.m.; located at the Steeple Building; (309) 927-3345.

Also in December, visit the *Julmarknad* (Christmas market), where cookie bake sales are a big draw, and also attend the *Lucia Nights,* where guests are served sweets by girls wearing traditional Swedish candle-and-greens head wreaths; (309) 927-3345.

Pork and Pie Country

If you're hankering for some serious sauce, stop by **Kewanee,** where the "world's best barbecue" is served for "ninety-six hours a year" during **Hog Days.** This is one of the oldest festivals in **Henry County,** with more than fifty years under its belt. But you'll have to loosen yours after you've sampled some of the best ribs, pork chops, and pork patties in the state. Event activities include a Hog Day Stampede (5K run for people), mud volleyball, and a "hoggatta regatta." The festival is held over the Labor Day holiday for several yummy days; located on Tremont Street between Third and Fourth Streets; (309) 852-2175; www.kewaneehogdays.com.

Want some pie with that pork? Drive southwest to **Aledo,** the "Rhubarb Capital of Illinois." And how can you argue with that proclamation when they sell over 2,000 lip-smacking-good, homemade rhubarb pies during the annual **Aledo Rhubarb Festival?** Besides live music, a craft show, book sale, and the "biggest leaf" contest, there's rhubarb sampling and free rhubarb seeds for aspiring rhubarb connoisseurs. Oh, and about those pies, they sell out quickly, so plan on showing up early. The festival is held the first weekend of June from Fri at 10 a.m. to Sat at 5 p.m.; located in downtown Aledo; (309) 582-2751; www.aledomainstreet.com.

Since Aldo is the county seat of **Mercer County,** the stately 1894 **Mercer County Courthouse** is the focal point of the town square and listed on the National Register of Historic Places. Admire the exterior stonework and then take a peek inside the lobby. The courthouse is located at 100 S.E. Third Street; (309) 582-7711.

Next head across the street to book yourself into one of the more unique sleeping arrangements in the state: The **Slammer Bed and Breakfast** is a place where you can "spend the night in jail"—that is, the former Mercer County Jail, which was built in 1909 to house prisoners close by the county courthouse. Now converted into nine sleeping quarters, the Slammer also features breakfast served inside a jail cell and a tour of the ominous Padded Cell, and you can spend your time searching the well-stocked vintage books of the Law Library before you break out of the joint. The Slammer is located at 309 S. College Ave.; (309) 582-5359; www.theslammer.net.

As you drive down Aledo's main thoroughfare, you'll think time has frozen. The late-1800s buildings are classics in architectural design; and there's an old-fashioned clock on a pole sitting guard smack-dab in the middle of the roadway at the intersection of Chestnut Street. The 1910 **Aledo Opera House** was restored in 2002 and still shows movies. The Aledo is located at 108 S.E.; (309) 582-7210.

TOP ANNUAL EVENTS

JANUARY

Bald Eagle Days
Rock Island
(309) 788-5912

MAY

Fulton Dutch Days Festival
Fulton
(815) 589-2616

Annual Wildflower Pilgrimage
Starved Rock State Park, Utica
(815) 667-4726

JULY

Sauk Valley Fly-In Air Show
Dixon
(815) 284-3361

Annual Steam Threshing and Antique Show
Freeport
(800) 369-2955

Ottawa's Riverfest
Ottawa
(815) 433-0161 ext. 31

AUGUST

DeKalb Corn Festival
DeKalb
(815) 748-2676

SEPTEMBER

Autumn Pioneer Festival
Belvidere
(815) 547-7935

OCTOBER

Sycamore Pumpkin Festival
Sycamore
(815) 899-3157

NOVEMBER

Julmarknad
Bishop Hill
(309) 927-3345

The *Mercer County Historical Society* maintains three buildings, including a one-room schoolhouse and the *Essley-Noble Museum,* which stands next to the town's popular recreation area called *Fenton Park.* Visitors will see a collection of American toys, clothing, antique farm implements, and exhibits of early county life. The county genealogy library is housed here also. The museum is open Apr to Oct on Wed, Sat, and Sun from 1 to 5 p.m.; donations are requested; 1406 S.E. Second Street; (309) 582-2280.

Soprano Jenny Lind was known as the "Swedish Nightingale" when she arrived to tour America as a headliner for P. T. Barnum. In 1850 she became the benefactor for the Augustana Lutheran Synod of America, donating more than half of the funds required to build a church for the Illinois Swedish community. The church was named the *Jenny Lind Chapel* in her honor. It's a small but stunning white building minus the steeple that typically adorns the rooftop of such early churches. The steeple was omitted because the lumber was needed to build coffins to bury members of the community who had succumbed to a cholera epidemic. Today the chapel is listed on the National

Register of Historic Places and serves as a museum as well as a sanctuary for special events. The museum is open from May 1 to Oct 31, daily from 9 a.m. to 5 p.m., and summer vesper services are held during June, July, and August on Sunday at 7 p.m.; special events include Christmas services, a Christmas Community Walk, and the annual Julotta; located at the southwest corner of Sixth and Oak Streets in Andover; (309) 521-8501; http://jennylindchapel.org.

There are numerous parks and recreational areas to choose from in *Henry County,* but the *Johnson-Sauk Trail State Park* has a most unique greeting post: Near the entrance is one of the last remaining barns of its type in the state. Called *Ryan's Round Barn,* it was built by Dr. Lawrence P. Ryan, a Chicago brain surgeon who for a variety of reasons, including the thought that it would be tornado proof, spent over $9,500 in 1910 to build this three-story barn. This is a true round barn (not polygonal), and the interior woodwork in the roof, convex exterior, and detailed interior silo is just breathtaking. The Friends of Johnson's Park Foundation maintain and repair the barn and offer guided tours. The barn is open May through Oct, and visitors are welcome on the first, third, and fifth Sun of the month from 1 to 4 p.m.; located off SR 78 at the well marked park entrance, 28616 Salk Trail Rd., Kewanee; (309) 853-5589.

The history of *Rock Island* is about as dramatic as can be, with its discovery in 1675 by explorers Jacques Marquette and Louis Joliet, the role it played during the Black Hawk War, and the introduction of the railroad to this area of the state. Positioned between the Mississippi River and the *Rock River,* this island was the centerpiece for steamboat travel and commerce, attracting nearly two thousand vessels that docked here during the decades between 1820 through 1850.

It was Colonel George Davenport who first settled here in 1816 as an military man assigned the task of securing the far wilderness for the benefit of the U.S. government. The plan was to fortify a safe haven that would attract pioneers. Davenport turned into a businessman while completing his mission and built a fine home that became a trade center. Today the 1833 Federal-style *Colonel Davenport House* has been restored, and exhibits tell the tale of early conflicts, lifestyle, and fur trading. Note: Because *Arsenal Island* is government property, a photo ID is required of all individuals age sixteen and older who enter the premises. The house is open May through Oct, Thurs through Sun from noon to 4 p.m.; admission is $5 for adults, $3 for students and seniors, and $10 for families; located at the end of Hillman Avenue on Arsenal Island (originally named Rock Island); (309) 786-7336; www.davenport house.org.

Stop at the *Rock Island Centennial Bridge Visitor Center* to rent bicycles or gather brochures before heading out on a self-guided tour. The center

Child's Best Friend

Rock Island youngsters Eddie and Josie Dimick died tragically on the same day in October 1878 after a bout with diphtheria. Rex, the family's dog, joined the grieving parents at the funeral and every day afterward traipsed directly to the Chippiannock Cemetery to keep guard beside his dear charges. Upon his death, and because animal burials were not permitted at the cemetery, Eddie and Josie's parents received permission to place a life-size carving of Rex beside the children's grave. The **Rex the Loyal Dog** *statue* is just one of the stops on the cemetery tour; call ahead to schedule a tour. The cemetery is open 8 a.m. to dusk; 2901 Twelfth St.; (309) 788-6622; www.chippiannock.com.

is open Thurs through Sat from 10 a.m. to 6 p.m.; 102 Fifteenth St.; (309) 786-2417. Bike along the *Great River Trial,* which parallels the Mississippi River for about 60 miles, or just take advantage of the miles of two-lane bike trials around Rock Island. There are also numerous walking tours on Rock Island, and pamphlets are available at the visitor center and the *Rock Island Public Library* at 401 Nineteenth St.; (309) 732-7323.

Tour the *Broadway Historic District,* which includes over five hundred elaborate Queen Anne, Greek Revival and Italianate structures dating from 1854 to 1915. On the Sunday after Mother's Day, attend the annual *Broadway Tour of Homes,* where five restored houses are open for visitors and costumed docents mingle as residents did in the nineteenth century, while horse and buggies and trolleys provide rides.

In this district, you may wander upon a *Great Unveiling;* this is a spring ritual in which residents and volunteers strip away the "updated" exteriors of their homes to reveal the original siding and woodwork formerly covered by vinyl or aluminum siding substituted during modern renovations. As you walk the streets, look for signs announcing which homes are undergoing this exterior correction.

The *Rock Island Arsenal* was originally established in 1863 as a Confederate prison. Today it is used by the *U.S. Army Armament, Munitions, and Chemical Command* and is the largest arsenal in the Western Hemisphere. The location, in the middle of the Mississippi River, was well planned, with the water providing a natural buffer and security for what is called *Arsenal Island.* Since this is a government facility, proper photo ID is required of all visitors age sixteen and older.

The *Black Hawk State Historic Site* encompasses the *Black Hawk Forest,* open daily from sunrise to 10 p.m. depending on the weather. There are points of interest at this site such as the *Hauberg Indian Museum.* Guests will learn about the Black Hawk War and view Indian artifacts and full-size replicas of both summer and winter homes used by native Salk tribes in Illinois. The site is open Mar through Oct, Wed through Sun from 9 a.m. to noon and 1 to 5 p.m., and Nov through Feb, Wed through Sun from 9 a.m. to noon and 1 to 4 p.m.; 1510 Forty-sixth Ave.; (309) 788-0177.

Also here is the *Singing Bird Nature Center,* which maintains a research area for bird enthusiasts. The building features large windows that overlook bird-feeding stations so visitors can view unaware birds feasting away in their natural surroundings. Hours vary and visitors are asked to call ahead at (309) 788-9536; www.blackhawkpark.org.

Like Rock Island, *Moline* and sister city *East Moline* are part of the *Quad Cities* (the others are Davenport and Bettendorf, Iowa, and yes, it's more like five cities than four) that have pulled resources to form a vibrant business and entertainment center for residents in the area. Moline is the city that John Deere built when he moved his self-scouring plow manufacturing operation here from Grand Detour because of Moline's proximity to the Mississippi River. Actually, the Mississippi is an integral part of the quality of life for residents, and a fifty-million-dollar construction renaissance has revitalized the riverfront and its allure with modern buildings, popular restaurants, and shops located along the *John Deere Commons.*

deere incorporated

By 1876, John Deere was producing more than 60,000 plows a year. In 1868 he incorporated the company under the name Deere and Company, and in 1876, the company registered its classic trademark, the leaping deer.

Begin at the *John Deere Pavilion,* where you can view agricultural exhibits. The facility is designed like a barn, but extensive use of glass windows gives it a contemporary feel. The museum is open Mon through Fri from 9 a.m. to 5 p.m., Sat from 10 a.m. to 5 p.m., and Sun from noon to 4 p.m.; admission free; 1400 River Dr., Moline; (309) 765-1000; www.deere.com/en_US/attractions/pavilion/index.html. Then, if you're into souvenirs, head across the street to the *John Deere Store,* where you'll find lots of those miniature John Deere tractor toys, plus clothing, books,

climbon

Visitors to Moline's John Deere Pavilion are invited to "climb on"— an invitation for anyone who's ever dreamed of taking a seat in a brand new tractor or combine to climb aboard. Antique rides are off-limits, though, so look but don't touch!

and knickknacks, all sporting the company's familiar green and yellow color combination and that cute jumping deer. The store is open Jan and Feb, Mon through Sat from 10 a.m. to 5 p.m. and Sun from noon to 4 p.m., and Mar through Dec, Mon through Fri from 10 a.m. to 6 p.m., Sat from 10 a.m. to 5 p.m., and Sun from noon to 4 p.m.; 1300 River Dr.; (309) 765-1007.

By now you must be ready for a sugar fix, so travel next to ***Lagomarcino's Confectionery,*** where for more than a century this family-owned shop has served its trademark golden sponge candy coated with rich dark chocolate. Take a seat in one of the antique mahogany booths and treat yourself to a 1920s soda-fountain specialty: a Green River phosphate. The hot-fudge sundae is another favorite, and comes with a side pitcher of hot fudge so you can be assured of a rich, chocolaty mouthful with every bite. The shop is located at 1422 Fifth Ave., Moline; (309) 764-1814; www.lagomarcinos.com.

Places to Stay in Northwestern Illinois

DEKALB

Best Western DeKalb Inn and Suites
1212 W. Lincoln Way Hwy.
(815) 758-8661
www.bestwestern
illinois.com

Magnuson Inn
1314 W. Lincoln Hwy.
(815) 747-8713
www.magnusonhotels.com

DIXON

Comfort Inn
136 Plaza Dr.
(815) 284-0500
www.comfortinn.com

Quality Inn and Suites
154 Plaza Dr.
(815) 288-2001
www.qualityinn.com

ELIZABETH

Dinner and Dreams Guest House
120 W. Main St.
(815) 858-2357
www.dinneranddreams
inc.com

FREEPORT

Baymont Inn
1060 Riverside Dr.
(815) 599-8510
www.baymontinns.com

Country Inn and Suites— Carlson
1710 S. Dirck Dr.
(815) 233-3300
www.countryinns.com

GALENA

Aldrich Guest House
900 Third St.
(815) 777-3323
www.aldrichguest
house.com

Best Western Quiet House and Suites
9923 US 20 West
(815) 777-2577
www.quiethouse.com

Chestnut Mountain Resort
8700 W. Chestnut Rd.
(815) 777-1320
www.chestnutmtn.com

Country Inn and Suites
11334 Oldenburg Lane
(815) 777-2400
www.countryinns.com

DeSoto House Hotel
230 S. Main St.
(815) 777-0090
www.desotohouse.com

**Eagle Ridge Inn
and Resort**
444 Eagle Ridge Dr.
(815) 777-5000
www.eagleridge.com

**Galena Log Cabin
Getaway**
9401 W. Hart John Rd.
(815) 777-4200
www.galenalogcabins.com

Hellman Guest House
318 Hill St.
(815) 777-3638
www.hellmanguest
house.com

Pine Hollow Inn
4700 N. Council Hill Rd.
(815) 777-1071

Queen Anne Guest House
200 Park Ave.
(815) 777-3849
www.queenanneguest
house.com

LANARK

Standish House
540 W. Carroll St.
(815) 493-2307

MOLINE

Days Inn & Suites
6910 Twenty-seventh St.
(309) 762-8300
www.daysinnmoline.com

La Quinta Inn
5450 Twenty-seventh St.
(309) 762-9008
www.lq.com

Quality Inn and Suites
6920 Twenty-seventh St.
(309) 762-1548
www.qualityinn.com

**Radisson on John Deere
Common**
1415 River Dr.
(309) 764-1000
www.radisson.com/molineil

MORRIS

Day's Inn and Suites
80 Hampton Rd.
(815) 942-9000
www.daysinn.com

Holiday Inn
222 Gore Rd.
(800) 230-4134
www.holidayinn.com

MOUNT CARROLL

Prairie Path Guest House
1002 N. Lowden Rd.
(815) 244-3462

MOUNT MORRIS

White Pines Inn
6712 W. Pines Rd.
(815) 734-7297
www.whitepinesinn.com

OREGON

**Pinehill Inn Bed and
Breakfast**
400 Mix St.
(815) 732-2067
www.pinehillbb.com

PRINCETON

AmericInn of Princeton
2120 Claude Bailey
Parkway
(815) 872-5000
www.americinn.com/
hotels/il/princeton

Econo Lodge
2200 N. Main St.
(815) 872-3300
www.econolodge.com

ROCKFORD

**Clock Tower Resort and
Conference Center**
7801 E. State St.
(815) 398-6000
www.clocktowerresort.com

Fairfield Inn and Suites
7651 Walton St.
(815) 398-7400
www.marriott.com

Hampton Inn
615 Clark Rd.
(815) 229-0404
www.hamptoninn1.hilton
.com

Howard Johnson Hotel
309 Eleventh St.
(815) 397-9000
www.hojorockford.com

ROCK ISLAND

Four Points Sheraton
226 Seventeenth St.
(309) 794-1212
www.starwoodhotels.com

**Victorian Inn Bed &
Breakfast**
702 Twentieth St.
(309) 788-7068
www.victorianinn
bandb.com

SHEFFIELD

Chestnut Street Inn
301 E. Chestnut St.
(815) 454-2419
www.chestnut-inn.com

SYCAMORE

Stratford Inn
355 W. State St.
(815) 895-6789
www.stratfordinnhotel.com

SELECTED VISITORS BUREAUS AND CHAMBERS OF COMMERCE

Illinois Bureau of Tourism—Travel
Information
(800) 2-CONNECT

Blackhawk Waterways Convention
and Visitors Bureau
201 N. Franklin Ave.
Polo, 61064
(815) 946-2108

Galena-Jo Daviess County
Convention and Visitors Bureau
101 Bouthillier St.
Galena, 61036
(877) 464-2536

Rockford Area Convention and
Visitors Bureau
102 N. Main St.
Rockford, 61101
(815) 963-8111

Quad Cities Convention and
Visitors Bureau
1601 River Dr., Suite 110
Moline, 61265
(309) 277-0937

Stephenson County Convention and
Visitors Bureau
4596 US 20 East
Freeport, 61032
(815) 233-1357

UTICA

**Starved Rock State Park
Lodge**
SR 178 and SR 71
(815) 667-4211
www.starvedrocklodge
.com

Places to Eat in Northwestern Illinois

FREEPORT

Beltline Cafe
325 W. South St.
(815) 232-5512

GALENA

Bubba's
300 N. Main St.
(815) 777-8030

Fried Green Tomatoes
213 N. Main St.
(815) 777-3938
www.friedgreen.com

Log Cabin
201 N. Main St.
(815) 777-0393
www.logcabingalena.com

Market House Restaurant
204 Perry St.
(815) 777-0690
www.markethouse
tavern.com

Perry Street Brasserie
124 N. Commerce St.
(815) 777-3773
www.perrystreetbrasserie
.com

MOLINE

River House Bar and Grill
1510 River Dr.
(309) 797-1234
www.riverhouseqc.com

ROCKFORD

**Great Wall Chinese
Restaurant**
4228 E. State St.
(815) 226-0982

EASTERN ILLINOIS

Rivers and Trails

Vermilion County is green; between the three state and three county parks located here, there are over 15,000 acres of recreation space. The largest city is the county seat of **Danville,** which was settled by workers who mined salt some 4 miles east. As early as 1801, salt had become the area's favored industry, and today, at the intersection of Lafayette and North Gilbert Streets, visitors can stop by the **Lincoln/saltworks marker,** which is on a waist-high wall built of stones from Abraham Lincoln's Danville law office. The wall is topped with a large black salt kettle from a nearby salt mine.

To learn more about the county's origins, begin your visit at the **Vermilion County Museum** complex located behind the marker. The museum building is a brick replica of the county's first courthouse, built in 1833, and contains exhibits depicting an early schoolhouse, coal mine, and the office Lincoln shared with Ward Hill Lamon. Throughout the month of July, the museum hosts the popular **Midwest Heritage Quilt Show.**

Also on the property is the 1855 **Fithian Home,** residence to legislator and physician Dr. William Fithian. The home is

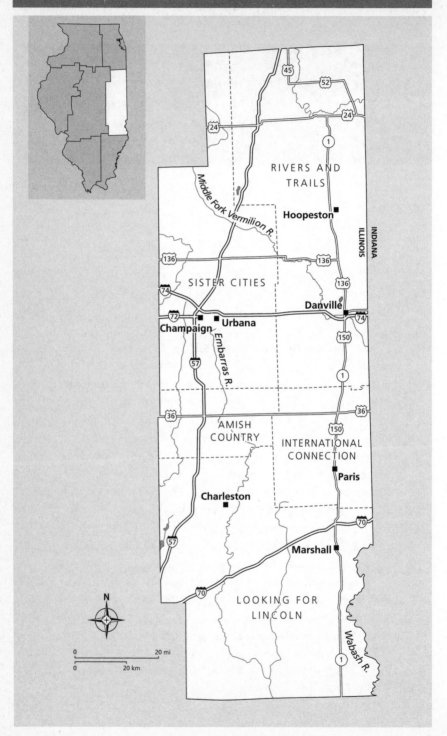

EASTERN ILLINOIS

RIVERS AND
TRAILS

Hoopeston

ILLINOIS
INDIANA

SISTER CITIES

Middle Fork Vermilion R.

Danville

Champaign
Urbana

Embarras R.

AMISH
COUNTRY

INTERNATIONAL
CONNECTION

Paris

Charleston

Marshall

LOOKING FOR
LINCOLN

Wabash R.

N

0   20 mi
0   20 km

on the National Register of Historic Places and verified as a Lincoln site. As a friend of Lincoln, Fithian opened his home to the future president and, as trite as it might sound, Lincoln slept in the canopy bed that is on display here and campaigned from the second-story balcony during his U.S. Senate run. The home is open Tues through Sat from 10 a.m. to 5 p.m.; admission is $4 for adults, $1 for children ages twelve through seventeen, and free for children under age eleven; 116 N. Gilbert St.; (217) 442-2922; www.vermilioncounty museum.org.

In downtown *Lincoln Park* you'll find the restored 1850 *Lamon House,* which was home to the cousin of Lincoln's law partner and currently serves as a living-history museum run by the *Vermilion County Museum Society.* The quaint, one-story, Greek Revival–style cottage is thought to be the county's oldest remaining frame house. The house is open May through Oct, Sun from 1:30 to 4:30 p.m.; they also have special hours during Christmas, so call ahead; 1031 N. Logan Ave.; (217) 442-2922; www.lamonhouse.org.

Each summer the museum society hosts the *Scent of July Garden Walk,* where between six and ten homes in the *Lincoln Park Historic District* open their beautifully landscaped gardens or front porches for visitors to explore; it's a fund-raiser that supports the renovations needed at the Lamon House. The event is usually held the third Sat of July; admission is $12 per person.

The *Vermilion County War Museum* is housed in the former Carnegie Library building, constructed in 1903. The building has been restored and is worth the price of admission itself. The museum covers 14,000 square feet and is a center of tribute as much as a collection of artifacts. Exhibit topics begin with the Revolutionary War. The museum is open Tues through Fri from noon

AUTHOR'S TOP FIVE PICKS

Country Cheese and More
Arthur
(217) 543-3544

The Heartland Spa
Gilman
(800) 545-4853

Lincoln Log Cabin State Historic Site
Lerna
(217) 345-1845

Kickapoo State Park
Oakwood
(217) 442-4915

University of Illinois
Urbana-Champaign
(217) 333-1000

to 3 p.m. and Sat from 10 a.m. to 4 p.m.; admission is $2 for adults, $1 for children ages seven through eighteen, and free for children age six and under; 307 N. Vermilion St.; (217) 431-0034; www.vcwm.org.

If you need quick refreshment, try the **Custard Cup,** a longtime local landmark that specializes in super-creamy frozen custard. And don't ask for ice cream when you order! The Custard Cup is located at 2507 N. Vermilion St.; (217) 443-0221.

For an evening of fine dining, visit **The Heron,** a supper club unlike those found up north. Housed in a historic Danville building, the woodwork is divine and the front-entry Palladian window is about as antique as you can get with its wide, Tiffany–style panes. After your gourmet meal, stick around for the great jazz. Dinner is served Wed through Sat from 5:30 to 9:30 p.m.; 34 N. Vermilion St.; (217) 446-8330; www.danvilleheron.com.

If you'd rather look for the live kind (of herons that is), visit **Heron County Park,** where man-made wetlands create a choice waterfowl attraction. The wetlands are found on the northern tip of **Lake Vermilion** and were developed by raising the water level about 5 feet. Stroll the **wetland boardwalk,** a unique 950-foot wooden walkway that floats atop the water's surface; then stop at the observation tower to get a bird's-eye view of the eagles and hawks nesting or resting in the surrounding bald cypress trees. Both the boardwalk and tower are handicapped accessible, making this wonderful nature getaway suitable for all ages. Bring your binoculars! The park is open from dawn to dusk; 22296-A Henning Rd.; (217) 442-1691; www.vccd.org/giheron.htm.

At the east edge of central Illinois is the county's second largest town, **Hoopeston.** This is corn central. For nearly seventy years, Hoopeston has hosted the annual **Sweet Corn Festival,** and you might think it'd be like other corn festivals in the state, but it's not. At this one you won't leave hungry,

Corn Art

As you circle Hoopeston's **McFerren Park,** keep your eyes open for what might be the tallest cornstalk in the nation that's not technically a cornstalk. Titled **Tribute to the American Farmer,** this agricultural sculpture is 16 feet high and was designed by area artist Dana Thomas, who was assisted by many local businesses and townspeople in bringing the vision to form. Originally used as "field art" for the 2003 Farm Progress Show, it was moved to its current location shortly afterward. Keeping with the farming theme, the artwork is constructed of materials commonly found on a working farm; the cornstalk's leaves are metal, the corn kernels are tractor-tire treads, and the main stalk is wood.

Lost Trail

As you head south from Rossville along SR 1, watch for an old brick church with a traditional steeple just to the east of the roadway. This is *Mann's Chapel,* built in 1857 and the oldest church in Vermilion County. It was restored in the 1950s, and although it lacks modern conveniences such as heat, restrooms, and electricity, there is a working pump organ that makes this location a picturesque place for weddings from April to October. Otherwise, the building isn't open for tours, so plan on taking exterior photographs.

Nearby is an original 1833 *Hubbard's Trail mile marker,* a well-weathered stone that might be easily overlooked, as it stands unceremoniously within visual distance of the chapel, when the corn isn't too high in the field that separates the two. The former Indian trail ran between Fort Dearborn in Chicago and Vincennes, Indiana, and was also known as Hubbard's Trace at the time when fur trading emerged as valuable commerce across the Illinois Territory. In 1833 the state converted the path into an official roadway, and it was eventually paved to accommodate automobiles, reinforcing its use as a main artery between Danville and Chicago.

because everyone gets a free corn on the cob, cooked, buttered, and salted to perfection. It's worth the drive just to see how they cook over fifty tons of corn during this corn extravaganza. It starts with an antique John Deere engine, a conveyer belt, husking machine and rollers, cold water, and an authentic steam engine heating boiling kettles, and then there's cooking, dumping onto a table, seasoning, and finally gobbling. You'll have to attend to catch all the details in between. Of course, there's a parade, and a carnival, demolition derby, and lots of other food, too. But there's one event during this festival that's rather unexpected: It's the *National Miss Sweetheart Pageant,* and no, this isn't a little kid contest. This is a nationally sanctioned pageant, and no less than eight former participants have gone on to become Miss America. Events run for five days over the Labor Day holiday; located at McFerren Park off of South Dixie Highway (SR 1) and West Penn Street; (217) 283-7873; www.hoopeston.org.

About 7 miles south on the Dixie Highway (SR 1), you'll come to the village of *Rossville,* which has literally risen from the ashes. In 2004 the downtown suffered a major fire that damaged nearly a quarter of the historic buildings. Today, more than twenty antiques and gift stores again line the main street, reviving the theme "The Village of Unusual Shops." But there are some historical venues of note here, too.

The *Rossville Depot Railroad Museum* was built in 1903, but today it's been renovated to reflect the 1950s. This isn't a typical depot museum brimming with maps and wallpapered with photographs. Every inch of this space is well used in what is dubbed "railroadiana" decor; there's a working telegraph with keys and sounders in the operator's bay, all sorts of lanterns, a 4-foot-high engine replica, and a bass drum (yes, that's right); and my guess is that the reason this place isn't filled with stacks of out-of-date train schedules is probably because it's managed by die-hard railroad enthusiasts from the *Danville Junction Chapter of the National Railway Historical Society.* Don't miss the *Baggage Room,* where over 1,000 feet of track carries HO trains through accurate-to-scale towns. The museum is open Memorial Day through Labor Day and summer holidays, Sat and Sun from noon to 4 p.m.; 210 E. Benton St.; www.danvillejct.org/museum.html.

The *Rossville Historical Society Museum* features three floors of local history, with displays depicting an 1890–1900 school, jail, doctor's office, pharmacy, and military artifacts. The museum is open Tues and Sat from noon to 4 p.m.; donations are requested; 108 W. Attica St.; (217) 748-6045.

Canine lovers will get a lick out of Rossville's *Dog Days of Summer* annual dog show and parade, held the first Sat of Aug. Admission is charged on a per-dog basis for adults; the fee for children ages twelve and under is $3; (217) 260-4700.

Sister Cities

The neighboring cities of *Urbana* and *Champaign* are home to the *University of Illinois,* the largest institution of higher learning in the state, with over forty-one thousand students in attendance. The university's successes in research and innovation, particularly in science, computing, engineering, and technology, have garnered this area of the state the nickname "Silicon Prairie." There are many places of interest on campus, but be aware that security rules may limit your access.

With that in mind, visit the *Krannert Art Museum* to experience its collection of fine art, sculpture, and ancient art. More than 130,000 people visit the museum yearly. A truly fascinating exhibit here falls under the topic of intermedia art, which combines traditional canvas work with computer-generated images. Also visit the *Kinkead Pavilion* wing of the museum, where over 9,000 works stand in the permanent collection. The museum is open during the regular school semester, Tues through Sat from 9 a.m. to 5 p.m. and Sun from 2 to 5 p.m.; closed on Mon; admission is $3 per person; 500 E. Peabody Dr., Champaign; (217) 333-1861; www.kam.uiuc.edu.

twothumbsup

Urbana native Roger Ebert began reviewing movies in 1967. In 1975 he became the first film critic to win the Pulitzer Prize for Criticism.

Vintage Barns

Since the University of Illinois was chartered as one of the nation's first land-grant colleges, its roots are settled in agricultural experimentation, which includes all aspects of farming. One area of early study focused on the most efficient and useful designs of barns; this gave rise to the construction of round barns that eventually gained popularity in the Midwest. Three examples still sit in a cluster in the **University of Illinois Experimental Dairy Farm Historic District.** They are identified as the 1908 **Twenty-acre Dairy Barn,** the 1910 **Dairy Horse Barn,** and the 1912 **Dairy Experiment Barn;** each rendition improved upon the former one to optimize dairy production. These barns are listed on the National Register of Historic Places and although they aren't open for tours, they're a novel site as you drive by. The barns are located at 1201 St. Mary's Rd. in Urbana.

The **Spurlock Museum** features five galleries focusing on ancient civilizations such as Egypt, East Asia, Mesopotamia, Southeast Asia, and Oceania. Special events include performances by dancers and musicians reflecting those cultures. The museum is open during the regular school semester, Tues from noon to 5 p.m., Wed through Fri from 9 a.m. to 5 p.m., Sat from 10 a.m. to 4 p.m., and Sun from noon to 4 p.m.; closed on Mon; admission is $3 per person; 600 S. Gregory St., Urbana; (217) 333-2360; www.spurlock.uiuc.edu.

Another unique university museum is the ever-expanding **Sousa Archives and Center for American Music,** which contains the world's largest compilation of original John Philip Sousa music manuscripts, plus period uniforms and historical instruments. The center is open Mon through Fri from 8:30 a.m. to 5 p.m., but tour appointments are recommended; admission is free; located in the **Harding Band Building** at 1103 S. Sixth St., Champaign; (217) 244-9309; www.library.illinois.edu/sousa.

footballfirst

Records show that the University of Illinois was the first in the nation to institute a football homecoming celebration. It was held on October 15, 1910, and what a day it was for the Illini; they beat the University of Chicago by 3-0, and broke a nine-year losing streak with Chicago.

When a town is dependent on a student body for economic survival, it's common to find excellent meal deals in surrounding eateries. Here are recommendations from people in the know.

Possibly the best Chicago-style deep-dish pizza outside the Second City's borders is served at **Papa Del's.** Expect to use silverware to eat it, and plan on leaving enough time in your schedule because these pies take forty-five minutes to bake. The restaurant is located at 206 E. Green St., Champaign; (217) 359- 7700. For a customized pizza or sandwich, try **Za's Italian Café,** where the menu is designed by you; healthy eaters and green-conscious patrons will appreciate Za's whole wheat and organic items and the money-back option if you return with your formerly used Za's drinking cup. This is a great family place and they've expanded to two Champaign locations; 1905 N. Neil St., (217) 356-5347, and 2600 W. Springfield Ave.; (217) 355-4990; zasitaliancafe.com.

You might have to wait for an hour to get in, but **Dos Reales** is authentic Mexican with generous portions, and prices that fit a starving student's budget. Try the chicken quesadilla, cheese dip nachos, and mango margaritas. Located at 1407 N. Prospect Ave.; (217) 351-6879.

For the more exotic palate, indulge in the beautifully crafted sushi at **Miko Restaurant.** The prices are a bit higher here, but the ambience makes it perfect for special occasions. If you're looking for entertainment, ask to be seated at a teppanyaki table, where the chef will cook your selections before your eyes. The restaurant is located at 407 W. University Dr., Urbana; (217) 367-0822; www.mikorestaurant.com.

Another more refined casual dining choice is **Silvercreek,** where the menu is seasonal, the breads are fresh baked on site, and the rustic decor strikes a perfect combination. The in-house pastry chef creates dessert special-ties daily; don't hesitate to try their fantastic version of Death by Chocolate. Silvercreek is located at 402 N. Race St., Urbana; (217) 328-3402; www.courier silvercreek.com/silvercreek.

There are also plenty of area attractions that aren't associated with the uni-versity. One example is the historical building that's home to the **Champaign County Historical Museum.** Once an office of the 1856 Grand Prairie Bank of Urbana, the **Cattle Bank Building** is thought to be the oldest business building in town. Keeping with that theme, there are bank-related exhibits here as a well as a research library. The museum is open Sat and Sun from noon to 5 p.m., but please call ahead if you're coming from a distance; dona-tions are requested; 102 E. University Ave., Champaign; (217) 356-1010; www .champaignmuseum.org.

A great place for the kids is the **Prairie Farm at Centennial Park.** Here you'll find a replica of a turn-of-the-century farm with barns, a pond and pas-ture, and a flower garden. The usual menagerie of farm animals is present and there's a separate petting-zoo area. Reminder: No open-toed shoes, bare feet, or sandals are allowed, as the animals might mistake toes for nibbles. The farm is open Memorial Day through Labor Day, daily from 1 to 7 p.m., but the pet-ting area is open daily from 3 to 5 p.m.; admission is free; 2202 W. Kirby Ave.; (217) 398-2583; www.champaignparkdistrict.com/facilities/pfarm.

For more fresh air, stop at the *Curtis Orchard,* where the smell of apple blossoms will tickle your nose. The store carries over thirty varieties of apples, and in the fall you can pick your own in the orchard. There's also a pleasant cafe on-site, and pies, cobbler, donuts, and fudge are sold in the bakery. Feed the animals, or for a nominal fee get lost in the corn maze; take a pony ride or attend special events on weekends that include live music and entertainment. Guarding the orchard near the parking area is a *giant metal Indian statue* posed with his bow in

popcorn on wheels

The Champaign County Museum owns a *Cretors popcorn truck,* which was built in 1919 but modified over the years. The original steam popper has been replaced with an electric cooker, and the 1910 Ford Model T truck chassis has been switched to a more dependable 1967 Chevrolet; the modifications allow this machine-on-wheels to attend town events.

place and the arrow ready to strike. This landmark was built by Herb Drews in 1949 as an advertisement for a Danville company. In 1994 the Curtises purchased the sculpture and moved it to this site. The orchard is open from late July to Oct, Mon through Sat from 9 a.m. to 6 p.m. and on Sun from 11 a.m. to 6 p.m., and Nov through mid-Dec, Mon through Sat from 9 a.m. to 5:30 p.m. and on Sun from 11 a.m. to 5 p.m.; 3902 S. Duncan Rd., Champaign; (217) 359-5565; www.curtisorchard.com.

The *Champaign County Forest Preserve District* manages six forest preserves and designated waterfowl areas, but several have venues of special note. At the *Lake of the Woods Forest Preserve,* visitors are treated to the *Mabery Gelvin Botanical Garden,* where extensive plantings of native flowers and fauna are arranged in lovely gardens that are perfect for an afternoon stroll. Since specimens are marked with identification signs, this is a learning experience as well. Another garden contained here is the *Miriam H. Davis Enabling Garden,* which is geared toward those in wheelchairs or with special needs, as the raised flower beds allow easy viewing of the herbs, waterfall, and blooming flowers. The *All-American Selections Display* features bedding plants popular throughout the nation. The preserves are open from 7 a.m. to sundown; admission is free; 109 S. Lake of the Woods Rd., Mahomet; (217) 586-4389.

Also on these grounds is the *Early American Museum,* a living history settlement where costumed volunteers demonstrate the everyday activities of early settlers, such as dipping candles, quilting, making soap, and spinning wool. The museum is open Mar through Dec, daily from 1 to 5 p.m., with additional summer hours from June through Aug, when it opens at 10 a.m.

TOP ANNUAL EVENTS

MAY

Sheep to Clothing, Lincoln Log Cabin State Historic Site
Lerna
(217) 345-1845

JUNE

Raggedy Ann Friendship Gathering
Arcola
(800) 336-5456

Taste of Urbana-Champaign
Champaign
(217) 398-2550

SEPTEMBER

Sweetcorn Festival/National Sweetheart Pageant
Hoopeston
(217) 283-7679

Broomcorn Festival
Arcola
(800) 336-5456

University of Illinois football games
Champaign
(217) 333-3470

OCTOBER

Harvest Frolic, Lincoln Log Cabin State Historic Site
Lerna
early Oct
(217) 345-1845

Mon through Sat; donations are requested; 600 N. Lombard St., Mahomet; (217) 586-2612; www.earlyamericanmuseum.org.

The *Champaign County Audubon Society,* in conjunction with the Champaign County Forest Preserve District, sponsors *Migration Fest* at the *Homer Lake Forest Preserve.* Participants of all ages are treated to a variety of activities, including hikes, storytelling, crafts, and up-close and personal visits with live raptors. The festival is held at the end of Apr, from 1 to 5 p.m.; admission is free; Homer Lake Forest Preserve, 2573 S. Homer Lake Rd., Homer; (217) 896-2455; www.ccfpd.org.

North and slightly east of Urbana is the village of *Rantoul,* which was established in 1890 and named in honor of Robert Rantoul, president of the Illinois Central Railroad. This was a place where travel by land merged with travel by air, and today the railroad is still running but the airport isn't. The former buildings of the now-closed Chanute Air Force Base are rented by a variety of companies. The *Chanute Air Museum* operates on these grounds, and those interested in the history of U.S. and Illinois aviation can enjoy the many exhibits about early flight pioneers, air squadrons, and Octave Chanute (1832–1910), whom some refer to as the "father of American aviation." Check out the military aircraft and underground missile silo, too.

The ***Rantoul Historical Society*** maintains display space on this campus, featuring memorabilia of early life in Rantoul as well as artifacts from World War II. Note: The parking lot is across the street from the museum. The society is open Mon through Sat from 10 a.m. to 5 p.m. and on Sun from noon to 5 p.m.; admission is $10 for adults ages fourteen and up, $8 for seniors, $5 for children ages five through thirteen, and free for children under age five; 1011 Pacesetter Dr.; (217) 893-1613; www.aeromuseum.org.

During the summer months you might see a lot of orange and blue around Rantoul. That's because the town becomes ***Camp Rantoul*** when the ***Fighting Illini Football Team*** and entourage arrive for preseason practices. Watch for signs, players, coaches, and television crews; practices are open to the public, but the times change depending on the weather. Preseason practices are held in early August with most beginning after 2 p.m.; located at the ***Bill Seeber Memorial Soccer Complex,*** 300 W. Flessner Ave.; signs may direct you from Gray Avenue and Doolittle Boulevard; (217) 893-0461; http://myrantoul.com.

It's possible that some of Santa's best retired stock are living at ***Hardy's Reindeer Ranch.*** Well, that's what you can tell the kiddies. These beautiful creatures are from Alaska and the first two were originally imported to Illinois as a way to advertise the ranch's Christmas tree farm, but the family loved them so much that they've expanded the herd to over fifteen. Visitors are invited to tour the reindeer's living area and meet them close up. There's a gift shop at the ranch as well as a banquet hall, and a calendar of special event weekends. The ranch is open Aug and Sept, Mon through Sat from 10 a.m. to 6 p.m. and on Sun from 1 to 6 p.m.; Oct, Mon through Sat from 10 a.m. to 8 p.m. and on Sun from 1 to 8 p.m.; and Nov and Dec, Mon through Sat from 10 a.m. to 7 p.m. and on Sun from 1 to 7 p.m.; there are also special hours around the Christmas holiday; admission for the reindeer tour only is $3 for each person and includes a snack to feed the reindeer, while other activities are charged on a per-use basis; 1356 County Rd. 2900 North; (217) 893-3407; www.reindeerranch.com.

Perfect Union

It was a happy marriage between the villages of Urbana and Rantoul and the railroad that guided the U.S. War Department to select this location for a U.S. air base. The skilled engineers and hopeful pilots from the student body of the nearby University of Illinois sealed the deal, and the Chanute Field opened in July 1917, becoming home to some of the new U.S. Air Force fliers and their machines. The affair lasted for more than seventy-five years until the government closed the facility in 1993.

Gotta Laugh

You can't say that the people in the far southeastern corner of **Moultrie County** don't have a good sense of humor. After all, the hamlet of **Gays** is famous for, of all things, the **Historical Two-Story Outhouse.** Not only is it a tourist attraction, but it sits as the featured star in the town's little **Goodwin Park.** It was built in 1872 as a privy for the emporium and second-story apartments owned by shopkeeper Samuel Gamill. The original store building was demolished in the 1980s, but the outhouse remained, after being championed by local preservationist citizens. The rooms seat four, two up and two down, and an ingenious design directs the upstairs waste behind the back wall, giving those on the first level peace of mind. The building isn't open for tours, but it's suitable for a photograph or two. The outhouse is located at 1022 Pine St., Gays.

Just down the street is **Gifford,** a little bitty town with a huge venue for horses and more. **Gordyville USA** is a sprawling, 160,000-square-foot building sitting smack-dab in the middle of over forty-acres of prime cornfields. So what do farmers (and families) do in the winter when not much is happening 'cause there's snow on the ground? They participate in or attend horse shows, indoor rodeos, barrel racing, auctions, flea markets, tractor-pull competitions, and farm-equipment and antique shows. This place accommodates over 700 portable stalls and has become the Midwest's premier indoor horse-show and activity center. Now that'll keep your mind off those snowdrifts! Check their Web site or call for calendar updates; admission varies with events; located at 2205 CR 3000 North, off Route 136 East; (217) 568-7117; www.gordyville usa.com.

Land of Quilts and Funny

In this era of fast cars and freeways, it's always a bit jarring to come upon a slow-trotting horse pulling a modest black buggy. The Amish have called Illinois home since the 1830s, and today most live in the counties of Douglas and Moultire. To visitors they seem like an enigma, but in recent years many Amish have made strides to open their culture to outsiders. Through the **Illinois Amish Interpretive Center** in **Arcola,** guests can learn about the Amish lifestyle by taking one of seven different **Amish Country Tours;** itineraries include sharing a traditional meal inside an Amish home, riding in an Amish wagon, or visiting an Amish woodworker's business. The center offers something for every interest and budget. Also on-site are the only **Amish Museum** in the state and a gift store. The museum is open Mon through Sat from 9 a.m.

to 5 p.m.; admission to the museum is $5 for adults, $4 for seniors, $3 for children ages six through thirteen, and free for children under age five; tours vary in price; 111 S. Locust St.; (888) 452-6474; www.amishcenter.com.

Next, stop at **Rockome Gardens,** where the word "rock" takes on a new meaning; because of all the attractions and events here, this is one of those "gotta see it to believe it" kinds of places. Rockome Gardens began as the brain-child of Arthur and Elizabeth Martin, who purchased the property in 1930 as a vacation haven. Mrs. Martin pictured gardens gracing the land, so her compassionate businessman husband directed his workers to create the stonework on the property as a way to keep paying his workers during the Great Depression.

Reopened in 2006 under new management, the focus here is still decidedly old-fashioned and family friendly. Artisans demonstrate making soap and throwing pottery; the village includes a blacksmith shop, ice-cream parlor, schoolhouse, petting zoo, and a train that chugs into the park's fifteen-acres of "backwoods." Visitors often finish the day with a rib-sticking meal at the **Rock-ome Restaurant,** where they have daily specials and delicious fried chicken.

horsepower

Illinois Amish drive black buggies outfitted with government-required LED lights, reflective tape, and an orange caution triangle. Amish families typically own multiple buggies, and the average speed of a one-horse ride is less than 10 miles per hour.

Cowboy Camp runs most Saturdays, and for $65 aspiring cowpokes can practice roping and rodeo skills, then share a hearty meal around a campfire. There are a whopping seventeen special events during the year, including a **Blue Grass Festival** (third week of Aug), **Pioneer Days** (second week of July), and the **Family Band Weekend** (end of May). Rockome is open May 1 to Oct 31, daily from 10 a.m. to 6 p.m., with some exceptions on Sun, depending on event scheduling; during Nov and Dec the park is closed, but entry is free if you're going to the **Country Heritage Craft Store** and the **Heart and Home Store,** which are open Thurs though Sat from 10 a.m. to 4:30 p.m. so patrons can purchase holiday gift baskets and Amish baked goods. Regular park admission is $8 for adults, $6 for seniors, and $4 for children, with additional fees for some special events and activities such as horseback riding, kayaking, pony rides, and fishing; 125 N. CR 425 East, Arcola; (217) 452-6474; www.rockome.com.

In downtown Arcola you'll find dozens of antique, gift, and novelty-type stores housed in vintage buildings. As you walk around town, you're bound to come across the **One and Only Hippie Memorial,** a 62-foot-long physical manifestation of the life and times of Bob Moomaw. He wasn't a hippie himself, but he ascribed to the era's pot-stirring rhetoric, although he rejected the

New Skin

While in downtown Arcola, take special note of the building located at 107 E. Main St. In 2009 the owner needed a way to repair the facade of his 1910 structure, which had been modified with a generic metal front in the 1950s after a terrible fire. With the assistance of the Illinois Historical Preservation Agency, a perfect Mesker Brothers metal facade was discovered about 40 miles away in the town of Stewardson, where an 1893 opera hall was slated to be demolished. The "transplant" was a success; the cast-iron columns and fancy work have returned the Arcola building to its former glorious self. The distinctive Mesker pediment crowning the top carries a salute to its former life with the words "Opera Hall" prominently visible. In September 2009, the town held a ceremony to dedicate the renewed building.

pot smoking that went with it. He was a rare philosopher and artist, and his work dominates the bulk of the space at Arcola's *Oak Street Parklet.* Across the way on Chestnut Street is a second park called *Always Remember,* which is dedicated to "a date that will live in infamy," December 7, 1941, when the Japanese attacked Pearl Harbor, as well as September 11, 2001. A time capsule is embedded inside the large globe that is the focal point of this monument; it is to be opened on Memorial Day in 2052.

In 1859 the big cash crop for this area was broomcorn, and Arcola celebrates this long heritage by holding an annual *Broomcorn Festival,* which features demonstrations of broom making, a flea market, craft show, homemade food, and a popular parade featuring the Arcola Lawn Rangers, a precision marching group that uses lawnmowers as props. The festival is held the weekend after Labor Day; contact the Arcola Chamber of Commerce at the Historic Train Depot, 135 N. Oak St.; (217) 268-4530; www.arcolachamber.com.

If you're in need of a good nights sleep while buried under an Amish quilt, consider booking a room at one of two establishments in town. The *Arcola Flower Patch Bed and Breakfast* has been featured in magazines and newspapers and is famous for its amazing seven-course breakfast. It also serves high tea by reservation to the general public. If it's on the menu, don't miss the Royal Coconut Cake. The Flower Patch is located at 225 E. Jefferson St.; (217) 268- 4876. The *Diamond House Bed and Breakfast* is a sister establishment that also features plentiful

betchadidn't know...

Broomcorn is a sorghum tall grass that doesn't produce ears of corn. Instead, it's a seed-bearing ornamental grass that dries into natural bristles especially suitable for use in natural-bristle brooms.

breakfasts, plus a gourmet six-course dinner that is open by reservation only to the general public. The Diamond House is located next door at 229 E. Jefferson St.; the reservations phone number and Web site are shared with the Flower Patch, (217) 268-4876; www.arcolaflowerpatch.com.

The small town of **Arthur** sits about 15 miles northwest of Arcola; a large population of Old Amish Order lives here, too, and is an influence on the community's culture. It's estimated that over 200,000 visitors stop in this friendly place during the year; in fact, the town's slogan is "You're a stranger only once." Start at the **Arthur Visitors Center,** where staff will provide free advice, maps, and details about happenings in the area. The center is located at 106 E. Progress St.; (800) 722-6474 or (217) 543-2242; www.amishcountry illinois.com.

cartoonlegend

Illinois born cartoonist John B. Gruelle spent his first nineteen years growing up in Arcola. His big break came when he won a $2,000 prize and a contract to work as a cartoonist on the *Mr. Tweedle Deedle* comic strip for the *New York Herald.* A prolific writer and an extraordinary illustrator, Gruelle is best known as the creator of Raggedy Ann and Raggedy Andy.

Perhaps you'd like to arrange a tour of local farms and businesses through the cooperative exchange called the **Amish Country Tours (ACT).** This service has a wide selection of options, from self-guided audio tours to themed itineraries, to accommodate your time schedule or interests. They can also arrange meals in Amish homes and lodging. Amish Country Tours is open Mon through Sat from 9 a.m. to 5 p.m.; prices depend on the activities you select; 138 S. Vine St.; (888) 321-9663; www.acmtours.com.

If you're into quilts and quilting, this area of the state is a great place to bring your fabric list or fill your hope chest. There are plenty of stores selling fabric, patterns, and quilting supplies; if you're not into sewing, consider purchasing a quilt from one of the consignment shops or ordering a custom-made quilt here.

Every year the **Amish Country Quilt Show** attracts more than a hundred entries, and large crowds enjoy the displays and shopping. The show is held the third week of Apr, Wed through Sat from 10 a.m. to 4 p.m.; admission is $3; located at the Arthur Community Building, 120 E. Progress St.; (217) 543-2287; www.illinoisamishcountry.com/events/quilt_show.htm.

The Amish are expert cheese artisans, so it makes sense that every fall Arthur hosts the **Amish Country Cheese Festival.** It's hard to miss the two 300-pound cheese wheels sitting alongside the tasting booth; visitors are treated to free cheese and crackers every day of this three-day party. Besides the parade, crafts show, and live entertainment, the festival features some major events, including the *International Cheese Curling Championships* and the *National Cheese Eating Championships,* where contestants are given an impressive one-pound block of Colby cheese, a bottle of water, and five minutes to gobble their way into the record books. By the end of the day, if you haven't had your fill of cheese, stop by one of Arthur's many Amish cheese shops to purchase more. The festival is held over Labor Day weekend in downtown Arthur; contact the Arthur Amish Country Information Center at (800) 722-6474; www.arthurcheesefestival.com.

Looking for Lincoln

As you travel through this next section of the state, you'll find a concentration of Lincoln-related sites. Honest Abe was born in Kentucky, but this area of Illinois was his stomping ground—the place where he essentially grew from a young man making his way in business to become a lawyer and finally the sixteenth president of the United States.

Follow Lincoln's footprints by starting at the visitor center at the *Lincoln Log Cabin State Historic Site.* During their older years, Lincoln's father, Thomas, and his second wife, Sarah Bush Lincoln, lived in this modest two-room cabin on these eighty-six acres. Lincoln himself never resided here, though. He was already gaining recognition as a practicing Springfield lawyer, but he did visit his parents, and this authentically furnished 1837 cabin, kitchen building, log barn, and smokehouse give visitors an idea of their lifestyle.

The *Stephen Sargent Farm* is also on these grounds, having been relocated from its original site about 10 miles south of the Lincoln's cabin. Costumed volunteers demonstrate 1840s Illinois prairie farm life, and special-event weekends include visits by actors portraying Lincoln and his family.

The *Volunteer Pioneer Fall Celebration* is a festival that celebrates sports of that era, and volunteers from both the Sargent and Lincoln farms participate in period games such as rail-splitting, skillet toss, and log sawing; there's also music, craft demonstrations, and sales, as well as a traditional barn dance. The celebration takes place on a weekend in October; see the Lincoln Log Cabin's Web site for details. The state historic site is open daily from 8:30 a.m. to dusk for walking the grounds; the farm buildings are open May 1 to Labor Day, daily from 9 a.m. to 5 p.m., and Nov through Feb, Wed through Sun from 9 a.m. to 4 p.m.; admission is free; 402 S. Lincoln Hwy., Lerna; (217) 345-1845; www.lincolnlogcabin.org.

Follow the signs 1 mile north to the *Moore Home State Historic Site* to view the 1856 frame home of Lincoln's stepsister, Matilda Moore; this is the house where Lincoln shared a last goodbye with his stepmother before leaving Illinois to assume the presidency in Washington, D.C. The refurbished home features lovely stenciling and is furnished with period pieces. The grounds are open from 9 a.m. to 5 p.m., but the home is open limited hours, so call for specific times and dates; admission is free; 400 S. Lincoln Hwy.; (217) 345-1845; www.lincolnlogcabin.org/moore.htm.

Traveling along the Lincoln Highway you'll see an all-brick country church just southwest of the town of *Campbell.* In the nearby yard is the *Thomas Lincoln Cemetery* and the final resting place of Lincoln's father, Thomas, and stepmother, Sarah. There are many Civil War veterans here also, and other graves that are quite old and marked with weathered stones. The *Shiloh Presbyterian Church* was built in 1881 and no longer has an active congregation, but the structure provides a beautiful country church backdrop as it sits in an open field. The grounds are open daily from dawn to dusk; located 1 mile west of the Lincoln Log Cabin State Historic Site; (217) 345-1845.

The city of *Charleston* serves as the county seat for *Coles County* and maintains one of the most stunning county courthouses in the state. The 1898 limestone-block Romanesque structure commands an entire street corner, and a center clock tower sits above various angles and peaks in its complex roofline; in 1978 the building was placed on the National Register of Historic Places. Of course, Abraham Lincoln practiced law here. The courthouse is open Mon through Fri from 8:30 a.m. to 4:30 p.m.; 651 Jackson Ave.; (217) 348-0501; www.charlestonillinois.org.

Sitting in Charleston's *Morton Park* is a replica of the *Liberty Bell* that was dedicated in 1976 as part of city's celebration of our nation's bicentennial; it's one of just two such replicas in the state. The park is located on Lincoln

In the Middle

Although it was originally called the *Five Mile House* because it was located 5 miles from the *Coles County Courthouse* in Charleston, today, with changes in roads, the distance between this brick, one-story house and Charleston is more like 3.7 miles. Constructed between 1830 and 1940, over the years this house was a residence, a stagecoach stop, and tavern. It's said that Lincoln visited the owner, who was one of his friends during the time when he rode the law circuit. In 1998 a massive push to restore the two-room cottage with a kitchen addition kicked into high gear, and after years of valuable findings through archaeological study, the home is now part of a living-history museum with limited hours. The house is open on selected weekends from Apr to Oct; located at the junction of SR 16 and SR 130; (217) 348-0430; www.fivemilehouse.org.

Avenue (SR 16). If you'd like to hear it ring, make Charleston your Fourth of July destination, as the replica chimes it's lofty sound during a special ceremony at the *Red, White, and Blue Festival.* Of course, in keeping with the Americana theme, there are hot dogs, hamburgers, and a free concert on the park lawn, so bring your chairs. The festival is held the Fourth of July weekend; admission is free; located in Morton Park on Route 16/Lincoln Street; (217) 348-0430.

To memorialize Charleston's role in the fourth Lincoln-Douglas debate on September 8, 1858, the town donated a portion of the east side of the *Coles County Fairgrounds* for the *Lincoln-Douglas Debate Museum.* Although the seven debates are spotlighted by each of the debate-hosting cities, this museum is different in that it covers all of the 1858 senatorial debates. The exhibit features hands-on displays and an interactive film and audio presentation that invites participation from all age groups. Fairground hours are dawn to dusk; the museum is open daily from 9 a.m. to 4 p.m.; 413 W. Madison Ave.; (217) 348-0430.

Charleston is the home of *Eastern Illinois University,* which provides a number of cultural offerings to the public. One place of note is the *Tarble Arts Center,* which contains the *Paul Sargent Art Gallery.* Changing displays of fine art keep this gallery interesting and fresh, and April exhibits feature the artwork of graduating seniors. From Dec to Feb, the center hosts a popular juried event open to all Illinois residents who are artists. The gallery is open Tues through Fri from 10 a.m. to 5 p.m., Sat from 10 a.m. to 4 p.m., and Sun from 1 to 4 p.m.; admission is free; Ninth Street and Cleveland Avenue; (217) 581-2787; www.eiu.edu/~tarble.

The hamlet of *Ashmore* sits about 3 miles east of Charleston, and an unusual tribute towers here in *Abe's Garden;* it's called the **World's Largest Lincoln Statue,** and who wants to argue with that? Even the owner of the

Name-Calling

People in Charleston are patriotic, and politics has always been a hot topic among the residents. The town was firmly planted behind Abraham Lincoln as the embattled president struggled with the War Between the States, so when Southern sympathizers called "Copperheads" approached Union Soldiers and residents, a battle ensued, culminating in nine deaths and at least a dozen injuries. The event became known as the *Charleston Riot,* and the *Charleston Riot Historic Marker* stands at the courthouse square on the corner of Sixth Street and Jackson Avenue to commemorate it. One block west of the marker, at 520 Jackson Ave., is a mural depicting the incident.

Lincoln Springs Resort, where this giant stands, isn't gambling a guess of this statue's stature, but estimates range from 50 to 70 feet tall. By comparison, a 6-foot-tall man doesn't come anywhere near Abe's kneecap. This version of Abe is rail thin and really has a face that only a mother could love, but he stands confidently, nonetheless, commanding the dozen or so chain-saw carvings at his feet that depict his life and include Civil War generals Ulysses S. Grant and Robert E. Lee. The resort also features an eighteen-hole miniature golf course and a state-of-the-art gaming area called The Game Nexus. They also serve great barbecue at the Smokehouse Restaurant. The resort is open Mon though Sat from 11 a.m. to 9 p.m. and on Sun from 11 a.m. to 2 p.m.; the miniature golf course closes at 6 p.m.; 9699 N. CR 2000 East, Ashmore; (217) 345-3424; www.lincolnspringsresort.com.

When driving around this area, you'd never expect to come upon one of the creepiest places in the state. The paranormal activities at *Ashmore Estates* have been featured in numerous newspapers and magazines, and even spotlighted in documentaries on the Syfy channel. In 1916 the forty eight-room mansion served as the poorhouse for indigent farmers and later became a home for the mentally infirm. But is this place really haunted or is it the work of some seventy performance artists who make it their business to scare the socks off of visitors? You'll have to decide for yourself, if you dare. Tour schedules vary, but they begin at 7 p.m., with the last tour of the night starting at 10 p.m.; 22645 E. CR 1050 North, Ashmore; (217) 512-9499; www.hauntedcharleston.net or www.ashmoreestates.net.

Within its borders, *Mattoon* has two beautiful lakes: *Lake Mattoon,* which is owned by the city and features a beach, marina, and boating, and *Lake Paradise,* which has a "no wake" restriction but is a favorite with anglers. Mattoon also has a couple of unusual sites, too.

Start with the *Original Burger King*—no, not that Burger King. This place was owned by Gene Hoots, who in 1954 trademarked the Burger King name for his new eating establishment. However, in Florida there was another Burger King that challenged his right to use the name, since they'd received a federal trademark for it. The courts let Mr. Hoots keep his restaurant's handle even though his trademark was approved only by the State of Illinois. And so it stands today. The sign is decidedly retro, the walls are wood paneled, and the burgers are not charbroiled. While you're there, try one of the Hooter Burgers. Gee, hopefully he's trademarked that name, too! The restaurant is located at 1508 Charleston Ave.; (217) 224-8122.

Across from *Lytle Park* there stands a giant ice-cream cone; there's no doubt about what they sell from the windows of this advertising novelty. And although the raised letters on the fiberglass cone say "Twistee Treat," this

OTHER ATTRACTIONS WORTH SEEING IN EASTERN ILLINOIS

William M. Staerkel Planetarium
Champaign

Middle Fork National Scenic River
Oakwood

Danville Stadium
Danville

Mann's Chapel
Rossville

place is called **Rhodeside Custard,** named after the owners, whose name is Rhodes. Stop here for a cool treat, but beware that they're only open seasonally. Rhodeside is located at 404 S. Thirty-second St.; (217) 234 7449.

More than twenty-five years ago, **Lender Bagels** opened an operation in Mattoon, and what began as a promotional event for the community has ended up being a delightful celebration called **Bagelfest.** The three-day festival features live music from national headlining groups, the crowning of a bagel queen, bingo, a carnival, and a 5K Run for the Bagel. The highlight is free breakfast. Stop at the **Demars Center** right there in **Peterson Park** to pick up your free bagel and coffee at 10 a.m., and then dodge to your seat along the parade route to enjoy your morning treat to the sounds of marching bands. The festival is located at Peterson Park, 500 Broadway; (217) 258-6286.

The county seat of **Clark County** is the picturesque town of **Marshall.** Seven properties in Marshall are listed on the National Register of Historic Places, and you may cross one of them as you come into town. The **Stone Arch Bridge** was built in 1831 at a time when construction methods depended on the skills of workmen rather than supplies. In fact, this bridge was built without mortar, and you're bound to pass over it if you come into town from the west on Archer Avenue, which is also called the National Road.

The **Clark County Historical Society** owns and maintains the **Clark County Museum,** which is housed in the 1837 **Manly-McCann House.** Uri Manly was Marshall's first postmaster and ran the post office from one of the rooms of his home. The house is open by appointment; 402 S. Fourth St.; (217) 826-8087.

To learn about all the historic homes in the area, stop at the **Marshall Log Cabin Visitors Center** where staff will direct you. Take a moment to admire this building before you leave, as it's a restored log cabin that was saved from **Snyder,** Illinois, and relocated to this location. The center is open Mar to Oct, Tues through Fri from 10 a.m. to 3 p.m.; 114 S. Michigan Ave.; (217) 826-2034.

Heading to southwestern Clark County, you'll find the town that sweet crude built. *Casey* is the first Illinois location where oil was discovered. Today oil wells continue to operate around the outskirts of town. But that's not the point of celebration here. This is where Illinois' official state snack food is celebrated at the annual *Casey Popcorn Festival.* Besides an official crowning at the Little Miss and Mr. Baby Pageant, there's a car show, entertainment, and the big draw of free popcorn served all day. The festival is held for three days over Labor Day weekend; admission is free; Fairview Park; (217) 232-2676; www.popcornfestival.net.

The *Casey Softball Hall of Honor and Museum* also houses the *Illinois ASA Softball Hall of Fame* and features local and statewide greats in the game of fast-pitch softball. They've been actively playing here since the 1930s. The museum is open on Sat from 9 a.m. to noon; admission is free; located at Fairview Park, Casey; (217) 932-5911.

Richard's Farm Restaurant is a popular Casey eatery, and if you're craving pork, you're in luck—their house specialty is a one-pound chop with all the trimmings. The locals will tell you to go with the buffet, especially on Sat from 5 to 8 p.m., when it's all about seafood. The atmosphere is rustic in this refurbished barn, but the service is friendly, and the meals are hearty. The restaurant is open Tues through Sun; call for reservations; 607 NE Thirteenth St.; (217) 932-5300; www.richardsfarm.com.

For Saturday night entertainment, stop at the *Casey Auction* to bid for all sorts of stuff, including collectibles, furniture, estate items, and antiques. Warning: This place is pure rustic, old-fashioned country. Auctions are held on Sat at 5:30 p.m. and Sun at 1 p.m. At the *Auction House Diner* you can treat yourself to a 50 cent bottomless cup of coffee. Casey Auction is located at 19 S.W. First St.; (217) 932-6186; www.caseyauction.net.

International Connection

Now on to *Paris,* but here the focal point is another stunning building, rather than the Eiffel Tower; as the county seat, Paris hosts the 1891 *Edgar County Courthouse,* which stands center stage in its downtown. It looks more like a castle, but for the statue of Themis, the goddess of justice, perched atop. Restored murals painted on the inside walls are original and depict the 1893 Chicago World's Columbian Exposition and a visual version of Shakespeare's *Merchant of Venice.* The courthouse is located at 115 W. Court St.

The *Bicentennial Art Center and Museum* is housed in the 1828 *Milton K. Alexander home.* Milton served as an officer in the Black Hawk War as part of the Illinois Mounted Volunteers. The artwork is from notable Illinois and Midwest artists. The museum is open Tues through Fri from 10 a.m. to 4 p.m.; admission is free; 132 S. Central Ave.; (217) 466-8130; www.parisart center.com.

Calling itself the "Honeybee Capital of the Nation," Paris is home to the annual *Honeybee Festival,* which opens with the crowning of the Queen Bee and coordinates with the Paris High School Homecoming, so get ready for some football. It's a full three days of activities including a parade, car show, arts fair, and plenty of reasons to buy and eat honey. The festival is held on the fourth full weekend in Sept; (217) 465-4179; www.honeybeefestival.org.

Oh, and in case you're wondering about the origin of this town's name, it wasn't a tribute to the city in France, the City of Lights (that place where people fall in love). Local lore says that this Paris received its name because someone carved "Paris" into a large oak tree in what is now the center of town, probably back in the 1840s. Not so romantic after all.

Places to Stay in Eastern Illinois

ARCOLA

Arcola Flower Patch Bed and Breakfast
225 E. Jefferson St.
(217) 268-4876
www.arcolaflowerpatch
.com

Comfort Inn
610 E. Springfield Rd.
(217) 268-4000
www.comfortinn.com

ARTHUR

Arthur's Country Inn
785 E. Columbia St.
(866) 527-2385

CHAMPAIGN

Comfort Inn
305 W. Marketview Dr.
(217) 352-4055
www.comfortinn.com

Courtyard by Marriott
1811 Moreland Blvd.
(217) 355-0411
www.marriott.com

Hampton Inn
1200 W. University Ave.
(217) 337-1100
www.hamptoninn.com

Hilton Garden Inn
1501 S. Neil St.
(217) 352-9970
http://hiltongardeninn1
.hilton.com

CHARLESTON

Queen Anne's on 7th Street Bed and Breakfast
899 7th St.
(217) 345-1288
www.queenanneson
7th.com

DANVILLE

Fairfield Inn by Marriott
389 Lynch Dr.
(217) 443-3388
www.marriott.com

Sleep Inn and Suites
361 Lynch Dr.
(217) 442-6600
www.sleepinn.com

URBANA

Hanford Inn and Suites
2408 N. Cunningham Ave.
(217) 344-8000

Holiday Inn
1003 Killarney St.
(217) 328-0328
www.holidayinn.com

Illini Union Guest Rooms
1401 W. Green St.
(217) 333-3030
http://union.illinois.edu/
services/hotel/default.aspx

SELECTED VISITORS BUREAUS AND CHAMBERS OF COMMERCE

Illinois Bureau of Tourism—Travel Information
(800) 2-CONNECT

Arthur Association of Commerce
106 E. Progress St.
Arthur, 61911
(217) 543-2242

Champaign County Convention and Visitors Bureau
1817 S. Neil St., Suite 201
Champaign, 61820
(800) 369-6151

Danville Area Convention and Visitors Bureau
100 W. Main St., No. 146
Danville, 61832
(217) 442-2096

Ramada Urbana
902 W. Killarney St.
(217) 328-4400
www.ramada.com

Places to Eat in Eastern Illinois

ARCOLA

Dutch Kitchen
127 E. Main St.
(217) 268-3518

Rockome Restaurant
125 N. CR 425 East
(217) 268-4106

CHARLESTON

Panther Paw Bar and Grill
1412 Fourth St.
(217) 345-7849
www.pantherpawbar.com

URBANA

Crane Alley
115 W. Main St.
(217) 384-7526

Kennedy's at Stone Creek
2560 Stone Creek Blvd.
(217) 384-8111
www.kennedysatstonecreek.com

CENTRAL ILLINOIS

Capital Battles

The central swath of Illinois contains the most familiar city in the state: Springfield. It was the last home of Abraham Lincoln and is the current state capital. But there were two capitals before Springfield. Kaskaskia in far southwestern Illinois served as the seat of government for the Illinois Territory, and then for the state of Illinois from 1818–1820. Vandalia held the honors from 1820 to 1837.

In **Vandalia** today, visitors can walk the hallways of **the Old State Capitol** where Douglas and Lincoln and other early lawmakers gathered to form the state laws. This striking, white Federal-style building was constructed in 1836 and used until 1839, when the governing bodies moved to Springfield. The ceilings are high, the curved staircase is impressive, and the renovated building seems to echo with footsteps from the past. The Old State Capitol is open Tues through Sat from 9 a.m. to 5 p.m.; admission is free; 315 W. Gallatin St.; (618) 283-1161; www.vandaliaillinois.com/oldstatecapital.html.

Immediately across the street from the old capitol building is a statue called **Sitting with Lincoln.** It's a life-size bronze

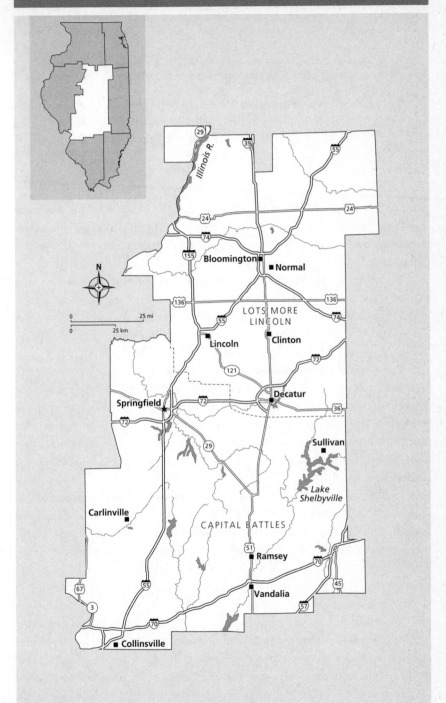

N

0 _____ 25 mi
0 _____ 25 km

Illinois R.

29
39
55
24
24
74
155
Bloomington ■
■ Normal
136
136
LOTS MORE
LINCOLN
55
74
Lincoln ■
■ Clinton
72
121
Decatur ■
Springfield ★
72
36
72
29
Sullivan ■
Lake
Shelbyville
Carlinville ■
CAPITAL BATTLES
51
Ramsey ■
70
Vandalia ■
45
57
67
3
55
70
■ Collinsville

Pioneer Women

On the southeast corner of Vandalia's old capitol grounds stands the 18-foot-tall, pink-hued, Missouri-granite **Madonna of the Trail** statue, which honors the strong but tender pioneer mothers who daringly crossed the country by wagon train. In 1911 the Daughter's of the American Revolution (DAR) pushed for a memorial to recognize these women. Nationally, twelve of these sculptures stand from coast to coast, marking the path along the original National Road from Maryland to California.

sculpture of Abraham Lincoln relaxing on a stone bench with his stovepipe hat lying nearby. This image was designed by Decatur, Illinois, artist John McClarey, and because there's enough space, visitors can sit next to the president.

Enjoy the fast pickin' of guitars and banjos on the capitol grounds during the two-day **Blue Grass Festival.** Stop by for food, street dancing, a craft show, free family outdoor movie, and great tunes. The festival is held on the Fri and Sat of Father's Day weekend in mid-June; admission is free; located on the lawn of the Old State Capitol, 315 W. Gallatin St.; (618) 283-1161.

The **Fayette County Museum** is housed in an 1860s Presbyterian Church. The Gothic design is uncommon for a church of that era. The displays include household items, school materials, a reed organ, children's antique clothing, plus Civil War and Lincoln artifacts. The museum is open Mon through Sat from 9:30 a.m. to 4 p.m.; Apr through Dec, it is also open on Sun from 1 to 4 p.m., closed Jan through Mar; donations are requested; 301 W. Main St.; (618) 283-4866.

Outside of the **Vandalia Tourist Information Center,** remember to pause at the **Farmers Monument.** This black granite statue is beautifully etched with images memorializing the contributions, sacrifices, and dedication of prairie farmers. For additional information about local landmarks, stop inside the tourist center, where you can obtain maps and directions. The center is open Mon through Sat from 9 a.m. to 4 p.m. and on Sun from 1 to 4 p.m.; 1408 N. Fifth St.; (618) 283-2728.

To celebrate its early farm heritage, downtown Vandalia salutes those golden kernels on **Corn Days,** a festival that includes lots of corn, barbecue, and music, plus a "Corn-y joke-telling contest," haystack scramble, and a community-wide yard sale. Don't miss the free horse-drawn hayrides; you'll need to get in line early. The festival is held the last weekend of Sept; admission is free; located in downtown; (618) 283-8751; www.vandaliamainstreet.com.

As you travel northeast you'll come into **Effingham County** and the city of **Effingham,** which is the county seat. The downtown is full of shops and antiques stores, and more than fifty eateries in the surrounding area offer something for everyone, from fast food to casual grills and upscale steak houses.

There's no worry that you'll miss this next entry, as it's 198 feet tall and can be seen from quite a distance away. The white **Cross at the Crossroads** is even illumined at night. It was built on the ground in segments; then each piece was hoisted and assembled by cranes. The construction was completed in July 2001; ironically it was dedicated on September 16, 2001, just days after the September 11 terrorist attacks. The cross is encompassed by a walkway with the Ten Commandments, a visitor center, and a chapel. The cross is open May to Oct, daily from 10 a.m. to 7 p.m., and Nov to Apr, daily from 10 a.m. to 4 p.m.; admission is free; located at the intersection of I-57 and I-70; (217) 347-2846; www.crossusa.org.

One of the state's largest lakes is **Lake Shelbyville.** The 11,100-acre body of water spans 20 miles between the town of **Sullivan** on the north end and **Shelbyville** on the south, with numerous towns and hamlets surrounding the perimeter.

dragonbreath

If your name is Beowulf, your dragon is waiting for you on the outskirts of Vandalia at the corner of Veterans Parkway and Rock Island Avenue. This roughly 30-foot-tall **Fire-Breathing Dragon** is ready for action if you have a dollar token to get him started. Just head to the store across the street to secure the magic coin that will make this guy spit fire. Who knows his purpose, but he stands in front of an old-fashioned windmill, so maybe he's the keeper of the water supply.

Art Walk

As you stroll Effingham's main business district during the summer, you'll notice an array of art. This is called the **Sculpture on the Avenues** outdoor exhibition, where more than thirty objects created by well-known artisans are on display. Begin your tour at 201 E. Jefferson St. in front of City Hall, where you will find one of the city's permanent exhibits, titled **Flame of Hope.** This is the work of the renowned sculptor **Leonardo Nierman,** and it was commissioned in 1997 by the Effingham Community Committee for the Arts to be the centerpiece of the first art show. Brochures for the walking tour can be found at a display in front of City Hall and at local hotels and businesses. For more information visit www.visiteffing hamil.com.

Dishpan Hands

Everyone who hates hand-washing dishes should pay homage to Shelbyville. It was here that local socialite Josephine Cochran (1839–1913) got so fed up with the servants breaking her fine china that in 1886 she developed an automatic dishwasher of her own design. Her company was the forerunner of the KitchenAid Corporation. A small monument explaining her achievement stands in front of her former Shelbyville residence. The *Josephine Cochran Home* was built in 1863 and features a hip roof and an unusual rounded or barrel-vaulted gable with a peekaboo window. This home is privately owned and not open for tours, but you can stop to read the plaque and admire the architecture. The house is located at 148 S. Broadway.

Each year, five of the larger towns encircling the Lake Shelbyville shoreline band together for a rather unusual event—the *Spores 'n' More Morel Mushroom Festival.* Shelbyville, Sullivan, Windsor, Bethany, and Findlay rotate the honor as main host for the official "Morel Hunt" and auction, while the others coordinate companion activities including plenty of food and music. The festival is held in late Apr on Fri and Sat; be forewarned that the mushroom hunt starts at 7 a.m. sharp; admission is free; for a schedule, contact the Shelbyville Office of Tourism, 315 E. Main St., Mon through Fri from 9 a.m. to 4 p.m.; (217) 774-2244; www.lakeshelbyville.com.

There's plenty of great architecture in Shelbyville, including the *Shelbyville County Courthouse,* which was built in 1879 and features four turrets marking each corner of the building. Statues of the goddesses Liberty and Justice welcome those who climb the front steps. Inside, historic paintings can be viewed, including one by American artist and Illinois native Robert Root (1863–1937). Visitors are permitted to tour the building when court is not in session. The courthouse is open Mon through Fri from 8 a.m. to 4 p.m.; 301 E. Main St.; (217) 774-4421.

Truly a special remnant of a bygone era, the 1903 multisided *Chautauqua Auditorium* in *Forest Park* has served as the venue for major community socials and events; politicians such as William Jennings Bryan and fire-and-brimstone preachers like Billy Sunday spoke here. The building is thought to be the only one of its kind in the world. During the Christmas holiday season, the structure is bedecked with carousel horses. The building is located at 655 E. North Ninth St.; (217) 774-5531.

Another building of note is the *Shelbyville Public Library,* which was dedicated in 1905 and financed by Andrew Carnegie as part of his push to expand the U.S. library system. Architectural details, inside and out, were preserved during a 1995 renovation, and visitors are welcome to enjoy the handsome oak archways, original fireplace mantels, and Roman pillars during regular hours. The library is open Mon through Fri from 9 a.m. to 7 p.m. and on Sat from 9 a.m. to 1 p.m.; 154 N. Broadway; (217) 774-4432; http:// shelbyville.lib.il.us.

Step back to the era of sock hops and poodle skirts at the *Boarman BelAir Museum,* where ten 1950s classic cars await your admiration. Established in 2005 as an extension of a lifelong hobby, the museum also features classic '50s decor and memorabilia, too. The museum is open Mon through Fri from 8 a.m. to 7 p.m. and on Sat from 8 a.m. to 7 p.m.; 224 W. Main St.; (217) 774-4919.

The town of Shelbyville can most likely be viewed from space during its annual *Victorian Splendor Light Festival,* where more than 400 displays are lit by thousands of lights. Open from late Nov to early Jan, the party begins in downtown Shelbyville on the Friday after Thanksgiving with a parade, decorated stores, tours of the candlelit courthouse, and serenades by a bell choir.

AUTHOR'S TOP TEN PICKS

Springfield
(800) 545-7300
www.visit-springfieldillinois.com

Cahokia Mounds
Collinsville
(618) 346-5160
http://cahokiamounds.org

Vandalia Statehouse State Historic Site
Vandalia
(618) 283-1161
www.state.il.us/hpa/hs/vandalia_statehouse.htm

Lake Shelbyville
Findlay
(217) 774-2244
www.lakeshelbyville.com

Horseshoe Lake State Park
Granite City
(618) 931-0270
http://dnr.state.il.us

Lincoln
(217) 735-2385
www.lincolnillinois.com

Fort Crevecoeur Park
Creve Coeur
(309) 694-3193
www.ftcrevecoeur.org

Scovill Park and Zoo
Decatur
(217) 421-7435
www.decatur-parks.org/zoo

Mari-Mann Herb Farm
Decatur
(217) 429-1404
www.marimann.com

Transportation Celebration
Effingham
(217) 342-4147

Next head to Forest Park, where amazing light displays will delight everyone. The trail passes through the **Eagle Creek State Park,** where lighted scenes portray themes such as Winter Wonderland, Winter Carnival, and Victorian Village. Consider touring by horse-drawn carriage or trolley. The park is open Sun through Thurs from dusk to 9 p.m. and Fri and Sat from dusk to 10 p.m.; donations are requested; contact the Shelbyville Office of Tourism, (217) 774-2244, www.lakeshelbyville.com.

The **Lewis and Clark State Historic Site** maintains a 14,000-square-foot museum divided into five segments that detail all aspects of the groundbreaking westward expedition, through short videos, narratives, journals, and maps. This location is Site One on the **Lewis and Clark Trail,** where the expedition team gathered to meet with the explorers and prepare for the journey that began in May 1804. One of the most impressive exhibits is a 55-foot-long, full-scale cutaway of a wooden keelboat like those used by the team. More than anything else, the boat gives visitors a sense of the danger they faced. Behind the museum is **Camp River DuBois,** where costumed docents prepare as the crew would have for the long journey ahead. The site is open daily during summer months from 9 a.m. to 5 p.m., and the rest of the year, Wed though Sun from 9 a.m. to 5 p.m.; admission is free; 1 Lewis and Clark Trail, Hartford; (618) 251-5811; www.campdubois.com.

Who was here before us? A visit to the **Cahokia Mounds State Historic Site** will answer that question. Before Columbus, this area of the flatlands along the Mississippi River was inhabited by an estimated 20,000 native North Americans. Archaeologists have uncovered a settlement so large that it covered more land than the city of London, England. The prehistoric people constructed massive dirt mounds that were used as home sites, burial grounds, and ceremonial sites. **Monk's Mound** is the largest such prehistoric structure in the U.S., rivaled only by similar mounds in Mexico. And then, in the blink of an eye, the mound builders were gone. Begin at the **Cahokia Mounds Interpretive Center Museum,** where murals, videos, and an impressive full-scale diorama unveil the lifestyle of these important early people. Then take the path to see the mounds; guided tours are available, as well as a self-guided tour with a brochure. Memorial Day to Labor Day, the grounds are open daily from 8 a.m. to dusk, and the museum daily from 9 a.m. to 5 p.m.; in winter the grounds are open Tues through Sun from 8 a.m. to dusk, and the museum Tues through Sun from 9 a.m. to 4 p.m.; admission is free; 130 Ramen St., Collinsville; (618) 346-5160.; cahokiamounds.org.

If you like your mustard spicy, then you have to visit the Horseradish Capital of the World right here in Illinois. The high-quality horseradish produced in **Collinsville** is so coveted that it's exported to Europe and China, where they really appreciate a good hot bite to their food. To celebrate its major crop, the town hosts the *International Horseradish Festival,* but this is more than a tingling taste-bud adventure: the activities include a root toss, root golf, a root-sacking contest, and the Horseradish Root Derby, all of which defy description here, so you'd better attend to see for yourself. The festival is held in early June on Sat and Sun; admission is free; located along downtown Collinsville streets; (618) 344-2884; www.horseradishfestival.com.

As a tribute to its Italian heritage, Collinsville also hosts *Italian Fest,* where there's a craft fair, live entertainment, grape stomping, and a cooking contest, but by far the most important event is eating. Authentic Italian food is on the menu, and there's nothing like the smell of bubbling tomato sauce in the morning. The festival is held the third weekend of Sept; admission is free; located in downtown Collinsville; (618) 344-2884; www.italianfest.info.

Various ethnic groups moved to this area to work in the coal mines back when "coal was king." To provide a venue for entertainment, relaxation, and camaraderie for the workers and their families, the union collected 1 percent of the employees' wages over the course of a year to fund the construction of a downtown building. Today the *Historic Miner's Institute* hosts movies, plays, and musical reviews. It's listed on the National Register of Historic Places, and renovations are ongoing. Call or check the Web site for current events; admission varies per event; 204 W. Main St.; (618) 344-0026; www .historicminersinstitute.org.

Before leaving Collinsville, don't forget to look up or else you'll miss one of the wildest roadside landmarks in Illinois—the *World's Largest Catsup Bottle.* Standing 170 feet tall, a massive "catsup" bottle belies its true purpose as a water tower. It was installed in 1949 as a promotional for a local bottler of Brooks "old original rich and tangy catsup." It's even listed on the National Register of Historic Places, but more importantly, it has its own fan club. The landmark is located at 800 S. Morrison Ave.; (618) 344-8775; www.catsup bottle.com.

During the summer this advertising monument becomes the focal point for the *Annual Brooks World's Largest Catsup Bottle Festival.* (The title of the event is as long as the tower is high!) Besides a car show, a hot dog eating contest (with catsup, of course) and lots of music, highlights of the celebration include the crowning of Little Princess Tomato and Sir Catsup. The festival is held in mid-July on Sun from 10 a.m. to 5 p.m.; admission is free; located at the American Legion grounds, 1022 Vandalia St. (SR 159); (618) 344-8775; www .catsupbottlefestival.com.

Edwardsville is third-oldest city in Illinois and was the preferred place of residence for many of the state's early movers and shakers; one such public

Park Here

Edwardsville is home to possibly the smallest official park in the state and nation. It's called the *Governor's Memorial Park,* and it's a scant 0.2 acres in size and features a boulder, a bench, and one shade tree. The bronze plaque lists the names of the five Illinois governors who've hailed from Edwardsville: Ninian Edwards, Thomas Ford, Edward Coles, John Reynolds, and Charles Deneen. The park is located at St. Louis and Randle Streets, beside the First Methodist Church.

servant was Benjamin Stephenson (1769–1822). As a U.S. congressman and personal friend of Illinois governor Ninian Edwards, Stephenson was well connected and respected politically. Stephenson County was named in his honor, although his home was in *Madison County* on a popular Edwardsville street. The house became a meeting place where politicians gathered to discuss the state's business and to socialize.

Today the *Colonel Benjamin Stephenson House* is prized as the oldest brick home in Edwardsville and is listed on the National Register of Historic Places. Visitors are greeted by costumed docents who show four of the home's rooms, which are decorated in period furnishings; especially note the beehive oven in the kitchen. There are rumors of ghosts walking these hallways, probably spurred by the 1825 murder that took place here; Stephenson himself died in the upstairs bedroom. The stories only add to this home's colorful history. The house is open Thurs through Sat from 10 a.m. to 4 p.m. and on Sun from noon to 4 p.m.; admission is $6 for adults, $3 for children ages six through twelve, and free for children ages five and under; 409 S. Buchanan St.; (618) 692-1818; www.stephensonhouse.org.

There's a neighborhood in Edwardsville called *LeClaire Village* that was built in the 1890s by entrepreneur N. O. Nelson as a prototype factory town with what he thought were idyllic housing and working conditions. Nelson hired architects to design one-story factory buildings that featured skylights, excellent lighting, and good ventilation, thinking that if he provided his Nelson Manufacturing Company employees with an upgraded work space, they'd return the favor with higher productivity. Nelson also built homes that workers could purchase for a fraction above his construction cost. A free education was offered at his school, *The Academy,* which still stands at 722 Holyoake Rd. The concept worked well until the Great Depression, and in 1930 Edwardsville annexed LeClaire into its borders. Today, the neighborhood is listed on the National Register of Historic Places and walking tours of the *LeClaire Historic District* are available through the Edwardsville/Glen Carbon Chamber of Commerce at 200 University Park Dr., Suite 260, Edwardsville; (618) 656-7600; www.edglenchamber.com/visitleclairetour.asp.

Each fall Madison County artists from Edwardsville and Alton coordinate the *Art East Tours,* an event where more than one hundred art professionals show their work at numerous locations throughout the two cities. This is a unique opportunity to meet the artists and enjoy pottery, metal, sculpture, photography, watercolors, ceramics, and mixed media artwork. The event is held the third week of Oct, Sat and Sun from 11 a.m. to 5 p.m.; admission is free; pick up a map of the locations in Edwardsville at the U.S. Bank, 101 N. Main St., Edwardsville, or in Alton at the Jacoby Arts Center, 627 E. Broadway Ave.

Before the Civil War, the city of *Alton* was mired in one of the most notable events in the fight against slavery. Activist and publisher Elijah Lovejoy (1802–1837) relocated his newspaper here after an angry mob destroyed his printing press in St. Louis. It wasn't long before he'd angered residents in Alton, and after weathering multiple attacks on his newspaper office, in 1837 a final and fatal gunshot killed him as protestors attempted to burn the building where he published his abolitionist newspaper. Some refer to this as the first blood of the Civil War.

Gentle Giant

Alton-born Robert Pershing Wadlow (1918–1940) began life as a normal-size baby, but by the time he died at age twenty-two he'd grown to be 8 feet, 11.1 inches tall, making him to this day the tallest man in history. Because he was known as quiet and kind, the town came to call him "Alton's Gentle Giant."

As he matured, it became more difficult to find clothing that fit him, so when the International Shoe Company offered to keep his size 37AA feet in leather shoes, he became a spokesperson for them, traveling crammed into the backseat of his father's automobile and making public appearances to advertise the company's products. Tragically, he died of an infection caused by a blister rubbed into his leg by the braces he required for walking; today that same bacteria can be treated with antibiotics. It's estimated that about 30,000 people attended his funeral, and he's buried in the Alton City Cemetery in a grave unmarked except for the words "At Rest."

The **Robert Pershing Wadlow Statue** stands in a park across the street from the Alton Museum of Art and History. The life-size figure is positioned in such a way that visitors can stand next to him and hold his right hand, much as a child would reach up to hold the hand of a parent; hence, the bronze fingers are quite shiny. **Robert Wadlow's Chair,** a bronze replica, is positioned nearby, and visitors often climb into it for a photograph. The statues are located at 2810 College Ave. (SR 140).

The *Elijah P. Lovejoy Memorial* can be visited at the historic *Alton City Cemetery.* It's a commanding monument created of granite and bronze, standing 93 feet tall and topped by a statue called *Winged Victory.* Visit the grave during normal cemetery hours from dawn to dusk; admission is free; 600 Pearl St.; (618) 462-1617.

A bust of Lovejoy and an original copy of one of his newspapers is on display at the *Alton Museum of Art and History.* The museum itself is noteworthy, as it is housed in *Loomis Hall* on the campus of *Southern Illinois University's* Dental School and is said to be the oldest educational building still used in the state. Other displays center on Alton's role in the Underground Railroad, vintage clothing, the Lewis and Clark expedition, and personal effects of Robert Wadlow. The museum is open Wed through Sat from 10 a.m. to 4 p.m.; admission is free; 2809 College Ave.; (618) 462-2763; www.alton museum.com.

Scotland has the Loch Ness Monster; Washington State searches for its Sasquatch; and Alton has sightings of the deadly, swooping *Piasa Bird.* This avian creature was first mentioned in the journals of Father Jacques Marquette in 1673; he made a sketch of an ancient image of a birdlike monster—with the face of a man and the tail of a dragon—painted on the cliffs towering above the Mississippi River. Indian lore tells of a giant man-eating bird that terrorized local tribes.

Interest in this story wanes off and on as sightings trickle in. The most recent tale goes back to 1977 when three area youngsters were supposedly attacked by the creepy bird; one of them was reportedly lifted into the air and then dropped after the boy's mother shrieked. Hmmm—well it's fun to ponder.

bigfish

In May 2005 a 125-pound blue catfish fought an Alton angler for more than 3 miles before accepting his fate; the catch is a Mississippi River world record.

But back to the Piasa portrait. Without protection from the elements and local mining operations, the original image was destroyed over time. A new Piasa Bird has been painted in its place and is visible from the Great River Road (SR 100). For detailed directions ask the friendly staff at the *Alton Regional Convention and Visitors Bureau,* which is open Mon through Fri from 8:30 a.m. to 5 p.m. and Sat and Sun from 9 a.m. to 3 p.m.; 200 Piasa St.; (618) 465-6676; www.visitalton.com.

A renovated 1899 furniture store is home to the *Jacoby Arts Center,* with over 40,000 square feet of display, classroom, and art-gallery space. Classes include lost arts such as papermaking from plants and Japanese binding techniques; many are only two or three hours long, so they're convenient for out-of-towners, but register ahead. A gift shop features products from skilled craftsman and artisans. The center is open Tues through Sat from 10 a.m. to 5 p.m. and Sun from noon to 4 p.m.; admission is free; 627 E. Broadway Ave.; (618) 462-5222; www.jacobyartscenter.org.

What kind of a wedding present would impress you? How about a 10,000-square-foot mansion? Industrialist Z. B. Job showed his romantic side when he gave the **Beall Mansion** to his bride in 1903. (Let's hope she liked it!) Presiding amid other impressive homes in what is referred to as the "Millionaire's Row" section of town, it features marble fireplaces with heavily carved wooden mantels, 11-foot-high ceilings, and Italian marble in most of the bathrooms. Today it is both a bed-and-breakfast and the **Beall Mansion Museum.** Tours of the three-story home are by appointment and run about thirty minutes; admission is $10 for adults, $7.50 for seniors, $5 for children ages three through twelve, and free for children under age three; 407 E. 12th Street; (618) 747-9100; www.beallmansion.com.

While a portion of downtown **Carlinville** is listed on the National Register of Historic Places, the city has an additional section of architectural gems spanning a 9-block square area unlike anywhere in the U.S. It's called the **Standard Addition** and it's the nation's largest concentration of vintage Sears, Roebuck and Co. catalog mail-order homes. To accommodate the influx of miners hired to meet production demands, the Standard Oil Company ordered 156 kit homes to ease the dire need for employee housing. Today, remarkably, 152 of those homes still remain. Tours can be arranged through the Carlinville Chamber of Commerce at 112 N. Side Sq.; (217) 854-2141; http://carlinvillechamber.com.

The **Macoupin County Courthouse** in Carlinville is a handsome building, and considering the cost, it should be. It was either government run amok or something sinister, but the final bill was well over $1.3 million, and that was in 1870. The striking limestone exterior and ironwork doors are impressive, but they're nothing compared to the spectacular, 191-foot-tall center dome. The building was designed by architect E. E. Meyers, and he also drafted the 1869 **Macoupin County Jail,** which is referred to as the "cannonball" jail because of its impenetrable construction; a cannon couldn't blow a hole in it and no prisoner could create a tool to cut through the thick fixed stones. Frankly, it looks like a medieval castle that belongs in Austria rather than here in this humble American town, but it makes a great background for a photograph. The jail is located at 215 E. Main St., and the courthouse stands across the street at 210 E. Main St.; (217) 854-3136.

The 1883 **Anderson Mansion** is home to the **Macoupin County Historical Society,** and besides eight marble fireplaces, an unusual front porch entry, and two bay windows, the most notable exhibit is a rare stained-glass window that was acquired from Chicago's 1893 World's Columbian Exposition. The mansion is open Mar through Nov, Wed from 10 a.m. to 2 p.m., and June through Aug, Wed from 10 a.m. to 2 p.m. and on Sun from 1 to 5 p.m.; donations are requested; 432 West Breckenridge St.; (217) 854-2850; www .macsociety.org.

With a population of around 5,000, **Staunton** is the type of small town that honors local residents with a sign and certificate for their outstanding front-yard landscaping. It might sound trite, but people here really do care about their surroundings, and they're friendly, too. Stop at the U.S. Post Office to see a richly colored oil painting by Ralph Hendricksen that was commissioned as part of the Works Projects Administration (WPA) program during the Great Depression. The mural was completed in 1941 and is titled **Going to Work.** The post office is located at 113 S. Edwardsville St.; (618) 635-2676.

Then travel back in time at *Henry's Rabbit Ranch Station and Visitor's Center,* which has been designated an "Official Roadside Attraction" by the *Illinois Route 66 Heritage Project.* The owners are dedicated Route 66 historians, and besides a welcome stop, they've created a mini-museum of Route 66 memorabilia featuring motel and gas-station signs, vintage trucks, and other vehicles such as Volkswagen Rabbits; oh, and there are lots of live rabbits here, too. The center is open Mon through Sat from 9 a.m. to 4 p.m. and on Sun when the mood hits; admission is free; 1107 Historic Old Rte. 66; (618) 635-5655; www.henrysroute66.com.

Macoupin County is another mining area, and in the southeastern part of the county is *Mount Olive,* where the *Union Miner's Cemetery* contains the graves of men who lost their lives digging coal and fighting for worker's rights. The septuagenarian organizer for the United Mine Workers of America (UMWA) and all-around activist extraordinaire Mary Harris Jones (1837–1930) is here, too, but people remember her by the name Mother Jones, the Miner's Angel. The *Mother Jones Monument* marks her resting place. Before she died, she said she wanted to be buried beside her boys. Here you will find

Regular or Premium?

You'll feel as though you're in a time warp when you drive into the *Soulsby Shell Station;* that's because this is the oldest gas station along Old Route 66, having serviced traffic passing along here since 1926. The vintage gas pumps are really fun to see. A nonprofit group currently owns the place with the hope of preserving it for future generations. The gas station is located at 201 S. Old Rte. 66, Mount Olive.

a granite obelisk bearing a medallion with her likeness. Flanking it are two larger-than-life statues of coal miners with sledgehammers. Mount Olive native son "General" Alexander Bradley, another UMWA organizer rests here also. The cemetery is located at 700 N. Lake St.

Lots More Lincoln

The town of **Lincoln** has the rare honor of being named for Abraham Lincoln before he was elected president. In fact, Lincoln himself christened the town in his own name by using the juice of a watermelon during an impromptu ceremony in August 1853, on the day when the first lots were sold. Today you're likely to see "Lincoln" walking the streets, attending community events, and even reenacting the watermelon town christening. When he practiced law in this area, his office was in the hamlet of **Postville,** the first location of the **Logan County Courthouse.**

In the interest of preservation, Henry Ford purchased the **Postville Court-house** in 1929 and relocated it to Dearborn, Michigan. Years later, Logan County residents raised funds to build a replica on the original grounds as part of their 1953 centennial celebration. Today the faithful two-story reproduction is open for tours. As in Lincoln's day, the courtroom is on the second floor.

Every year county residents cele-brate with an **Abraham Lincoln Birth-day Party,** which is held the Saturday before his February 12 birthday. The courthouse is open Mar through Oct, Tues through Sat from noon to 5 p.m., and Nov through Feb, Tues through Sat from noon to 4 p.m.; admission is $2 for adults and $1 for children; 914 Fifth St.; (217) 732-8930; www.postvillecourt house.com.

inventive president

Lincoln was granted U.S. Patent No. 6,469 in 1849 for his invention of an inflatable device to enable boats to cross over rocky shoals, making him the first and only presi-dent to own a patent. The idea might have become a success if he'd taken time to market it rather than enter into politics.

By the way, the **Watermelon Statue and State Historic Marker,** which consists of a slice of "water-melon" and a plaque painted with a depiction of the watermelon christening ceremony, can be seen at 101 N. Chicago St. And if you'd like to see another interpretation, visit the **State Bank of Lincoln,** where a life-size bronze statue titled **The Christening** depicts Lincoln, the cut watermelon, and the cup from which he poured the juice. Lincoln's signed **life mask and plaster hand molds,** as made by sculptor Lenard Volks, are here also. The bank is open

Mon through Fri from 8:30 a.m. to 5 p.m. and on Sat from 8:30 a.m. to noon; admission is free; 111 N. Sangamon St.; (217) 735-2326.

Another local Lincoln statue sits upon the world's largest covered wagon, according to the *Guinness Book of World Records*. The **Railsplitter Covered Wagon** not only weighs five tons, but Lincoln himself is a sizable 350 pounds and 12 feet tall just from his waist up. Interestingly, he's not distracted by oncoming traffic because his eyes are glued to the law book in his hand. (Would that be considered texting 1850s style?) Area businesses take turns hosting this mammoth statue, and in late 2009 it was moved to the grounds of the Best Western Lincoln Inn, at 1750 Fifth St.; (217) 732-9641.

The **Lincoln/Logan County Chamber of Commerce** sponsors the **Lincoln Art and Balloon Festival,** where over thirty hot-air balloons glow, launch, and land over a two-day event. The activities are hosted by the town and **Logan County Airport.** Downtown you'll find crafts, food, and a flea market. The festival is held in late Aug; admission is free; 1351 Airport Rd.; (217) 735-2385; www.lincolnillinois.com/abf.aspx.

If you happen to negotiate a ride on one of those hot-air balloons, try to get a bird's-eye view of the top of the **Lincoln City Hall,** because there's a **City Hall Phone Booth** up there! Originally, the telephone was installed as part of the civil defense plan during World War II; later it was manned as a weather-watching station. It caused quite a ruckus when the booth was nearly removed permanently while City Hall underwent much-needed roof repairs. Townsfolk protested, citing the booth as a favorite city landmark and—power to the people—they won. From the ground it's best seen looking up from the corner of McLean and Broadway Streets. City Hall is located at 700 Broadway St.; (217) 735-2815; http://cityoflincoln-il.gov.

One of the most Lincolnesque celebrations in the state is the **Abraham Lincoln National Railsplitting Festival** sponsored by the **Logan County Railsplitter's Association.** Ongoing since 1970, the event features amateurs and professionals in separate competitions; the professionals are vying for the title of "National Championship Railsplitter." Each competition is governed by official rules (who knew there were rules for chopping wood?) and contestants from several states swing their axes in hopes of winning the prize. Besides the main event, there's chain-saw carving, a quilt show, Civil War ball, old-time live music, and storytelling. There are even workshops on making bread and apple butter and cooking in a Dutch oven. The festival is held the third weekend of Sept, starting Sat at 10 a.m. and ending Sun at 3:30 p.m.; admission is $3 per day or $5 for the weekend for ages 13 and up, and free for children age twelve and under; located at the Logan County Fairgrounds off North Jefferson Street; (217) 735-2385; www.railsplitting.com.

TOP ANNUAL FESTIVALS

SPRING

Maple Syrup Time
Springfield, Feb–Mar
(217) 529-1111

The American Passion Play
Bloomington, before Easter
(309) 829-3903

JUNE

Horseradish Festival
Collinsville
(618) 344-2884

Illinois Shakespeare Festival
Bloomington, late June to mid-Aug
(309) 438-8974

JULY

Logan County Fair
Lincoln, late July to early Aug
(217) 732-3311

AUGUST

Illinois State Fair
Springfield
(217) 782-6661

SEPTEMBER

Marigold Festival
Pekin
(309) 346-2106

Apple 'n' Pork Festival
Clinton
(217) 935-6066

OCTOBER

Boo at the Scovill Zoo
Decatur
(217) 421-7435

NOVEMBER

Christmas on Vinegar Hill
Mt. Pulaski
(217) 792-3222

Victorian Splendor Light Festival
Findlay, late Nov to early Jan
(800) 331-4479

DECEMBER

Christmas Market
Carlinville
(217) 854-2141

When in *Atlanta* stop at the octagonal 1908 *Atlanta Public Library,* which is listed on the National Register of Historic Places. Remember those old-time wooden book stacks and that hard furniture? It's still here and worth a peek for memory's sake. Downstairs is part of the *Atlanta Museum,* with exhibits and collections of local history; visit during library hours. The library is open Tues, Wed, and Fri from 12:30 to 4 p.m., Thurs from 12:30 to 8 p.m., and Sat from 9 a.m. to 4 p.m.; 100 N.W. Race St.; 217-648-2112.

Two points of note before you leave the library. You may have noticed that only part of the museum is located downstairs. That's because the collection has expanded so much that they've opened the *Atlanta Museum Annex,* which is housed in a former bank building, constructed in 1856, along Arch Street. Also, take note of the *Atlanta Clock Tower* that stands in front of the library. This timepiece was salvaged from the tower at the Atlanta

High School building and requires hand-winding three times a week to keep it running on time.

The *J. H. Hawes Grain Elevator Museum* operated along Atlanta's Vine Street from 1904 to 1976. Today it's listed on the National Register of Historic Places and is the only completely restored wooden grain elevator in the state. If you can tolerate climbing stairs, sign up for a tour here; it's worth the trek up the seven flights of turned staircase leading to the cupola. Look for the hand-braided rope that commands the movement of the elevator's pulleys. You'll also see how the scale house weighs the grain. The museum is open seasonally in June, July, and Aug on Sun only from 1 to 3 p.m.; donations are requested; 300 Vine St.; (217) 648-2056; www.haweselevator.org.

As you drive away from town, don't forget to give thumbs up to the 19-foot giant holding a hot dog; yes, it's another one of those crazy 1960s-era fiberglass guys. This fellow is nicknamed *"Tall Paul,"* but his formal moniker is the **Bunyon Statue,** spelled with an "o" instead of an "a," as per his original owner from Cicero, Illinois, who didn't want to infringe on another restaurant's Paul Bunyan mascot. When the Cicero hot dog stand closed, the people of Atlanta were able to rescue this giant for their stretch of Route 66. The statue is located along Arch Street. Or if you're heading out of town on South Street, wave goodbye to the *Smiley Face Water Tower* as you leave.

Mount Pulaski was the original Logan County seat until 1853, when the town of Lincoln was tapped for the honor. However, the *Mount Pulaski Courthouse* where Abraham Lincoln tried cases still stands in the Mount Pulaski square. The Greek Revival–style redbrick building has been renovated to appear as it did in 1847, and the wooden flooring in the second-story courtroom is the same that Lincoln strode as he defended his clients before the judge and jury. The courthouse is open Tues through Sat from noon to 4 p.m.; admission is free; 113 S. Washington St.; (217) 792-3919; http://mtpulaski il.com.

Designated as the county seat of *Tazewell County,* the town of *Pekin* takes pride in its past and has one of the most active genealogical societies in the state. The *Tazewell County Genealogical and Historical Society Library* is staffed by trained volunteer researchers ready to assist visitors. If you can prove that you're a direct descendant of an original Tazewell County settler, they'll present you with a wall certificate. The library is open Mon, Thurs, and Fri from 9 a.m. to 1 p.m., Tues from 9 a.m. to 1 p.m. and 7 to 9 p.m., Wed from 9 a.m. to 4:30 p.m., and Sun from 2 to 4:30 p.m.; admission is free; located at the Ehrlicher Research Center, 719 N. Eleventh St.; (309) 477-3044; www.tcghs.org.

As the "Marigold Capital of the World," Pekin's big community event is the annual *Marigold Festival,* which is sponsored by the *Pekin Chamber of Commerce* and takes place when the city's favorite flowers are at the height of bloom. Besides a parade, queen contest, food, and free music, citizens and businesses enter their beautiful marigold gardens in the Grow for the Gold contest; this makes driving around town part of the attraction. The festival is held over Labor Day in mid-Sept; admission is free; located along downtown streets; (309) 346-2106; http://marigoldfestival.blogspot.com.

East Peoria is home to *Fon du Lac Farm Park,* a peaceful, 1920s-type farm with antique farm equipment, a quaint school house, and fun additions like a slide on the silo side of the little barn. There's also a museum and a petting zoo; the farm animals roam the grounds and visitors are permitted to interact with them. The park is open June through mid-Oct, Tues through Sun from 10 a.m. to 3:30 p.m.; admission is $2.00 for adults and $1.50 for children; 305 Neumann Dr.; (309) 694-2195; www .fondulacpark.com.

Next, cool off at the *Fon du Lac Park District's* latest offering, *Splashdown.* It's more like blast off, as there are plenty of fast-moving water slides, a splash and play pool, and a tube ride down a lazy river. Best of all, the three-acre water park is 100 percent handicapped accessible, making it user friendly for most everyone. Splashdown is open seasonally, June through Sept, Mon through Fri from 11 a.m. to 6 p.m.

jawbreaker

Pekin's Mechanical Baking Company is one of three nationwide that still produces "hardtack," that tooth-breaking biscuit eaten by Civil War soldiers and still coveted by reenactors today. The soldiers cracked it with their rifle butts or with a rock and referred to it as "eatable leather."

and weekends from 11 a.m. to 6 p.m.; admission is $8 for adults and $6 for children, and prices are discounted after 3 p.m. every day. 1 Eastside Dr.; (309) 694-1867; www.fondulacpark.com.

As a tribute to the French explorers who traversed this area of the state, volunteers have resurrected *Fort Crevecoeur Park* in the town of *Creve Coeur.* The current fort stands where LaSalle's did, on the eighty-nine-acre outpost that was his 1680s central hub. Costumed interpreters share their knowledge of those long-ago days through demonstrations and discussion. The park holds two events of note: The *Spring Rendezvous* takes place in mid-May and the *Fall Rendezvous* in late Sept. Both events feature the dramatic arrival in canoes of actors dressed as French militia in buckskin. The park is open Apr 1 to Oct 31; admission is free; 301 Lawnridge Dr., Creve Coeur; (309) 694-3193; www.ftcrevecoeur.org.

Much like Urbana and Champaign in Eastern Illinois, the towns of **Bloomington** and **Normal** are connected by geography, history, and general politics. Men of great influence resided here in the 1840s, such as Bloomington's own Judge David Davis. As a longtime law colleague, mentor, and friend of Abraham Lincoln, Davis became the man who boosted Lincoln into the limelight during the 1860 Republican Convention in Chicago. After Lincoln took the presidential oath, it wasn't long afterward that Davis received a coveted appointment to the U.S. Supreme Court.

Today, the **David Davis Mansion State Historic Site** provides an inside look at the life and customs of Lincoln's close friend. Completed in 1872 and dubbed "Clover Lawn," Davis's thirty-six-room, Italian-inspired architectural stunner boasts eight marble fireplaces, rich woodwork, and velvet draperies befitting the upper-crust of Victorian society. The mansion is open Wed though Sun from 9 a.m. to 5 p.m., with forty-five minute tours running from 9:30 a.m. to 4 p.m.; admission is $4 for adults and $2 for children; donations are requested for tours; 1000 E. Monroe Dr., Bloomington; (309) 828-1084; http://daviddavismansion.org.

To complement the home, Davis's wife, Sarah, commissioned the addition of a European "starburst"–style garden with flowing brick walkways and manicured hedges; some of the plants currenty in the garden are from original cuttings. View this and other area gardens during the **Glorious Garden Festival—Garden Walk** held on the third Fri and Sat of June from 9 a.m. to 5 p.m.; admission is $15 for adults and $7 for children; purchase tickets at the David Davis Mansion drive-up garden booth at 1000 E. Monroe Dr.; (309) 828-1084.

The grounds of another mansion are used each year for the **Illinois Shakespeare Festival,** where professional actors and students from **Illinois State University** perform in the modern, 438-seat, open-air theater at **Ewing Manor.** Donated by Hazel Buck Ewing in 1969 as a venue for cultural events, the Tudor mansion makes a lovely backdrop as richly costumed actors recite their lines. This festival has received international recognition. Performances in the Romanesque-style theater run Tues through Thurs and on Sun beginning at 7:30 p.m., and on Fri and Sat at 8 p.m.; individual ticket prices range between $16 and $40; the box office is located at 48 Sunset Rd.; (309) 438-8974; http://thefestival.org.

nojumbojet

The Tilbury Flash racing plane was built in Bloomington in 1932 by Owen Tilbury, a twentysomething student at what was then Illinois State Normal University. It's called the world's smallest plane, and pilots who flew her reported that the air pressure from other planes could push her around much like a boat bouncing in another's wake.

OTHER ATTRACTIONS WORTH SEEING IN CENTRAL ILLINOIS

Beer Nuts Products
Bloomington

Miller Park Zoo
Bloomington

Prairie Aviation Museum
Bloomington

Children's Museum of Illinois
Decatur

Andersen Prairie
Pana

Dana-Thomas State Historic Site
Springfield

Daughters of Union Veterans of the Civil War Museum
Springfield

Illinois State Capitol
Springfield

Illinois State Museum
Springfield

Lincoln Memorial Garden
Springfield

Lincoln National Home State Historic Site
Springfield

Old State Capitol State Historic Site
Springfield

Oliver Parks Telephone Museum
Springfield

Washington Park Botanical Gardens
Springfield

Every spring over three hundred volunteers gather to perform in a polished production that celebrates the life of Jesus Christ called the *American Passion Play.* It's a community tradition that's continued yearly since 1924. The show schedule coincides each year with Easter, and performances begin at 2 p.m.; admission is $20 per person; the play is presented at the *Bloomington Center for the Performing Arts,* 600 N.E. St.; (309) 829-3903; www.american passionplay.org.

Much of Bloomington's downtown area has been listed on the National Register of Historic Places, and the centerpiece of the district is the *Old McLean County Courthouse.* The building, completed in 1903, features an American Renaissance–style exterior; there's heavy carving on the cornices and pediments, and the copper dome in the center of the building is spectacular. The *McLean County Historical Society Museum* is housed here, with over three floors of displays featuring household, military, farm, and Indian artifacts. Admittedly, there's a cult following for one exhibit: the orange racing plane called the *Tilbury Flash.* The museum is open Sept to May, Wed through Sat and on Mon from 10 a.m. to 5 p.m., and on Tues from 10 a.m. to 9 p.m.; admission is $5 for adults, $4 for seniors, and free for children; 200 N. Main St.; (309) 827-0428; www.mchistory.org.

It's been called the best in the Midwest; the **Third Sunday Market** is more than a flea market. This event brings together more than 450 dealers who specialize in a wide variety of antiques and collectibles, from postcards and cut glass to dolls and vintage furniture. The market is held May to Oct on the third Sun of every month, rain or shine, from 8 a.m. to 4 p.m.; admission is $6 for adults $6 and free for children ages thirteen and under; located at the Interstate Center, 2301 W. Market St.; (217) 202-2847; www.thirdsundaymarket.com.

Need a snack? How about trying Bloomington's hometown favorite: **beer nuts.** The glazed red-skin peanuts have been manufactured with a secret recipe right here since 1937 by a family-owned and operated business. The 100,000-square-foot production plant isn't open to the public, but you can take a video tour at the **BEER NUTS Production Plant and Company Store.** Maybe there'll be a tasting, too. The store is open Mon through Fri from 8 a.m. to 5 p.m.; admission is free; located at 103 N. Robinson St.; www.beernuts.com.

But don't bring those nuts to this next venue, because these critters are on special diets. The **Miller Park Zoo** is a bustling place. Besides viewing rare and endangered species, you can ask questions of the zookeepers. The **Tropical America Rainforest** features twenty species of free-flying birds; some of the other exhibits showcase sun bears, red pandas, lemurs, sea lions, river otters, and bald eagles. The zoo is open daily from 9:30 a.m. to 4:30 p.m. (closed Christmas and Thanksgiving); admission is $5.00 for adults, $3.50 for children ages three to twelve and seniors, and free for children under age three; 1020 S. Morris Ave.; (309) 434-2250; www.cityblm.org/zoo.

The restored 1864 **Funk Prairie Home** is located in the town of **Shirley,** and it's the homestead of former Illinois senator and businessman Lafayette Funk. The home is open for tours, and it's really a grand farmhouse. This is also the location of the **Funk Gem and Mineral Museum,** which grew from the hobby of Lafayette Funk II. The "Hall of Gems and Minerals" display is impressive and thought to be the largest private collection of rare gems, fossils, and minerals in the state. You won't miss the museum building because it's covered with an estimated thirty-tons of sparkling-in-the-sun rocks and mica, and antique sleighs sit on the grounds. The Funk Prairie Home is open Mar through Dec, Tues through Sat from 9 a.m. to 4 p.m.; admission is $2 for adults and $1 for children; 10875 Prairie Home Lane; (309) 827-6792.

siruporsyrup

Illinois is one of just seventeen states that produce maple syrup, and is the farthest west sugaring location. The word *sirup* is defined as the product before it is boiled to create sugaring; syrup is the final cooked product.

The **Funks Grove Pure Maple Sirup** store is out this way, too. "Sirup," as they spell it, is generally available from Mar through August, as well as "maple sirup candy" and novelties. Visit in early spring to see the catch buckets collecting tree sap. The farm entrance is marked with a sign. Hours vary, so call ahead. The farm is located at 5257 Old Rte 66; (309) 874-3360; www.funkspuremaplesirup.com.

Clinton is the county seat of **DeWitt County** and in this area of the state, agriculture is really big business. This town also has a Lincoln connection and it commissioned a life-size **Abraham Lincoln Sculpture** by artist A. L. VanDenBergen. It was dedicated in 1931 and stands in **Mr. Lincoln's Square,** which is a nice small-town park. It's reported that in 1848 this is where Lincoln quipped, "You can fool all the people some of the time and some of the people all the time, but you cannot fool all the people all the time."

The restored **C. H. Moore Homestead** is now home to the **DeWitt County Museum.** While standing in the home's vaulted ceiling library, it's possible to picture C. H. Moore and his former law partner Abraham Lincoln enjoying political discourse while sitting among the walls of books. The homestead is open Apr through Dec, Tues through Sat from 10 a.m. to 5 p.m. and on Sun from 1 to 5 p.m.; admission is $3 for adults and $1 children; 219 E. Woodlawn St.; (217) 935-6066; www.chmoorehomestead.org.

The museum sponsors the **Apple 'n' Pork Festival,** featuring stick-to-the-ribs home cooking with plenty of smoked ham, pork sandwiches, apple fritters, river-rat potatoes, and apple cider. Over 300 craft and flea-market dealers set up shop, and there's live entertainment and free museum tours, too. This festival began in 1969, and in recent years it's estimated that more than 70,000 have attended the two-day event. The festival is held the last weekend of Sept; located at the C. H. Moore Homestead; (217) 935-6066; www.chmoorehomestead.org.

bearbeginnings

The Staley Bears were the precursor to the Chicago Bears. Decatur's A. E. Staley Company organized the team in 1920 and hired George S. Halas as coach. When the company failed to raise money for a second season, Halas moved the squad to Chicago.

Decatur is the county seat of **Macon County** and home to **Milliken University.** The Italianate **Milliken Homestead** was built in 1876 by university benefactor James Milliken. After the death of his wife, the house was used as a hospital during the 1918 flu epidemic and an art institute before being renovated to its former glory to be used as a home museum. Many of the Millikens' original furnishings are on display here, and when you tour the home take note of the stained and etched windows. The home is open Apr through

Oct on the last Sun of each month, from 2 to 4 p.m.; admission is $2 for adults and 50 cents for children; 125 N. Pine St.; (217) 422-9003.

The *Richard J. Oglesby Mansion* was the home of three-term Illinois governor Oglesby, who was also a supporter of Lincoln; he was in attendance at the deathbed of the fallen president. This home was built in 1874 and contains many original Oglesby family possessions, including a complete library collection. In the Italianate-style home, there are seven fireplaces, multiple verandas, and a commanding walnut staircase. The mansion is open June through Oct, Wed and Sat from 1 to 4 p.m., and Mar to Nov, on the last Sun of the month, from 2 to 4 p.m.; admission is $2; 421 W. William St.; (217) 429-9422.

The ten-acre *Scovill Children's Zoo* houses more than 500 animals in natural-looking settings that seem to blend with the walkways and buildings. Take a ride on the *Endangered Species Carousel,* which features thirty carved and authentically painted animals on the verge of extinction; or hop on the *Z.O. and O. Express* for a 1-mile jaunt around Lake Decatur. The train locomotive is a small-scale replica of an actual 1863 steam engine. The zoo is open May through Aug, daily from 10 a.m. to 7 p.m., and Apr, Sept, and Oct, daily from 10 a.m. to 4 p.m.; admission is $4.75 for adults, $3.75 for seniors, and $3.00 for children; there are additional fees for the carousel and train rides; 71 S. Country Club Rd.; (217) 421-7435; www.decatur-parks.org/zoo.

dacturdoodads

Krekel's Kustard is as well known for its crispy-on-the-edge burgers as it is for the cow on the roof and the Chickenmobile, a 1970s Cadillac with a chicken head and tail sprouting from the roof and trunk. Look for these local icons at the four Krekel's Kustard locations in Decatur.

Chances are you've never heard of Hieronymus Mueller, but chances also are that you've come in contact with his inventions every day. He was a German immigrant in the 1850s, by trade a gunsmith, and by virtue of his ingenuity, an industrialist whose innovations garnered him more than 500 U.S. patents, including one for the water faucet, another for the spark plug, and yet another for roller skates. The story of his life and all he created can be seen at the *Hieronymus Mueller Museum,* which is open Thurs through Sat from 1 to 4 p.m.; admission is $2.00 for adults and $1.50 for children age seventeen and under; 420 W. Elderado St.; (217) 423-6161.

If you've ever wanted to see an Indianapolis 500 pace car, your dream can come true if you visit the *Chevrolet Hall of Fame Museum.* The showroom is filled with classic Chevys and race cars, those heart-stopping Camaros, and Chevrolet memorabilia from the 1920s to the present. If you get

Center Stage

Don't miss a visit to Decatur's *Central Park,* where the *Transfer House* now stands surrounded by fountains and mature trees. In 1895 this red-roofed shelter was in the middle of traffic, literally, as it sat in the center of the intersection of Main Street *and* Main Street (that's not a typo), in what was called *Lincoln Square.* It was here that electrified streetcars and interurbans dropped patrons needing to transfer to another streetcar. When a 1962 highway project required a road expansion, the building was relocated to its current perch, and it has been adopted as Decatur's official landmark.

hungry while you're here, stop at the *Dreamer's Diner* on-site; in fact, the windows of the restaurant look right into the showroom so you can browse as you eat. Sweet! The museum is open Tues through Sun from 10 a.m. to 6 p.m.; admission is $7 for adults and free for children age 12 and under if accompanied by an adult; 3635 US 36 East; (217) 791-5793; www.chevrolet halloffamemuseum.com.

The *Macon County Historical Society* has converted an old brick school building into the *Macon County History Museum and Prairie Village* complex. The grounds include the rustic log cabin that served as the area courthouse. Lincoln practiced law here, and after touring this space you'll appreciate the rough conditions faced by circuit lawyers during the 1830s and 1840s. The museum is open Tues through Sat from 1 to 4 p.m.; admission is $2 for adults and $1 for children age twelve and under; (217) 422-4919; 5580 N. Fork Rd.; www.mchsdecatur.org.

Meribeth King started a hobby herb garden in her yard back in 1970; today it's grown into a full-time operation called the *Mari-Mann Herb Company* and her herbs are spanning the globe in worldwide distribution. Everything here is Earth-friendly. Tour the gardens, stop at the gift and health food store, or make reservations for a high tea or brunch. The company is open Mon through Sat from 9 a.m. to 5 p.m. and on Sun from noon to 5 p.m.; 1405 Mari-Mann Lane; (217) 429-1404; www.marimann.com.

And last, but not in any way the least, is the city that is most synonymous with Abraham Lincoln: *Springfield.* Because there are so many things to do and see in this town, it could fill an entire book on its own. Of course, your tour should include the *Lincoln Home National Historic Site,* the only home Lincoln owned and shared with his wife and family. In order to tour the home, you must obtain a ticket from the *Lincoln Visitor Center.* The center is open daily from 8:30 a.m. to 5 p.m.; admission is free; 426 S. Seventh St.; (217) 492-4241; www.nps.gov/liho.

Be aware that tickets for the Lincoln Home go quickly, so if by chance you miss the cutoff for tours, you can still take away a sense of the neighborhood, circa 1860, as the four blocks surrounding the Lincoln Home have been preserved to appear the way they did in Lincoln's day. Stroll the brick streets of the *Lincoln neighborhood* and admire the restored exteriors of the homes tucked behind traditional white picket fences; then pause at the *Heirloom Garden,* where flowers and plantings that were popular in the 1860s bloom and flourish today. The neighborhood is located at South Eighth and East Jackson Streets; (217) 492-4241; www.alplm.org/home.html.

emptynest

The Lincolns rented their Springfield home with the anticipation that they'd retire there after his presidency, but after Abraham Lincoln was assassinated in 1865, Mary never returned. The two-story Quaker-brown residence remained in the family until 1887, when son Robert bequeathed ownership to the state.

Another must is the *Abraham Lincoln Presidential Museum and Library,* where interactive exhibits make it possible to meet the man face-to-face with "Holavision," video, and animatronic technology. This museum will require time to tour, as you're bound to become engrossed. The museum is open daily from 9 a.m. to 5 p.m.; admission is $10 for adults ages sixteen to sixty-one, $7 for seniors age sixty-two and up, and $4 for children ages five to fifteen; 212 N. Sixth St.; (217) 782-5764; www.alplm.org.

The *Lincoln Tomb* at *Oak Ridge Cemetery* is covered in white granite, and statues of soldiers from each of the military branches of the era stand sentry along the first tier. Visitors are permitted to walk through the tomb's interior rooms, which are lined with marble and plaques that bear the words of many of Lincoln's most famous speeches. The final resting place of Lincoln, his wife, Mary Todd Lincoln, and three of their sons is also available for viewing. The Lincoln Tomb can be viewed from May to Labor Day, Mon through Sun from 9 a.m. to 5 p.m.; after Labor Day through Nov, Tues through Sat from 9 a.m. to 5 p.m.; Dec through Feb, Tues through Sat from 9 a.m. to 4 p.m.; and Mar through Apr, Tues through Sat from 9 a.m. to 5 p.m.; admission is free; 1441 Monument Ave.; (217) 782-2717; www.state.il.us/hpa/hs/lincoln_tomb.htm.

Also of note in the Oak Ridge Cemetery is the *Illinois Vietnam Veterans Memorial,* which honors those Illinois heroes who died or were declared missing in the service of their country during the Vietnam War. The black-granite marble is stark; there are five pillars that represent the branches of the U.S. military, and they merge to hold an eternal flame. The memorial can be viewed during regular cemetery hours, Apr to Oct, daily from 7 a.m. to 8 p.m., and Nov through Mar, daily from 7 a.m. to 8 p.m.; admission is free; 1441 Monument Ave.; (217) 782-2717.

And how about one last Lincoln for the road? Try the rather "interesting" version of the man, sans beard, that stands in front of Gate One at the *Illinois State Fairgrounds.* His boots are laced tight, his ax is poised for some serious chopping, and frankly, he looks like one of those fiberglass guys we've been following around Illinois. The 30-foot-tall statue is titled, appropriately, **The Rail Splitter,** and it was created in 1967 by Carl W. Rinnus, a Springfield native. The statue is best viewed during daylight; admission is free if you're outside the gate; located at 801 Sangamon Ave.; (217) 782-6661.

Places to Stay in Central Illinois

BLOOMINGTON-NORMAL

Baymont Inn and Suites
604 IAA Dr.
Bloomington
(309) 662-2800
www.baymontinns.com

Best Western University Inn
6 Traders Circle
Normal
(309) 454-4070
www.bestwestern
illinois.com

Chateau Hotel
1601 Jumer Dr.
Bloomington
(309) 662-2020
www.chateauhotel.biz

Comfort Suites
310B Greenbriar Dr.
Normal
(309) 452-8588
www.comfortsuites.com

Hampton Inn West
906 Maple Hill Rd.
Bloomington
(309) 829-3700
http://hamptoninn1
.hilton.com

Holiday Inn Express
1715 Parkway Plaza
Normal
(309) 862-1600
www.hiexpress.com

Signature Inn
101 S. Veterans Parkway
Normal
(309) 454-4044
www.jamesoninns.com

DECATUR

Country Inn and Suites Hotel
5150 Hickory Point
Frontage Rd.
(217) 872-4202
www.countryinns.com

Days Inn
333 N. Wyckles Rd.
(217) 422-5900
www.daysinn.com

Hawthorn Decatur Hotel Suites
2370 Mt. Zion Rd.
(217) 864-9311

Holiday Inn Express
5170 Wingate Dr.
(217) 875-5500
www.hiexpress.com

PEKIN

Concorde Inn and Suites
2801 E. Court St.
(309) 347-5533
www.concordeinn.net

Holiday Inn Express
3615 Kelly Ave.
(309) 353-3305
www.hiexpress.com

SHELBYVILLE

Shelby Inn
816 W. Main St.
(800) 342-9978
www.theshelbyinn.com

SPRINGFIELD

Comfort Suites
2620 S. Dirksen Parkway
(217) 753-4000
www.comfortsuites.com

Courtyard by Marriott
3462 Freedom Dr.
(217) 793-5300
www.marriott.com

SELECTED VISITORS BUREAUS AND CHAMBERS OF COMMERCE

Illinois Bureau of Tourism—Travel Information
(800) 2-CONNECT

Bloomington–Normal Area Convention and Visitors Bureau
3201 Cira Dr., Suite 201,
Bloomington, 61704
(309) 665-0033

Collinsville Convention and Visitors Bureau
221 W. Main St.
Collinsville, 62234
(618) 344-2884

Decatur Area Convention and Visitors Bureau
202 E. North St.
Decatur, 62523
(800) 331-4479

Springfield Convention and Visitors Bureau
109 N. Seventh St.
Springfield, 62701
(800) 545-7300

Crowne Plaza Springfield
3000 S. Dirksen Pkwy.
(217) 529-7777
www.cpspringfield
.crowneplaza.com

Fairfield Inn
3446 Freedom Dr.
(217) 793-9277
www.marriott.com

Holiday Inn Express
3050 S. Dirksen Pwy.
(217) 529-7771
www.hiexpress.com

Mansion View Inn and Suites
529 S. Fourth St.
(217) 544-7411
http://mansionview.com

Pear Tree Inn, Drury Hotels
3190 S. Dirksen Pkwy.
(217) 529-9100
http://druryhotels.com

Places to Eat in Central Illinois

BLOOMINGTON

Bandana's Bar-B-Q
502 IAA Dr.
(309) 662-7427
www.bandanasbbq.com

Jim's Steakhouse
2307 E. Washington St.
(309) 663-4142
www.jimssteakhouse.net/
bmain.htm

COLLINSVILLE

Oatman House Tea Room
501 E. Main St.
(618) 346-2326
www.oatmanhousetea
room.com

LINCOLN

Blue Dog Inn
111 S. Sangamon St.
(217) 735-1743
www.bluedoginn.com

SPRINGFIELD

Maldaner's
222 S. Sixth St.
(217) 522-4313
www.maldaners.com

Saputo Twins Corner
801 E. Monroe St.
(217) 544-2523
www.saputos.com

Sebastian's Hideout
221 S. Fifth St.
(217) 789-8988
www.sebastians
hideout.com

WESTERN ILLINOIS

Mississippi Gem

The Mississippi River has been both friend and foe to the river town of **Quincy.** Because of the mighty river, Quincy enjoyed rapid growth in the 1800s, with the robust riverboat traffic that conducted business along her riverfront. On the other hand, despite sitting on bluffs overlooking the Mississippi, the town has repeatedly suffered flooding that has devastated the downtown area. It's a testament to the toughness of the people that the nearly 1,000 vintage structures and homes have survived the many floods. The **Quincy Downtown Historic District** alone boasts about one hundred of these prized buildings dating back to the 1850s. Just about every example of early and Victorian-era architecture can be admired along the city's streets, including Queen Anne, Greek Revival, Federal, Prairie, and Craftsman.

The downtown is generously landscaped with dogwood trees, and as they burst into bloom each spring, the city celebrates their beauty with the **Dogwood Festival.** Thousands attend this annual event, which features a parade, crafts fair, plenty of food and snacks, and an afternoon military band

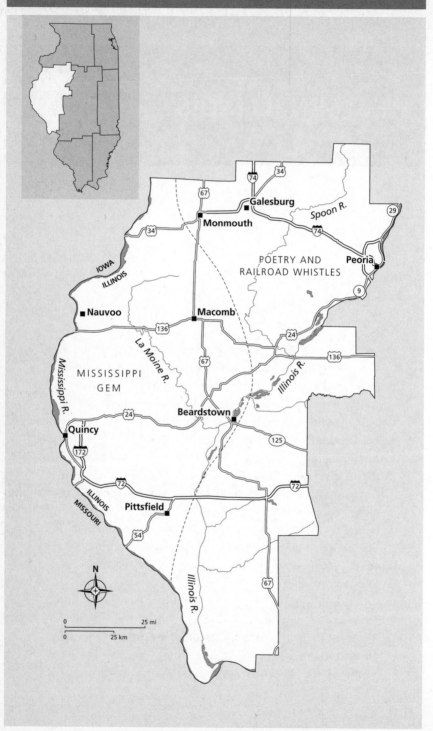

concert. When the sky cooperates with a bright blue backdrop, added to the blue hues of the Mississippi River, and the pink and white dogwood blossoms, it makes for one perfect color combination. The festival is held the first week in May; admission is free. ***Quincy Area Chamber of Commerce,*** (217) 222-7980; www.quincychamber.org.

No, a princess doesn't live up on that hill. But the ***Villa Kathrine*** has long intrigued people who spy it from afar, as the Moorish style of the 1900 building, with a turret and dome, gives it the appearance of a castle perched on a bluff overlooking the river. Today, this is the home of the ***Quincy Area Convention and Visitors Bureau,*** but the building is also available for tours. Stop here for brochures and suggestions of things to see, and before you leave don't forget to walk through the courtyard and visit the peaceful reflecting pool. The bureau is open Mon through Fri from 8:30 a.m. to 4:30 p.m.; admission for a tour is $3; 532 Gardner Expressway; (217) 224-3688; www.see quincy.com.

The first settler in this part of Illinois was New York native John Wood, who arrived to purchase land being sold through the Illinois Military Tract program. His first home was a one-room log cabin, but as his wealth and stature in politics grew, so did his homes. A two-story log cabin was traded in for the house now known as the ***Governor John Wood Mansion,*** which was completed in 1835 and is said to be the best example of Greek Revival architecture in this area of the state. Although Wood next commissioned an octagonal home, a crash in the real estate market caused him to abandon that property and remain in this fourteen-room abode. Today the governor's mansion contains many of his personal possessions. The ***Historical Society of Quincy and Adams County*** manages the property and provides tours. The mansion is open Apr through Oct, Mon through Sat from 10 a.m. to 2 p.m., and tours are conducted daily on the quarter hour; admission is $3.00 for adults and $1.50 for students; 425 S. Twelfth St.; (217) 222-1835; www .adamscohistory.org.

Quincy also has a history of unfailing hospitality; when thousands of Mormons were threatened with extinction if they didn't leave Missouri, the people of Quincy stood along the Mississippi's eastern shoreline armed with blankets and supplies for the outcasts as they escaped across the frozen river. The story was the same for fugitives running from slavery; the townsfolk openly supported and aided the Underground Railroad movement.

An organizer of the Quincy Underground Railroad at the time was Dr. Richard Eells, a physician and fierce abolitionist who was arrested for his participation in saving an escaped slave. His defense, under the Fugitive Slave Act, traveled all the way to the U.S. Supreme Court; by the time the high court ruled

AUTHOR'S TOP TEN PICKS

Lincoln's New Salem
State Historic Site
Petersburg
(217) 632-4000
www.lincolnsnewsalem.com

Wildlife Prairie State Park
Peoria
(309) 676-0998
www.wildlifeprairiestatepark.com

Village of Elsah
(618) 374-1568
www.elsah.org

Pere Marquette State Park
Grafton
(618) 786-3323
http://dnr.state.il.us

Quincy
(800) 978-4748
www.quincyil.gov

Bluffdale Vacation Farm
Eldred
(217) 983-2854
www.bluffdalevacationfarm.com

Nauvoo
(217) 453-6648
www.beautifulnauvoo.com

Carl Sandburg Birthplace
State Historic Site
Galesburg
(309) 342-2361
www.sandburg.org

Villa Katherine Park
Quincy
(217) 224-3688
www.adamscohistory.org/villa.html

The 1898 Duryea Motor Trap car
Peoria Public Library, Peoria
(309) 497-2000

in his favor, the good doctor had been long in his grave. *The Dr. Richard Eells House* has been renovated, and volunteers tell the story of this remarkable man during house tours. The house is open Feb through Nov, on Sat from 1 to 4 p.m.; admission is $3; 415 Jersey St.; (217) 223-1800.

When Richard Newcomb built his massive home in 1891, the 20,000-square-foot, thirty-three-room, Berea sandstone residence was the largest in Quincy. Today, the red terra-cotta turrets and inviting wraparound stone porch continue to beckon visitors inside. Luckily, because the *Newcomb Stillwell Mansion* is home to the *Quincy Museum,* the public is welcome to explore this exceptional property, including the first-floor Victorian parlor and living space, second-floor exhibits, and third-floor children's dinosaur and discovery museum. The museum is open Tues through Sun from 1 to 5 p.m.; admission is $3 for adults, $2 for students, and free for children under age five; 1601 Maine St.; (217) 224-7669; www.thequincymuseum.com.

The *Quincy Art Center* began operation from the carriage house of the *Lorenzo Bull Home,* but the popularity of the programs and exhibits required that the building be enlarged, although the inherent design of the carriage house remains. Besides rotating exhibits, there are classes and lectures. The center is open Tues through Fri from noon to 4 p.m. and Sat and Sun from 1 to 4 p.m.; admission is $3 for adults and $1 for seniors, students, and children; 1515 Jersey St.; (217) 223-5900; www .quincyartcenter.org.

jewelofatown

In the 1840s, because of its booming economy, population growth, commerce, shipping, and farming, Quincy earned the nickname the "Gem City."

The cars featured at the *Missis-sippi Valley Antique Auto Museum* run the gamut from the sublime to the wacky; examples include a 1911 Little and the Ford Roadster pickup seen on the country humor television show *Hee Haw*. A horse-drawn hearse is part of the nonmotorized display. The museum is open Memorial Day to Labor Day on Sun from noon to 4 p.m.; admission is $2 for adults and free for children under age twelve; located at Front and Cedar Streets in All-American Park on the bank of the Mississippi River; (217) 223-7909.

There are no signs that say "shhh" in the Romanesque Revival–style Old Public Library; that's because it now houses the *Gardner Museum of Architecture and Design.* Displays feature ornamental items that appeared in Quincy homes and churches before their demolition. But this 1888 structure, with a giant, pointed turret and local limestone exterior, is worth the visit alone. Don't forget to peek out the third-story windows for a terrific view of *Washington Park* and the Mississippi River. The museum is open Wed through Sat from 1 to 4 p.m.; admission is $3; 332 Maine St.; (217) 224-6873; www.gardnermuseumarchitecture.org.

Notable Quincy residents, including former Illinois governor John Wood and early pioneer John Tillson, are laid to rest in *Woodland Cemetery* on South Fifth Street. The cemetery originally contained the *Quincy National Cemetery,* a U.S. government–maintained burial plot for Civil War soldiers, before it was moved to Quincy's *Graceland Cemetery,* which is located just 1 block east of Thirty-sixth and Maine Streets. Consequently, interesting Civil War–era monuments remain on the Woodland grounds. The cemeteries are open daily from dawn to dusk.

Pittsfield is the county seat of *Pike County* and home to about 4,000 residents—and way more hogs than that. The city gladly accepts the mantle of "Pork Capital of the World," and an estimated half a million hogs head to American tables from this meatpacking city annually. To celebrate its livelihood, the town hosts the *Pig Days Festival,* where all sorts of activities pay tribute to the porkers, like the "Longest Pigtail Contest" and the "Hog Calling"

Holy Man

The grave of Father Augustine Tolton, America's first African-American Catholic priest, can be found in St. Peter's Cemetery in Quincy. Young Tolton, his mother, and sister made a daring escape from slavery by crossing the Mississippi River from the Missouri side. They were taken in by kind Quincy abolitionists, who arranged housing and education for the children.

Tolton matriculated at the Catholic school and graduated from Quincy College before entering a seminary in Italy. Upon his ordination in 1886, Father Tolton was sent back to the U.S. to serve the people of Illinois. He assisted for a time in Quincy before moving to a new church in Chicago. It was while tending to St. Monica's congregation that he suddenly fell ill and died in 1897. His grave is marked by a large, wooden cross immediately inside the front gate of the cemetery.

competition; there's also live music, an arts and crafts show, and of course, lots of pork. Try the pork sandwiches, barbecued pork, or the full pork chop dinner. The festival is held the second week of July, starting on Fri at 8 a.m. and ending on Sat at 9 p.m.; admission is free; located downtown on the square in front of the courthouse; (217) 285-2971; www.pikeil.org.

The *Pittsfield Fall Festival* is another event that's well attended. This community party includes a long parade, live entertainment, food vendors, and carnival rides. The festival is held for three days over Labor Day weekend; admission is free; located downtown on the square in front of the courthouse; (217) 370-9846.

Visitors to Pike County might want to plan their tour route after stopping at the *Pike County Visitors Center,* where staff can provide maps and directions; if you visit after hours, just step inside, as the foyer is open twenty-four hours and stocked with pamphlets. The center is open Mon through Fri from 8:30 a.m. to 5 p.m.; 224 W. Washington St., Pittsfield; (217) 285-2971; www.pikeil.org.

The visitor center sponsors the *Pike County Fall Color Drive* when the foliage along the byways peaks in a vibrant fall spectacular. It's not just a drive-by, but a festival-like event with contests and prizes, and music and food along the route. For a map contact the visitor center or download one from its Web site. The event is held the third week of Oct; (217) 285-2971; www.pikecolordrive.com.

The Pike County Historical Society also maintains the *Pike County Historical Museum,* which is housed in the *East School.* The building was designed by architect John Mills Van Osdel and is one of just two remaining examples of his work. Changing exhibits include china and dishware, furniture, vintage wedding gowns, a dray wagon, and a printing press. The museum is open from May to Oct 3, but hours are limited so visitors are asked to call ahead; admission is free; (217) 285-4618.

Called one of the most beautiful courthouses in Illinois, the old **Pike County Courthouse** was designed by architect Henry Elliott and features an octagonal design and chiseled stonework exterior. Visitors are welcome to view the interior, which includes stained-glass windows, a balcony, and curved staircases. The courthouse is open during regular business hours, from 9 a.m. to 4 p.m.

If you have a camper or RV, or would like to sleep in a cabin overlooking a lake, stop at **Pine Lakes Resort** for a change of pace. Besides swimming at the sandy beach along the forty-five acre lake from Memorial Day to Labor Day, you can rent rowboats, fish without a license, and participate in camp-wide games and activities. This is old-fashioned family fun. The resort is located at 1405 Lakeview Heights; (217) 285-6719; www.pinelakesresort.com.

How to fight mosquitoes? It's a common summer problem, especially when large bodies of water like the Mississippi and Illinois Rivers are nearby. The town of **Griggsville** has conquered the problem by becoming the "Purple Martin Capital of the Nation" and encouraging the birds to feast at will. Although there are other U.S. towns that claim the same title, it's Griggsville's industry that backs the claim; this is the home of Nature House, Inc., formerly the J. L. Wade Company, which manufactures purple-martin houses. While in town, look for the gold standard in birdhouses: The **Purple Martin High-Rise** is a 562-room apartment, if you will, that soars more than 70 feet into the air. There are other examples around town, too, so keep your eyes open. The birdhouse is located on Purple Martin Boulevard; (217) 833-2412; www.griggsvilleil.org.

The county seat of **Schuyler County** is **Rushville,** which was founded in 1825 and today has a modest population of around 3,000. The third-generation

Float Boat

The town of **Grafton** is one of those peaceful river towns where antiques and sandwich shops dot the streets. For a change of pace, ask the locals to point you in the direction of the **Grafton Ferry,** which is just north of the public boat ramp at SR 3. The fee is $7.50 one way, $3.00 for bikes, and $2.00 for pedestrians; and round-trips are discounted; call (618) 786-1855 for a departure schedule; www.graftonferry.com. Note: The ferry doesn't run if the river isn't cooperating!

'squitosolution

It's estimated that one purple martin eats 2,000 pesky mosquitoes a day, so Griggsville has installed over 500 purple martin houses throughout town. If each house hosts just one feathered tenant, then an estimated one million mosquitoes will be devoured per day. Of course martin houses are multi family dwellings, so mosquitoes don't have much of a chance here.

Schuyler County Courthouse sits on the southwest corner of the downtown **Rushville Square.** It was built in 1881 and features a square clock tower on the outside and a wooden staircase that mimics that square on the inside between floors. The courthouse is open Mon through Fri from 8 a.m. to 4 p.m.; 102 S. Congress St.; (217) 322-6226; www .schuylercountyillinois.com.

One of the more unusual museums in the state is the **Schuyler Jail Museum and Genealogical Center,** which combines county artifacts, a genealogical research library, and a tiny limestone jail cell from pioneer days. The center is open Apr 1 to Nov 1, daily from 1 to 5 p.m., and the rest of the year on Sat only, from 1 to 5 p.m.; donations are requested; 200 S. Congress St.; (217) 322-6975.

Some might say the town of Rushville will put a smile on your face. Well, that's been true for over ninety years, because it's here that the annual **Smiles Day Festival** takes place. The event honors a tradition begun in 1919 when townsfolk gathered to welcome home their World War I veterans. Today, every U.S. military veteran in attendance is considered an honorary parade marshal at 10:30 a.m. on Saturday morning, when more than a hundred units march in a whopping parade. The festival is held the third week of Sept on Sat; admission is free; located in Central Park; (217) 322-3003; www.smilesdayblog.com.

About 8 miles northeast of Rushville, an eco-friendly lodging experience awaits you at the **Peace of Earth Lodge.** This bed-and-breakfast will put you in the trees, literally, as all of the buildings are constructed to ensure unobstructed views of the surrounding woods. The main lodge features large windows, the two-room cabins have enclosed porches that look out on the trees, and the Tree House is elevated so the birds can join you for breakfast. The lodge is located on Ray Road (Highway 4), 8 miles northeast of Rushville; (217) 322-2865; www.peaceofearth.net.

The city of **Macomb** is home to **Western Illinois University** (WIU), which provides educational and cultural experiences for area residents as well as the more than 11,000 students who study here each semester. The university's **Leslie F. Malpass Library** is one of five campus libraries and is constructed in a pinwheel-like design with balconies and long hallways overlooking a six-story atrium. Be aware that security rules may be in effect and limit your visit. To avoid a parking ticket, it's also wise to get clearance from Parking Services at (309) 298-2705.

Vince Grady Field on the campus of WIU is transformed into a field of launches during the *Macomb Balloon Rally.* About thirty hot-air balloons take flight during this two-day event featuring a different theme each year. In between the balloon launches, there are concerts, a car show, and food, as well as coordinated activities in downtown Macomb. The event is held the second weekend of Sept; the mass ascension begins Fri at 6 p.m., the flights on Sat start at 6:45 a.m., and the return is at 6 p.m., followed by an enchanting night glow at 7:30 p.m.; admission is free; the field is located north of University Drive; watch for signs; (309) 833-1315; www.macombballoonrally.com.

One of Macomb's most notable homes is the *Old Bailey House,* built in 1887 by W. S. Bailey, who founded the Union National Bank. The Eastlake-style architecture is very recognizable from the street; inside, hardwood floors and the cherry staircase are of special note. Displays change frequently, covering topics from Victorian clothing to early Macomb life. The first floor is open for tours by the *McDonough County Preservation Society.* The house is open Mon through Fri from 9 a.m. to 5 p.m. and weekends by appointment; 100 S. Campbell St.; (309) 833-1727.

Barn-a-Rama

It's impossible not to notice the many farms dotting the countryside as you pass through areas like Macomb and McDonough Counties. The *Macomb Area Convention and Visitors Bureau* has turned antique barn-watching into a sport, providing detailed descriptions for those enthusiasts eager to locate all things gambrel, hipped, stick, or batten. Old Illinois barns were commonly built in the cross-gable style, meaning there is a gable on each of the four sides. But that's not the only type you'll find on this trip.

A rare "true round" barn, called the *Kleinkopf Barn,* was built in 1914 and is listed on the National Register of Historic Places. Most round barns are actually polygonal, while a "true round" has no straight lines. The *Kipling Barn* is a three-story 1920s specimen, complete with an internal grain elevator. An example of a square barn is the *Ausbury Barn,* built in 1918. Supposedly, the owner celebrated its construction with a rowdy barn dance.

Thirty barns, from seventy to nearly 140 years old, await your admiration on a driving tour put together by the bureau. Just remember to view the barns from your car, as none are open for tours and all stand on private property. For a map contact the Macomb Area Convention and Visitors Bureau at 201 S. Lafayette St.; (309) 833-1315; www.makeitmacomb.com.

The **McDonough County Courthouse** is the focal point of downtown Macomb. It was built in 1872 of limestone and red brick, and the oak and walnut wood interior is beautifully preserved. The courthouse is located at 130 S. Lafayette St.

The downtown area is converted into a street fair during the **Macomb Heritage Days Festival,** where residents and visitors enjoy live entertainment, a flower show, book sale, firefighters' water fight, parade, and the "Ugly Dog, Fat Cat Contest," which attracts canine and feline contestants from miles away. The festival is held the last full weekend of June; admission is free; located in downtown Macomb at Courthouse Square and Chandler Park; www.makeitmacomb.com.

At the far western part of the state, **Hancock County** follows the course of the Mississippi, which provides a perfect scenario for birding aficionados or for those who love a good country drive with perfect scenery. The city of **Carthage** is the county seat and home to the 1908 Greek Revival–style **Hancock County Courthouse.** This building features a pristine white exterior and a spectacular rotunda; stained-glass windows and murals splash color on the interior walls. At the time of its dedication, the courthouse was state of the art, with over 700 lightbulbs illuminating the rooms and hallways, and multiple indoor toilets. The courthouse is open Mon through Fri from 9 a.m. to 4 p.m.; 500 Main St.; (217) 357-3911; www.hancockcountycourthouse.org.

For the younger set, stop at the **Worlds of Wonder Playground,** or the "WOW Park" for short. Volunteers have constructed over 10,000 square feet of wooden structures in a fort-like setting. Try out the mazes and swings, and then visit the dragon and pirate ship, too. Adults can relax at the picnic shelter while watching their little ones find their way around this play haven. The playground is located at the corners of Locust and Adams Streets.

The **Hancock County Historical Society** runs the **Kibbe Hancock Heritage Museum,** which community members and staff affectionately refer to as "The Kibbe." The collection is thanks to the efforts of Dr. Alice Kibbe (1881–1969), a professor of biology at Carthage College. When Carthage College relocated to Wisconsin in the 1960s, she generously used her own funds to acquire the college's artifacts in order to preserve them for Hancock County. Her vision has served the county well, and the museum expanded in January 2009. The exhibits contain Civil War, World War I and II, and Indian artifacts, as well

earlyg.i.bill

Nearly all of the 800 square miles of Hancock County were designated as Military Land Tract bounty. Through a lottery, War of 1812 veterans could claim 160-acre parcels as a reward for their military service.

as Victorian clothing and textile displays, antique memorabilia, and a collection of rocks and fossils. The museum is open May through Oct, Mon through Sat from 10 a.m. to 4 p.m. and on Sun from 1 to 4 p.m., and Mar, Apr, Nov, and Dec, Mon, Wed, Fri, and Sat from 1 to 4 p.m.; closed Jan and Feb; admission is free; 308 Walnut St.; (217) 357-3119.

Across the street is the *Old Carthage Jail and Visitors Center,* where visitors can view a video to learn about the events on June 27, 1844, when two of the inmates held here were Joseph Smith and his brother Hyrum. A mob rushed the 1841 limestone structure and murdered the two men, changing the course of history for the Mormon congregation. A tour of the jail is included. The Smith brothers are depicted in a life-size bronze statue standing in the middle of the *Smith Memorial Garden.* The center is open in summer months, Mon through Sat from 9 a.m. to 9 p.m. and on Sun from 12:30 to 6 p.m., and during the winter, Mon through Sat from 9 a.m. to 5 p.m. and on Sun from 12:30 to 5 p.m.; admission is free; 307 Walnut St.; (217) 357-2989.

Beautiful Plantation

There was a particular site on the far western section of Hancock County and next to the Mississippi River that attracted settlers. It started out as an Indian trading village, then surged as a boomtown called Commerce until the bust of 1837 took away the dreams of the once-vibrant population. The town lay desolate until 1839, when Mormon founder Joseph Smith directed his religious community to settle on this promising acreage next to the Mississippi River. In fact, three sides of the town are bordered by the river like a horseshoe, and it's as though the water is holding the land in the crux of a flowing arm. Smith renamed the town *Nauvoo,* meaning "beautiful," and by 1845 it had been transformed into the second largest city in the state, with over 12,000 residents, lagging just behind Chicago. Political turmoil and the assassination of Joseph and Hyrum Smith led to a weakening of the Mormon community, as factions broke off and Brigham Young took command of the flock and directed that they head for freedom in Utah.

Today, historic Nauvoo is a bustling town centered on tourism, and although most people walking the streets are Mormons who gather here as pilgrims from worldwide locations, there's no proselytizing on the street corners, or anywhere else in town. Instead, all are welcome to learn about the harshness of 1840s-era pioneer life and the history of the people who settled here. To say there's a lot to do and see is an understatement; more than sixty buildings, museums, and visitor centers are open for tours, and since several

TOP ANNUAL EVENTS

FEBRUARY

Chocolate Festival
Galesburg
(309) 343-2485

MAY

Dogwood Festival
Quincy
(217) 222-7980

JUNE

Steamboat Festival
Peoria
(309) 676-0303

Railroad Days
Galesburg
(309) 343-2485

AUGUST

Nauvoo Grape Festival
Nauvoo
(217) 453-6648

SEPTEMBER

National Stearman Fly-In Days
Galesburg
(309) 343-6409

Prime Beef Festival
Warren County
(309) 734-3181

NOVEMBER

East Peoria Festival of Lights
East Peoria
late Nov–Dec
(800) 365-3743

DECEMBER

Nauvoo Christmas Walk
Nauvoo
(217) 453-6648

groups operate and own the various sites, it can take time to unravel all of it, so here are some highlights.

The *Nauvoo Historical Society* is a not-for-profit group that is completely independent of all religious groups and concentrates on preserving the history of Nauvoo, from the days of the earliest Indian settlements to the present, and they manage two house museums. The *Rheinberger Museum* sits in *Nauvoo State Park* and is the former residence of Alois Rheinberger, a viticulturist whose grapes still produce after more than 150 years. Remnants of his vineyard still thrive at this *Nauvoo State Park Museum,* and the public is welcome to see the original press and the wine cellar. The museum is open May 15 to Oct 15, daily from 1 to 4 p.m.; admission is free; located at SR North; (217) 453-2512 or (217) 453-6648; www.nauvoohistoricalsociety.org.

Next, visit the restored *Weld House Museum* for an eclectic assortment of artifacts, including nearly a thousand Indian arrowheads, agricultural and household goods, a Victorian wedding dress, and funeral curiosities. This was the home of Dr. John Weld from 1842 to 1846, and one of the more interesting tales about this house is that a later owner named Dr. Varney possibly cared for Chicago gangsters running from the law. The museum is open May 15 to Oct 15, daily from 1 to 4 p.m.; admission is free; 1380 Mulholland St.; (217) 453-6648.

The *Joseph Smith Historic Site* is maintained by the Community of Christ Church and is made up of four historic buildings and the *Smith Family Cemetery.* The cemetery is open around the clock. The *Smith Homestead* is a two-story log and frame home and the first residence built by John for his wife, Emma. The *Mansion House* was built in 1842, and even all these years later, it's obvious that the home was a handsome frame structure for this area of the country. It provided a larger living space for the Smith family, but also served as a hotel. The *Red Brick Store* was Smith's retail establishment. The *Nauvoo House* was never completed for its original purpose as a large, three-story gathering place; after Smith's death, Emma remarried and her new husband adjusted the size of the building to serve as a new family home. These sites are open May through Oct, Mon through Sat from 9 a.m. to 5 p.m. and on Sun from 1 to 5 p.m., and fewer hours during the rest of the year; a $3 preservation fee is charged; 865 Water St.; (217) 453-2246; www .cofchrist.org/js.

For a sweeping view of the countryside and a chance for some fresh air, board the *Inspiration Point Wagon Tour,* a forty-five-minute ride that overlooks the Mississippi River, or take the *Wagon Tour of Old Nauvoo,* an hour-long ride around town with pauses in front of notable buildings. If you're chilly, they'll provide quilts to warm you. Catch the free wagon rides at the corner of Partridge and Hibbard Streets, or ask for details at the *Historic Nauvoo Visitors' Center,* where you can also see a film about the settlement, view artifacts, and pick up brochures. Don't miss the center's peaceful *Monument to Women Garden.* The center is open Mon through Sat from 9 a.m. to

Tornado Tribute

The sky posed a familiar threat on April 19, 1927, and country school teacher Annie Keller recognized the signs of a tornado looming in the distance. She rushed the children inside the small Centerville school building and ordered everyone to take cover underneath their desks just as the wind surged, tearing away the school's roof and sending debris inside. Miss Keller was killed, but her sixteen charges survived thanks to her quick actions. A pink marble monument pays tribute to her courage; the *Annie Louise Keller Memorial* was the work of Illinois sculptor Lorado Taft, and it stands in *Whiteside Park* in the center of the town of *White Hall.*

5 p.m. and on Sun from 12:30 to 5 p.m.; admission is free; located at Main and Young Street; (217) 453-2237; www.historicnauvoo.net.

Of course, the most striking building here is the faithful reproduction of the *Nauvoo Temple.* Dedicated in 2002, this temple stands in place of the original, which was destroyed more than one hundred years ago by arson and a tornado. The building was open for tours until it was dedicated; the interior is now considered sacred and only those of the Mormon faith are admitted. The temple is located at 50 N. Wells St.

Depending on your interests, you may want to make this an overnight trip, and there are many local places worth considering, but one that offers a unique experience is *Nauvoo Log Cabins.* These are authentic log homes that have been collected by the owner, dismantled piece by piece, and marked for reassembly at this site. Each cabin has a provenance that is shared with overnight guests, as well as all the creature comforts of heating and air-conditioning, kitchenettes with microwaves, satellite television, and high-speed Internet. I'd guess the long-ago owners would be confounded by all of it, but it makes for a pleasant stay while you're taking in the sights. Nauvoo Log Cabins is located at 65 N. Winchester St., Nauvoo; (217) 453-9000; www.nauvoologcabins.com.

For in-depth lists of bed-and-breakfasts, lodges, and eateries, visit the *Nauvoo Tourism Office* at 1295 Mulholland St.; (877) 628-8661; http://beautiful nauvoo.com.

Way back in 1938 the community started a celebration of its heritage with the *Nauvoo Grape Festival,* and the tradition continues today with a full slate of live entertainment, mingling pioneer actors, a car show, parade, music, and wine and cheese tasting. By the way, this area is famous for great blue cheese; you might want to bring a cooler to take some home. The festival is held on Labor Day weekend from Fri at 5 p.m. to Sun at 8 p.m.; located at Nauvoo State Park on SR 96 North; (217) 453-6648; www.nauvoo grapefestival.com.

Poetry and Railroad Whistles

Galesburg is the county seat of *Knox County* and was founded on a vision of higher education; in 1836 Presbyterian minister George Washington Gale selected this area of the state as the site on which he'd build a college. Today the four-year liberal arts *Knox College* stands as a lasting reminder of Gale's early commitment.

Galesburg native-son Carl August Sandburg was the first person to receive Pulitzer Prizes in two different categories, poetry and history. After passing away at his retirement residence in North Carolina on July 22, 1967, his ashes

Man of Words

Carl Sandburg's illustrious and extensive writing career is most remarkable, considering the rough start he had as a youngster growing up in Galesburg. At age thirteen he quit school to take odd jobs to support his family. About five years later he jumped a railroad car and headed west, living as a hobo riding the rails. This is where Sandburg says he gained his true education, learning about life and studying the human experience in small towns and cities along the road.

After military service during the Spanish-American War, Sandburg returned to Galesburg and enrolled at Lombard College, where he completed all but his last semester of study, falling short of a formal degree. His writing career zigzagged from writing poetry books to journalistic pieces. He worked as a reporter, a feature writer, and a political organizer. In 1914 several of his poems were published in *Poetry,* a nationally circulated magazine of critical acclaim. Worldwide audiences applauded his free-verse poetry books titled *Chicago Poems* and *Cornhuskers,* because they reflected the true voice of common people.

But it was an obsession with Abraham Lincoln that drove him to write his most important work: a biography series of Abraham Lincoln based on Sandburg's personal thirty-year collection of Lincoln memorabilia. He peppered the research with firsthand interviews of many of Lincoln's associates and people who had attended the Lincoln-Douglas debates in Galesburg during the Senate campaign of 1858. In 1926 he published *Abraham Lincoln: The Prairie Years,* but it wasn't until 1939 that he completed his first financial success and Pulitzer Prize winner, *Abraham Lincoln: The War Years.* He finished the extensive six volumes in just thirteen years.

Just over a decade later, Sandburg received his second Pulitzer Prize for his poetry book, *Complete Poems.* At age seventy he conquered another writing genre by penning his first and only novel, *Remembrance Rock.*

were returned to his birthplace in Galesburg and buried in a backyard park beneath a large stone aptly named for his novel, **Remembrance Rock.**

At the ***Carl Sandburg Historic Site,*** visitors can tour the quaint, three-room boyhood home and his burial place. Next door, the ***Carl Sandburg Visitor's Center*** has a small theater and gift shop, as well as hundreds of displays about Sandburg's life and writings. The Illinois Historic Preservation Agency maintains the home site, and the nonprofit ***Carl Sandburg Historic Site Association*** handles museum tours. The site is open Wed through Sun from 10 a.m. to 4 p.m., but call to verify, as limited funding has affected this museum's hours; admission is $3; 331 E. Third St.; (309) 342-2361; www.sandburg.org.

The Carl Sandburg Historic Site hosts the ***Songbag Concert Series*** in the barn at the rear of the Sandburg homestead. The music is acoustic, traditional, and folk, and single artists or small groups perform for about two hours. The series is held the last Saturday of the month, and concerts begin at 7 p.m.; admission is $3; 331 E. Third St.; (309) 342-2361; www.johnheasly.com.

When walking in downtown Galesburg, it's hard to miss the **Big Blue Chair.** Yes, go ahead—take a seat and have someone snap a photo; then send it to the **Galesburg Area Convention and Visitors Bureau** (CVB), where they'll post it on their Web site. And while you're at it, step inside the **Galesburg Visitors Center** (in the CVB office), located behind the chair, to get brochures, tour information, and advice from the staff. The bureau is located at 2163 E. Main St.; (309) 343-2485; www.visitgalesburg.com.

They'll probably send you in the direction of the **Seminary Street Historic Commercial District,** where a colossal redevelopment program has rejuvenated downtown Galesburg with unique shops, restaurants, and antiques stores behind the doors of beautifully restored nineteenth- and twentieth-century buildings. Located on Seminary Street; (309) 342-1000; www.seminarystreet.com.

The 1916 **Orpheum Theatre** is another renovated gem that is currently used as a performing-arts venue and community theater. Built by vaudeville-house architects C. W. and George L. Rapp, the building features all the wonderful grandiosity expected of such a place, from dramatic Corinthian columns and French Baroque medallions to exquisitely carved plaster friezes decorating the mezzanine. The theater is open Sept to May, Mon through Fri from 10 a.m. to 5 p.m., with tours by appointment; admission varies with events; 57 S. Kellogg St.; (309) 342-2299; http://theorpheum.org.

Aerobatics, wing walkers, and flour bombing are all a part of the mini air show demonstrations during the annual **National Stearman Fly-In Days,** when more than a hundred of these antique bi-wing trainers land near Galesburg. The event includes exhibits, entertainment, and food and is held for seven days during the second week of Sept; admission is free, but a fee of $1 each is charged for the tram ride to see the flight line of parked planes; located at the Galesburg Municipal Airport, 58 Illinois Rte. 164; (309) 343-2485 or (309) 343-6409; www.stearmanflyin.com.

The former Burlington Northern Railroad depot is now home to the **Galesburg Railroad Museum,** which features a close-up look at a Pullman parlor car and various other antique railroad cars located on the surrounding grounds, plus a nice display of railroad memorabilia inside the building. The museum is open May through mid-Oct, Tues through Sat from 10 a.m. to 4 p.m. and on Sun from noon to 4 p.m., and weekends only during off months; call ahead to confirm times because of the changing schedule; admission is $5 for adults, $2 for children ages eight to sixteen, free for children ages seven

and under, and $10 for a family pass; 211 S. Seminary St.; (309) 342-9400; www
.galesburgrailroadmuseum.org.

Each year the railroad museum and community throw a party of sorts
during the **Galesburg Railroad Days** celebration. Visitors are treated to a
model-train show and tours of the train yard; the city adds a street fair, carnival, pony rides, and food, while the **Galesburg Historical Society** pitches
in with a free **Tram Tour** of local historic sites. The event is held the fourth
weekend in June; admission is free; (309) 343-2485; www.galesburgrailroad
days.org.

Historic Walnut Grove Farm features a lot of yearly activities, but they'll
get you into the Christmas mood the first Friday through Sunday following
Thanksgiving Day. Meet with St. Nick, ride a horse-drawn wagon and enjoy
food and music of the season. Maybe you can pick out a Christmas tree, too.
Stay at the **Walnut Grove Farm Guest House Bed and Breakfast** and be
awakened by the morning sounds surrounding this nineteenth-century farm.
Walnut Grove is located at 1455 Knox Station Rd., Knoxville; (309) 289-4770;
www.walnutgrovefarm.com.

The town of **Monmouth** has its hero, too; Wyatt Earp was born here in
1848 and later became well known for his gun-slinging prowess as a deputy
U.S. marshal during the 1881 shoot-out at the OK Corral in Tombstone, Ari-
zona. His legend has been dramatized in television shows and movies. The
Wyatt Earp Birthplace Historical House Museum, listed on the National
Register of Historic Places, is outfitted with Earp family antiques and collectables. The rear yard has backdrops that simulate the scene in Tombstone,

Cruisin' with My Baby

It's only one night a year, and yet it probably draws more people to Warren County
than any other annual event: It's **Maple City Street Machines Cruise Night,** a mammoth car show that celebrates American's love affair with automobiles. The event is
sponsored by the Maple City Street Machines club, and remarkably, there is no entry
fee to show your car, and no admission fee to view everyone else's.

Recent shows have featured over 1,600 autos, ranging from new Corvettes to pristine Model Ts. Eager entrants often breeze into town before the streets are closed
at 8 a.m. Cars are parked as they arrive, snaking around the town square and north
and south along Monmouth's city blocks. It's estimated that over 25,000 people
attend, and by early evening live music and the smell of great cooking fill the air.
Don't miss the prize drawings and the 50/50 raffle that benefits a worthy local charity. The event is held the last Friday of July from 6 to 10 p.m.; Monmouth Chamber of
Commerce, (309) 734-3181; www.maplecitystreetmachines.com.

and each year during the **Wyatt Earp Day** celebration, costumed volunteers reenact the fateful event at the OK Corral. This is a privately owned homestead that is sometimes open and sometimes not, so it's best to drive by and see what's happening before knocking on the front door. As they say, they're "open in the summer from 2 to 4 p.m. and by chance." Located at 406 S. Third St.; (309) 734-3181.

Monmouth's history is steeped in clay; the pottery industry grew here, and businesses like the Western Stoneware Company employed Monmouth area potters for generations, but just shy of its one-hundredth anniversary in 2006, the company closed. However, in true American spirit, three employees reopened the enterprise shortly afterward under the name **W. S. Incorporated of Monmouth.** Today, the revitalized business maintains its long tradition of quality by creating handmade pottery. The phrase "mass production" is not in this company's vocabulary. Stop by its **pottery store** outlet and see for yourself. The store is open Tues through Sat from 10 a.m. to 4:30 p.m. and on Sun from noon to 4:30 p.m.; 1201 N. Main St.; (309) 734-6809; http://western stoneware.com.

Where's the beef? How about trying your luck at the **Warren County Prime Beef Festival,** where beef lovers gather in the city of Monmouth to celebrate red meat? There are all sorts of competitions here, from demo derby, to strong man, to fireman against fireman, plus a parade, pageant, car show, and beef show, but by far it's the Backyard BBQ Cook-off that gets everyone buzzing. Check the Beef Cook-Off tent for the schedule of free samples. The festival is held the weekend after Labor Day, Wed through Sat; admission is free; located at the northeast edge of Monmouth in the city park and on the airport grounds; watch for signs; (309) 734-3181; www.prime beeffestival.com.

Fulton County contains a most amazing treasure: Indian mounds dating between 3,000 B.C. and A.D. 12,000 are located here. Perhaps they are places of burial or worship, or sacred sanctuaries of tribal leaders. All of this might have gone undiscovered had it not been for the bounty land program of the Illinois Military Tract, which encouraged the settlement of the undeveloped Illinois Territory by veterans of the War of 1812. It was common for vets to sell their parcels to one another, and hence the bluff property came into the hands of William Dickson. Although he'd discovered artifacts while clearing the land for planting, it wasn't until his son, Dr. Thomas Dickson, took over the site that the true historical value became understood.

Today the Illinois State Museum complex, called the **ISM Dickson Mounds Museum,** contains a variety of experiences for visitors, including exhibits and hands-on displays inside the building, and outdoor opportunities

OTHER ATTRACTIONS WORTH SEEING IN WESTERN ILLINOIS

Old Carthage Jail and Visitors Center
Carthage

Par-A-Dice Riverboat Casino
East Peoria

Central Congregational Church
Galesburg

Stockade Soldier Citizen Museum
Galesburg

Lake Storey Recreational Area
Galesburg

Seminary Street Historic
Commercial District
Galesburg

Great Rivers Tour Boat Company
Grafton

Historic Barn Tours
Macomb

Metamora Courthouse State
Historic Site
Metamora

African-American Museum Hall
of Fame
Peoria

Peoria Chiefs
Peoria

Bradley University
Peoria

to view the mounds via hiking tours or from an observation point at the top of the museum building. The museum is open daily from 8:30 a.m. to 5 p.m., except Christmas, Thanksgiving, and New Year's Day; admission is free; 10956 N. Dickson Mounds Rd., Lewistown; (309) 547-3721.; www.museum.state.il.us/ismsites/dickson.

No matter the season, Fulton County is a lovely area for a drive. Pause to watch the water pouring over the spillway at the dam in **Bernadotte,** or stop for ice cream at any one of the other little towns along the route. If you're in the area in the fall, follow along the **Spoon River** for the annual **Spoon River Valley Scenic Drive.** This area of the state was memorialized in the works of American poet Edger Lee Masters, who wrote unmerciful stanzas about the flaws of the citizenry of his boyhood town of Lewistown and the surrounding area. The scenic drive winds through farmland and wooded areas, and the fifteen quaint towns along the way entertain visitors with festival-like events such as live music, demonstrations, carnivals, and food; more than two dozen museums and sites are open especially for this event. Begin your trip at any small town along the river. The event is held the first and second weekends in Oct; (309) 647-8980 or (309) 647-6074; www.spoonriverdrive.org or www.fultoncountytourism.org.

Petersburg is inexorably connected to the early hamlet of *New Salem,* because in the early 1840s an exodus from New Salem to the growing and bustling Petersburg caused the tiny town to fail. Today, Petersburg is the county seat of *Menard County* and home to over 2,000 residents, but New Salem exists only as a reconstructed historical village. Because of their proximity, it's convenient to tour both.

Starting in Petersburg, the obvious place to pause is at the *Menard County Courthouse Square,* where you'll see various plaques, statues, and signs of interest along the four exterior corners of the 1896 *Menard County Courthouse.* Stop on the second floor to view Lincoln documents displayed there. The courthouse is open during business hours; 102 S. Seventh St.; (217) 632-3201.

The *Menard County Historical Society Museum* is just down the street, and it displays various artifacts of county-wide interest and contains the genealogical library for the area. The museum is open Mon through Fri from 9 a.m. to noon and 1 to 4 p.m.; 125 S. Seventh St.; (217) 632-7363.

West on Jackson Street 1 block from the square, find the *Edgar Lee Masters Home and Museum;* this is where the poet and author of the *Spoon River Anthology* lived his boyhood years. The museum contains memorabilia of his life; although he's known as a prolific writer, he was also a lawyer who worked with Clarence Darrow. The museum is open Memorial Day through Labor Day, Thurs through Sat and on Tues from 10 a.m. to noon and 1 to 3 p.m.; admission is free; located at Jackson and Eighth Streets (217) 632-7363.

Perhaps the best way to travel between Petersburg and New Salem is by trolley. Board the *Stier Trolley Express* for its *Historical Petersburg Trolley Tours,* which feature a lively commentary of the area as you ride this cherished form of old-fashioned transportation. The trolley has seasonal hours only, running in spring and fall on weekends and in the summer Tues through Sun, every hour on the hour; admission is $9 for adults, $5 for children ages seven through twelve, and free for children under age six; board at the New Salem Visitors Center, 15588 History Lane; (217) 632-4000; www.stiertrolley express.com.

Lincoln's first serious foray into politics came while living in *New Salem,* where he ran a store and served as a land surveyor and the postmaster. Today the village has been reconstructed with houses, businesses, and support buildings constructed to reflect the 1830s; it's called *Lincoln's New Salem State Historic Site,* and visitors can see what the land looked like when Lincoln lived here. Costumed docents perform the chores required by nineteenth-century life, from spinning yarn, to cooking over an open hearth, to blacksmithing, with animals standing nearby. The site is open Mar 1 to Apr 15, Wed through

Sun from 9 a.m. to 5 p.m., and Apr 16 to Labor Day, daily from 9 a.m. to 5 p.m.; located at *New Salem Visitors Center,* 15588 History Lane; (217) 632-4000; www.lincolnsnewsalem.com.

A *Theatre in the Park* series is held at the Lincoln's New Salem State Historic Site during the summer in a 475-seat outdoor amphitheater. Performances have garnered many awards and vary in subject, but most emulate that of an old-time chautauqua, with country music, lectures, and light comedy presented in a friendly manner. The series is held from June through Aug, Fri and Sat at 8 p.m.; admission depends on the show; New Salem Visitors Center, 15588 History Lane; (217) 632-4000.

About 10 miles west of Peoria, you can walk on the wild side at the *Wildlife Prairie State Park.* The 2,000 acres are designed to give visitors the sense of a natural prairie habitat. Animals such as elk, cougar, and bison roam the grounds behind enclosures that mimic the Illinois prairie of generations ago. There are four fun lodging options here too: The Cabin on the Hill; The Train Caboose; Cottages by the Lake; and The Prairie Stables, all of which include two days' admission and almost all of the comforts of home. A train travels the park's rustic perimeter; tickets are an additional fee. Operating under the theme of "Education, Conservation, Recreation," the park offers a staggering 900 programs per year. Before you leave, stop by the snack shop for a bison burger. The park is open from Mar 1 to the middle of Dec, but call ahead because hours fluctuate with the weather and seasons; admission is $6.50 for those age thirteen and up, $4.50 for children ages four through twelve, and free for children under age three; 3826 N. Taylor Rd., Hanna City; (309) 676-0998; www.wildlifeprairiestatepark.org.

Playing in Peoria

It's the largest city on the *Illinois River* and the county seat of *Peoria County;* the town of *Peoria* is located in one of the first areas to be settled. Today it ranks sixth largest in the state, and continues to push forward with redevelopment along the riverfront.

To get a good sense of the town, contact the *Peoria Historical Society,* which offers four *trolley tours:* the River City Historical Tour, the All-American City Tour, the Old Peoria and Judge Tour, and the Springdale Cemetery Tour. The society also runs nine historic walking tours. Prices range from $8 to $12; 611 SW Washington Street; (309) 674-1921; www.peoriahistoricalsociety.org.

While downtown, stop to see *The Duryea,* one of the earliest gasoline-powered American automobiles. After gaining notoriety in 1895 when one of their prototype automobiles won the first American auto race, in downtown

testingground

The phrase "Will it play in Peoria?" comes from the Roaring Twenties, when vaudeville acts survived or flopped on the stages of Peoria's theaters. Producers trusted the people of Peoria because their likes, dislikes, and opinions tended to signal the national mood.

Chicago, brothers Charles and Frank Duryea came home determined to build cars in the garage of their *Peoria Heights* home. But lack of financing and other issues made things difficult for the pair and they eventually went in different directions, each moving to other states to work on their projects. Today, one of their first models is on display in the lobby of the *Peoria NEXT Innovation Center,* having spent many years prior at the *Peoria Public Library.* The Innovation Center home is short-lived, as eventually the car will take up residence at the Peoria Riverfront Museum, once that building is completed. The center is open regular business hours; admission is free; 801 W. Main St.; (309) 495-7238.

The *Lakeview Museum of Arts and Sciences* is the largest private museum in Illinois outside of Chicago. It is also one of only fifty U.S. museums that feature exhibits in both the arts and sciences. The art gallery contains an extensive permanent collection of folk art, Illinois quilts, and Illinois River decoys. Science exhibits tackle astronomy, geology, anthropology, and Illinois wildlife. *Children's Discovery Center* provides hands-on experiences for all ages, and a laser light show is presented in the planetarium. The *Guinness Book of World Records* has recognized the Lakeview Museum for its display of the world's largest scale model of the solar system. The museum is open Tues through Sat from 10 a.m. to 4 p.m. and on Sunday from noon to 4 p.m.; admission is $6 for adults and $4 for children, and the planetarium fee is $4.00

Woman of Stature

Bradley University has earned nationwide respect for its dedication to quality education, and it's thanks to Mrs. Lydia Moss Bradley (1816–1908) that the facility even exists. She was a wealthy widow, but frankly, it was her own business sense that turned the $500,000 inheritance she received from her beloved husband into a two-million-dollar estate that has ensured that this school is permanently endowed for the education of "the children." In 1897 she founded the Bradley Polytechnic Institute, and there's no doubt she'd be thrilled to see what her modest school has become today. As you walk the campus, look for the life-size *Lydia Moss Bradley Statue* standing in the middle of the commons walkway. She was a petite woman who accomplished great things. The university is located at 1501 Bradley Ave., Peoria; (309) 676-7611.

for adults and $3.50 for children ages three through seventeen; a combination admission fee for the museum and the planetarium is available; 1125 W. Lake Ave.; (309) 686-7000; www.lakeview-museum.org.

The *Peoria Park District* runs the *Peoria Zoo at Glen Oak Park,* where over one hundred species of animals roam and conservation is the topic of the discussion. Special displays highlight species native to Africa, Asia, and Australia, with new exhibits always planned and in the construction stage. The zoo is open daily from 10 a.m. to 5 p.m.; admission is $7.95 for those age thirteen and up, $7.50 for seniors, $4.25 for children ages three through twelve, and free for children under age two; 2218 N. Prospect Rd.; (309) 686-3365; www.peoriazoo.org.

Perhaps the best way to end your Peoria visit is aboard the **Spirit of Peoria** for a ride along the Illinois River on one of the only stern-driven paddle wheelers in the state. The boat is a faithful replica, and some of its fixtures, such as the vintage captain's bell and the brass communication tube, add to the boat's historic flavor. The captain provides commentary and history as you glide down the gentle waterway. Tours vary (from a two-hour ride, for example, to a dinner cruise or overnight stay), so availability and pricing will depend on your selection; 100 Water St.; (309) 637-8000; www.spiritofpeoria.com.

Places to Stay in Western Illinois

ELSAH

Green Tree Inn
15 Mill St.
(618) 374-2821
www.greentreeinn.com

Maple Leaf Cottage Inn
12 Selma St.
(618) 374-1684
www.mapleleafcottages
.com

GALESBURG

America's Best Value Inn
29 Public Sq.
(309) 343-9161
www.americasbestvalue
inn.com

Comfort Inn
907 W. Carl Sandburg Dr.
(309) 344-5445
www.comfortinn.com

Country Inn and Suites
2284 Promenade Court
(309) 344-4444
www.countryinns.com

Holiday Inn Express
2285 Washington St.
(309) 343-7100
www.hiexpress.com

Vista Lodge
565 W. Main St.
(309) 343-3191
www.vistarez.com

LEWISTOWN

Cottonwood Motel
805 S. Main St.
(309) 547-3733
cottonwoodmotel
.tripod.com

MACOMB

Days Inn
1400 N. Lafayette St.
(309) 833-5511
www.daysinn.com

SELECTED VISITORS BUREAUS AND CHAMBERS OF COMMERCE

Illinois Bureau of Tourism—Travel Information
(800) 2-CONNECT

Greater Alton/Twin Rivers Convention and Visitors Bureau
200 Piasa St., 62002
(618) 465-6676

Galesburg Area Convention and Visitors Bureau
2163 E. Main St., 61401
(309) 343-2485

Macomb Area Convention and Visitors Bureau
201 S. Lafayette St., 61455
(309) 833-1315

Peoria Area Convention and Visitors Bureau
456 Fulton St., Suite 300, 61602
(309) 676-0303

Quincy Convention and Visitors Bureau
532 Gardner Expressway, 62301
(217) 214-3700

Best Western Macomb Inn
1655 E. Jackson St.
(309) 836-6700
www.bestwestern.com

Olson Conference Center
Adams Street and
Western Avenue
(Western Illinois University
campus)
(309) 298-3500
www.student.services.wiu
.edu/occ

The Pineapple Inn
204 W. Jefferson St.
(309) 837-1914

NAUVOO

Hotel Nauvoo
1290 Mulholland St.
(217) 453-2310
www.hotelnauvoo.com

Nauvoo Family Inn and Suites
1875 Mulholland St.
(217) 453-6527
www.nauvoofamilyinn.com

Nauvoo Log Cabins
65 N. Winchester St.
(217) 453-3900
www.nauvoologcabins.com

NEW SALEM

Thomas Benton Gray House
36510 290th Ave.
(217) 285-2230
www.grayhousebb.com

PEORIA

Baymont Inn and Suites
2002 W. War Memorial Dr.
(309) 686-7600
www.baymontinns.com

Candlewood Suites at Grand Prairie
5300 W. Landon's Way
(309) 691-1690
www.petersenhotels.com

Comfort Suites
1812 W. War Memorial Dr.
(309) 688-3800
www.comfortsuites.com

Holiday Inn City Center
500 Hamilton Blvd.
(309) 674-2500
www.holidayinn.com/
peoria-dwtn

Hotel Père Marquette
501 Main St.
(309) 637-6500
www.hotelperemarquette
.com

Mark Twain Hotel
225 N.E. Adams St.
(309) 676-3600
www.marktwainhotel.com

Radisson Hotel Peoria
117 N. Western Ave.
(309) 673-8040
www.radisson.com

Red Roof Inn
1822 W. War Memorial Dr.
(309) 685-3911
www.redroof.com

PETERSBURG

The Oaks
510 W. Sheridan Rd.
(217) 632-5444
www.theoaksbandb.com

PITTSFIELD

Green Acres Motel
625 W. Washington St.
(217) 285-2166

QUINCY

Country Inn and Suites
110 N. 54th St.
(217) 222-8949
www.countryinns.com

Fairfield Inn by Marriott
4315 Broadway St.
(217) 223-5922
www.marriott.com

Places to Eat in Western Illinois

GALESBURG

Chez Willy's
41 S. Seminary St.
(309) 341-4141
www.chezwillys.com

Landmark Cafe
and Creperie
62 S. Seminary St.
(309) 343-5376
www.seminarystreet.com/
landmark

Packinghouse Dining
Company
441 Mulberry St.
(309) 342-6868
www.seminarystreet.com/
packinghouse

Sirloin Stockade
2200 N. Henderson St.
(309) 344-2011
www.stockadecompanies
.com

The Steak House
951 N. Henderson St.
(309) 343-9994

MACOMB

Sullivan Taylor Coffee
House
119 S. Randolph St.
(309) 836-7064
www.yourwinesellers.com/
SullivanTaylor.htm

NAUVOO

Grandpa John's Cafe
1275 Mulholland St.
(217) 453-2310
http://grandpajohnscafe
.com

Hotel Nauvoo
1290 Mulholland St.
(217) 453-2310
www.hotelnauvoo.com

PEORIA

Flagstone's Restaurant at
Radisson Hotel Peoria
117 N. Western Ave.
(309) 673-8181

Kelleher's Irish Pub
and Eatery
619 S.W. Water St.
(309) 673-6000
www.kellehersirishpub.com

Spirit of Peoria
100 Water St.
(309) 637-8000
www.spiritofpeoria.com

Red, Green, and White

For those familiar with the flat and open terrain of north central Illinois, the area encompassed in the state's southern region would surely seem out of character. The 948-acre **Red Hills State Park** contains the highest peak between St. Louis, Missouri, and Cincinnati, Ohio, and where there are hills there are ravines. Here the dense hardwood forest gives way to meadows, freshwater springs, and a lovely lake. When it comes to attracting wildlife, this place is perfection.

Hikers, cyclists, and equestrian will appreciate the trails graded at various skill levels, and handicapped routes make this park available to just about everyone. **Red Hills Lake** provides forty acres of water recreation, and boats can be rented at the concession pavilion. The **Chauncey Marsh Nature Preserve** is an extension of Red Hills, and visitors are treated to the thriving and rare **Wabash Border Marsh Ecosystem** that supports the fragile flowers and fauna within its 627 acres. The park is located at US 50, 1100 North and 400 E. Rural Rte. 2, Sumner; (618) 936-2469.

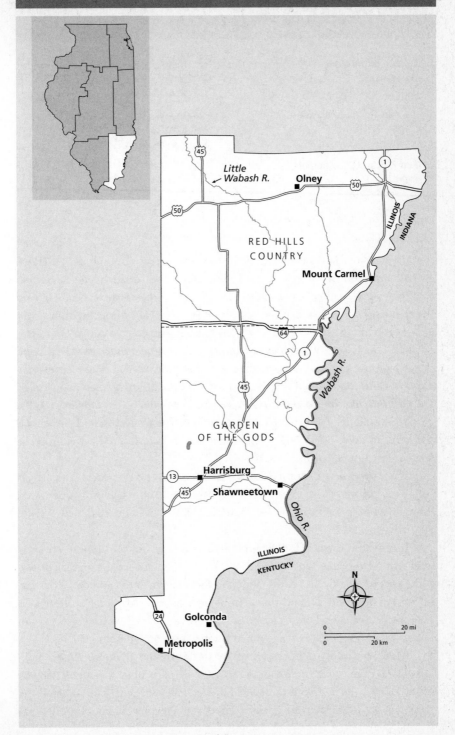

AUTHOR'S TOP FIVE PICKS

Garden of the Gods
Harrisburg
(618) 253-1070

Superman's Metropolis
Metropolis
(877) 424-5025

Cave-in-Rock State Park
Cave-In-Rock
(618) 289-4325

Rim Rock National Recreation Trail
Harrisburg
(618) 253-7114

Fort Massac Encampment
Metropolis
(618) 524-4712

If you're not into hiking or just need a respite, stop by the park's **Trace Inn Restaurant.** It's a meal with a view, since the restaurant is situated so that the ever-changing seasons and the Red Hills Lake below can be enjoyed through the large windows. The restaurant is open Tues through Sun from 11 a.m. to 8 p.m.; (618) 936-2352; www.redhillstraceinn.com.

The county seat of **Lawrence County** is **Lawrenceville** a town of around 5,000 that once thrived on the income of local oil fields. The stately **Lawrence County Courthouse** is the backdrop for the annual town celebration called the **Fall Festival on Courthouse Square.** There's live entertainment, food, a craft show and flea market, plus small town fun. The festival is held the second weekend in Sept, Fri through Sun; admission is free; located on courthouse square downtown; (618) 943-3516.

The **Lawrence County Historical Museum** houses local artifacts as well as a history of the town's early oil business. The museum is open Mon through Fri from 8:30 a.m. to 5:30 p.m.; donations are requested; 619 Twelfth St.; (618) 943-4317.

The nearby town of **St. Francisville** is known for its Chinese chestnut trees that were planted in 1967 and became the impetus for the annual **Chestnut Festival.** The event has expanded to include live entertainment, a parade, helicopter rides, prizes, and music from blue grass to gospel. The festival is held the first weekend of Oct for two days; admission is free; located in downtown; (618) 943-3516; www.lawrencecountyillinois.com/chestnutfest.

Wabash County is bordered on two sides by the **Wabash River,** making this a prime area for outdoor activity. In particular, the **Beall Woods State Park** is graced with massive, 120-foot tall trees and is nicknamed the "Forest of the Wabash." Here, virgin timber remains pristine and the 270 acres of primeval forest cuddle against the meandering Wabash River, making for spectacular views and hiking opportunities. Visitors can select from five designated trials rated easy to moderately easy and running from ½ mile to 3 miles in length. Note: Flooding can be a problem that closes these trails, so contact the office prior to hiking. The park is open daily from sunrise to 10 p.m.; closed Christmas and New Year's Day; 9285 Beall Woods Ave., Mount Carmel; (618) 298-2442.

bumpyride

Before you leave *St. Francisville,* check out the *Cannonball Bridge,* a former railroad bridge that spans the *Wabash River* and is sure to give you a wide-eyed expression as you drive across the rumbling wooden planks that act as the road surface. The cost is $1, and you won't soon forget the experience.

As the county seat of Wabash County, *Mount Carmel* is the scene of county business, with a decidedly modern county courthouse as the town centerpiece. Area and county history is on display at the *Wabash County Museum.* An active group of volunteer members of the *Wabash County Historical Society* organizes the changing exhibits, lectures, and research library. The museum is open Tues, Thurs, and Sun from 2 to 5 p.m.; donations are requested; 320 N. Market St.; (618) 262-8774; www.museum.wabash.il.us.

As you pass through Mount Carmel, you might hear the echo of a faraway horse and the call of "Hi-ho, Silver, away!" One of the first voices of **The Lone Ranger** radio series belonged to Mount Carmel native Brace Beemer (1902–1965). From almost the beginning, Beemer lived a life of adventure, having enlisted for duty during World War I at the tender age of fourteen. As far as he was concerned, his age was a minor fact, but not to his superiors; when he was wounded and his youthful secret discovered, he was promptly returned home from the battlefield and discharged from service. From 1941 to 1954 Beemer was tapped to play the radio voice of the masked cowboy who fought for justice. The modest frame home where he was born still stands at 930 Cherry St. in Mount Carmel. This is a private residence, so just drive by and tip your ball cap.

The historical society also sponsors a variety of fund-raising activities, including the popular annual *Spring Home Preservation Tour,* which features a changing selection of architecturally important homes. The tour is held mid-May from 1 to 5 p.m.; tickets are $10 each and can be purchased at the museum at 12:30 p.m. on the day of the event; 320 N. Market St.; (618) 262-8774; www.museum.wabash.il.us.

If you've got a taste for barbecue, attend Mount Carmel's *RibberFest,* where professional "ribbers" compete for national qualification in this officially sanctioned Kansas City Cook-Off contest. The eating begins at noon, so don't be late 'cause the ribs won't wait! The event is held the first weekend in Sept; it's free to watch, but not to eat; located on Market Street downtown; (618) 262-8378; www.cityofmtcarmel.com.

While you're in *Edwards County,* stop at the county seat of *Albion* to see one of the town's most interesting landmarks: the *Albion Pagoda.* Standing on the southwest corner of the courthouse square, the current structure was designed by noted architect W. E. Felix and constructed in 1914, although it is the third generation of pagodas built here; the original was installed in 1890 to protect a mineral water well.

Also, take note of the *Edwards County Courthouse,* a striking, traditional building that shares the grounds with a historic jailhouse, *Veteran's Memorial Arch,* and the dramatic *Angel of Hope Sculpture.* The courthouse is located at 50 E. Main St.; (618) 445-2016.

And join in the festivities of *Pork Day USA,* Albion's tribute to pork chops celebrated with a parade, free entertainment, a pageant, and plenty of grub. The event is held on Sat in early July; (618) 392-0925; http://southeast illinois.com.

Down the road, find the town of *Olney,* the county seat of *Richland County.* It's safe to say that Olney residents are nature minded. Besides white squirrels, these folks have *Bird Haven,* a unique environment that is part of the *Robert Ridgway Memorial Arboretum and Bird Sanctuary.* This

Grab a Spoon!

If you're anywhere in southeastern Illinois, you're likely to smell chowder. If you thought New England had the market cornered on chowder, then you're mistaken, because chowders are a long-standing tradition here.

Yes, chowder is a type of thick soup, but in this part of Illinois it's also the term used for community gatherings. And while they gather, they also eat. And, more often than not, they're eating chowder from family recipes that include water, potatoes, salt pork, and onions simmered in a huge cast-iron kettle. Some of these kettles hold seventy gallons of this flavorful mix. The difference between other chowders and those found in southern Illinois is the addition of tomatoes.

In 1958 the county commissioners anointed **Edwards County** the "Chowder Capital of the World," and apparently no one has challenged that proclamation, because it still stands. More than twenty chowder events are held in the county each year. The Mount Carmel Knights of Columbus holds their chowder feast in late Aug; (618) 262-8222. And the Albion Chowder is held in mid-June; (618) 445-2303.

Squirrely City

If you're trying to locate the town of *Olney,* just watch for the *white squirrels.* Yes, that's right—the town is teaming with the cute little critters that have as many stories behind them as they have nuts in storage.

There are two major theories about how the area became overrun with the unusual squirrels, but we'll leave the debates to the experts—the townsfolk who protect them with laws, fines, and regulations geared to people and pets that might do harm to the prized tourist attractions. So while in Olney, keep your pets on a leash, drive slowly so you don't run over a squirrel, and please, don't try to sneak one into your jacket pocket to take along as a souvenir. Let's just say it wouldn't be pretty.

The best time of day to see them is early in the morning, and the location of choice tends to be the downtown *Olney City Park* at SR 130, or any of the feeding stations placed throughout the neighborhoods.

was the summer home and then permanent residence of scientist, author, and renowned ornithologist Robert Ridgway (1850–1929). On these grounds he planted species not commonly found in Illinois to test the hardiness of the trees and fauna. Consequently, today there's a rich collection of plants to observe, plus there are over 18-acres of nature trials to explore. Birds are especially attracted to this refuge, making it a bird-watcher's delight. Although the home is gone, a replica of Ridgway's front porch stands on the site of the original cottage. The sanctuary is open from dawn to dusk; admission is free; located on East Fork Lake Road; (618) 395-7302.

The people of Olney wind down the summer and head into fall with the annual *Olney Arts and Crafts Festival.* Serious artists participate in this event, as this is a juried art show. There's live music and performing arts enter-tainment, plus plenty of great food. The festival is held the last Sat of Sept; admission is free; located downtown; (618) 395-7302.

And on Thurs, Fri, and Sat between Thanksgiving and Christmas, the town sponsors the *Olney Christmas Light Display,* which includes a remarkable 200 exhibits, all glittering amid 150,000 lights; (618) 395-7302.

West of Olney is the town of *Flora* in *Clay County,* and the people here have shown a remarkable dedication in restoring the *Flora B&O Depot* as one of their community projects. The office of the *Flora Chamber of Commerce* is located at the former Baltimore and Ohio Railroad depot, as well as a small museum and planned veterans memorial. The depot is open Mon through Fri from 9 a.m. to 4 p.m.; donations are requested; 223 W. Railroad St.; (618) 662-5646; www.florachamber.com.

OTHER ATTRACTIONS WORTH SEEING IN SOUTHEASTERN ILLINOIS

Albion Public Library
Albion

The Chocolate Factory
Dixon Springs

Lake Glendale Recreation Area
Dixon Springs

Smithland Pool
Golconda

Ohio River Recreation Area
Golconda

Lincoln Heritage Trail State Monument
Lawrenceville

Super Museum and Souvenir Store
Metropolis

Elijah P. Curtis Home
Metropolis

Merv Griffin's Theater
Metropolis

Harrah's Metropolis Casino
Metropolis

Lake Thunderhawk
Ozark

Cannonball Bridge
St. Francisville

Teutopolis Monastery Museum
Teutopolis

Moravian Church and Cemetery
West Salem

Stop to read the ***George Rodgers Clark Memorial Marker*** next to the depot. It's interesting to note that Clark's route across the Illinois prairie during the Revolutionary War was nearly identical to that of the current B&O Railroad tracks. The marker is located at 223 W. Railroad St.

You'll keep busy at the hundred-acre ***Charley Brown Park,*** which features playgrounds, two lakes, a dam, community pool, and golf course, plus over eighty campsites. Many, however, would say their favorite entertainment here is the ***Little Toot Railroad.*** Two small trains, one a diesel Tom Thumb reproduction and the other a 1959 steam-engine train, circle a 1-mile route over trestles, past water tanks, and through the scenic landscape. The Little Toot Railroad operates daily from May to Oct, and from Thanksgiving to Christmas during the Christmas in the Park celebration; admission is $4; located on Old US 50; (618) 662-5646; www.littletootrailroad.com.

Pillars and Salt

Saline County was named for ***Saline Creek*** and the many salt springs dotting this section of the state. Early on, salt mining was a major economic boost to this area. Today, the county is home to the largest underground coal-mining operation in the state. The county seat is **Harrisburg**, which calls itself the gateway to the **Shawnee National Forest** just to the south of the town.

One of the most remarkable sections of the forest is what is known as the **Garden of the Gods Wilderness;** it's a place where jutting rock pillars give visitors the sense that they're looking at sculptures, almost like those on the Polynesian Easter Island, rather than naturally cut formations. Garden of the Gods is located at 50 Hwy. 145 South, Harrisburg; (618) 253-7114.

betchadidn't know…

Salt was used in the tanning of animal hides, making it a required ingredient for pioneers and merchants active in the fur trade.

There's also civilization of sorts within this park; the **Saline Creek Pioneer Village** depicts life in Illinois from 1800 to 1840. Besides several historical buildings, there's a reproduction **Block House,** the **Pauper Cemetery,** and the 1877 **Pauper Farm,** which served as a county-run boarding house where indigent farmers could live if they fell on hard times. Today it houses a museum with local artifacts. The village is open Tues through Sun from 2 to 5 p.m.; admission is $3 for adults and $1 for children; 1600 S. Feazel St.; (618) 253-7342.

You're bound to be amazed at the striking historical buildings that overlook the downtown city square of **McLeansboro.** Of course, as the county seat of **Hamilton County,** the **Hamilton County Courthouse** is here, too, but it's a much more modern specimen compared to the **McCoy Memorial Library** building, which was built in 1884 as a family residence for the Cloud family. Today, the library is on the first floor, the **Hamilton County Museum** on the second, and the **Hamilton County Genealogy Center** on the third. Because it was once a home, many of the original fixtures, as well as the nine elaborate fireplaces, are intact and add to the Victorian ambience of the rooms. The building is open Mon through Thurs from 11 a.m. to 4 p.m. and Fri and Sat from 1 to 4 p.m.; closed on Sun; 118 S. Washington St.; (618) 643-2125.

Next, retreat down the street to the country hospitality of the **Innstead Bed and Breakfast,** where your sleep will be peaceful under handmade quilts and the breakfast will make you glad you stayed in town. The B&B is located at 400 S. Washington Ave.; (618) 643-2038.

Money and Mining

Today, **Old Shawneetown** is a quiet little village of about 300 people, and although it's also the county seat of **Gallatin County,** the lifestyle here is

Money's in the Mattress

In Old Shawneetown you'll see the 1840 Five Column Bank, which was the first bank chartered after the Illinois Territory became the State of Illinois. The building took longer to construct than it lasted in business, having failed by 1843. Various other financial enterprises used the building until 1942, when it was finally deeded to the state. It's currently owned by the Illinois Historic Preservation Agency as the **Shawneetown Bank State Historic Site,** and although it isn't open to the public, the exterior is worth admiring. The odd number of Doric columns is unusual on a Greek Revival structure, and the front limestone steps and facade still sport a high watermark, evidence of its being submerged during flooding by the Ohio River. The building is located at 280 Washington St.

peaceful and relaxed. But at one point the men who settled here had hoped it would become the financial capital of Illinois, thanks to the area's fast-paced trading in the salt industry. To that end, resident John Marshall offered his grand, two-story brick home for use by the Illinois Territory's first chartered bank. Today the building has been converted into the *John Marshall House Museum.* It stands on the banks of the Ohio River and serves as a record of frontier life, with early Illinois artifacts, murals, and exhibits relating to early banking. Make certain you check out the currency display of paper bills in denominations not used today, such as the seven-dollar bill. Volunteers from the *Gallatin County Historical Society* provide tours. The museum is open from Mother's Day to Labor Day, on Sat and Sun from 1 to 4 p.m.; donations are requested; located on First Street.

The area surrounding the town of *Rosiclare* was once the largest mining operation of fluorspar in the nation, and if words like inclusion, crystals, and calcites are in your vocabulary, then you need to visit the *American Fluorite Museum,* where a world-class fluorspar display won't disappoint. Housed in the headquarters of the former Rosiclare Lead and Fluorspar Mining Company, the museum displays numerous unusual fluorspar samples, mining tools, and scale mining models, too. The museum is open Mar through Dec on Thurs, Fri, and Sun from 1 to 4 p.m. and on Sat from 10 a.m. to 4 p.m.; admission is $3 for adults and $1 for children ages six through twelve; located on Main Street; (618) 285-3513.

Join the town for the annual *Fluorspar Festival,* which includes the *Cars along the Ohio Show,* featuring classic cars, trucks, and motorcycles, plus a parade, arts and crafts fair, kiddie carnival, and barbecue. Stay for the evening fireworks over the Ohio River. The festival is held the first Sat in Oct; admission is free; located in downtown Rosiclare; (618) 287-4333; www.hardincountyil.org.

Elizabethtown sits right next to the Ohio River, and the perfect place to enjoy a view of it is at the *River Rose Inn Bed and Breakfast,* where guests can pull up a chair underneath the magnolia trees and watch paddle wheelers rolling down the waterway. You can stay in the main house, which is a brick 1914 Greek Revival mansion, or select the Magnolia Cottage as your getaway. And there's a pool, too. The River Rose Inn is located at 1 Main St.; (618) 287-8811; www.shawneelink.net/~riverose.

A rose by any other name isn't the same in this case: Don't confuse the River Rose Inn with the *Rose Hotel,* which is located down the street and thought to be the state's oldest operating commercial inn. Although it's owned by the Illinois State Preservation Agency, today it's leased to a private party that also operates it as a bed-and-breakfast. The mansion was built in 1812 by early settler James McFarland (1776–1837) for use as a tavern before it became a popular hotel for river travelers. Everyone mentions the hotel's wide veranda overlooking the Ohio River, but the gazebo, which was constructed in 1882, will provide a lovely view as well. Tours are offered by appointment. The hotel is located at 10 Main St.; (618) 287-2872.

heavymetal

The mineral fluorspar acts as a fluxing additive that removes impurities and allows steel to be smelted at a lower temperature. By 1940, the mining of fluorspar and steel manufacturing had reached an all-time zenith. Hardin County produced nearly 50 percent of the needed supply.

Every year people here dress in period costumes from the Civil War era and dance in the streets as part of the *Hardin County Heritage Festival.* Witness a Civil War reenactment and a formal ball and get a laugh out of the Duck Race down the Ohio River. Those plastic toys can really move in that water. The festival is held the second Fri and Sat of Aug; located in downtown Elizabethtown; (618) 287-4333; www.hardincountyil.org.

River Ride

For a different way to navigate, board the **Shawnee Queen** *water taxi* at Rosiclare. The boat crosses the Ohio River and makes various stops at ports such as Golconda, Elizabethtown, and Cave-in-the-Rock. It's about a two-hour round-trip and reservations are required because of limited seating and river conditions. The water taxi operates from the second week of May to Nov 1, Tues through Sat from 6 a.m. to 6 p.m.; the fee depends on the destination; 190 Main St.; (618) 285-3342; www .ridesmtd.com.

TOP ANNUAL EVENTS

JUNE

Annual Superman Celebration
Metropolis
(877) 424-5025

OCTOBER

Golconda Fall Festival
Golconda
(618) 683-4317

Fort Massac Encampment
Fort Massac State Park
Metropolis
(618) 524-9321

NOVEMBER

Olney Community Christmas Light
Display
Olney
late Nov–Dec
(618) 395-7302

DECEMBER

Annual Tour of Homes
Metropolis
(877) 424-5025

And now on to the "fight for truth, justice, and the American way," as only a comic book character can promise. It's the motto of Superman, and if you have any chance of seeing him, surely your luck will be best in his hometown of *Metropolis.* In fact, he's on billboards, on the water tower, standing on the street corner, and sometimes walking around town. Check out the downtown phone booth that stands ready for his quick transformation. But you can be assured he won't be standing around the corner of Third and Ferry Streets; that's because someone has installed a "deadly" *Kryptonite Monument* there.

As the county seat of *Massac County,* Metropolis's town square features the *Massac County Courthouse.* It's a nice enough looking brick building built in 1942, but it's upstaged by a 15-foot-tall, painted bronze *Superman statue* standing in the side parking lot. And talk about pulling rank, the courthouse's official address is 1 Superman Sq. The Man of Steel's image can be seen in the windows of the shops and businesses that circle *Superman Square.*

Of course, true fans will be sure to visit the *Super Museum and Souvenir Store,* where just a fraction of one man's collection is on display. Over 20,000 artifacts, including the flight suit George Reeves wore under his leotards until the cables snapped one day and George crashed to the ground. And remember when Christopher Reeve created that stirringly beautiful "Fortress of Solitude" using that Kryptonian crystal? It's here, too. The museum is open daily from 9 a.m. to 5 p.m.; admission is $5 for adults and free for children under age five; 517 Market St.; (618) 524-5518; www.supermuseum.com.

The admission fee also covers entry to the *Americana Hollywood Museum,* which features memorabilia of popular entertainers such as Elvis, Marilyn Monroe, and John Wayne, as well as current stars. There's a western backdrop movie set, statues that you can pose beside for photographs, and a gift store, too. The museum is open Apr through Sept, daily from 9 a.m. to 6 p.m., and Oct through Mar, daily from 9 a.m. to 5 p.m.; admission is $5 for adults and free for children under age five; 108 W. Third St.; (618) 524-5975.

asuperwoman

Noel Neill played Lois Lane in the 1950s *Superman* television series, and over the years she's supported the Superman Celebration with her frequent attendance. To thank her, the city commissioned a life-size bronze statue of the "First Lady of Metropolis."

Of course, all of this super-ness requires a festival, so Metropolis hosts the annual *Superman Celebration,* which draws about 30,000 visitors from all over the world. Stars from various movie and television series that have a Superman connection, along with artists and writers from DC Comics, are often surprise guests at this event. Plus there's a real sense of fun here, with a street dance, movie screenings, crafts show and flea market, and several Superman contests. Don't miss the Fan Film competition. The celebration is held the second week of June; admission is free; located at Superman Square downtown; (877) 424-5025; www.supermancelebration.net.

About a block away from the center square is the 1879 *Elijah P. Curtis Home,* which is maintained as a house museum by the *Massac Historical Society.* Curtis, a lawyer and Civil War major, commissioned this two-story, Greek Revival, brick home for his young bride. The interior features especially striking woodwork and fine carpentry details. The house is open Sat and Sun from noon to 5 p.m., Mon from noon to 4 p.m., and Tues from 11:30 a.m. to 2:30 p.m.; donations are requested; 405 Market St.; (618) 524-5025.

Big Bag John

Before heading out of Metropolis, stop at the *Big John Grocery* to buy some picnic supplies and see *Big John.* No, he's not the store manager; he's the 30-foot-tall fiberglass giant standing out in front that's grinning from ear to ear as he lugs two bags of "groceries" to some unknown car in the parking lot. The grocery is locally owned and operated, but statues similar to this one tend to stand guard at popular southern food chains. Big John Grocery is located at 1200 E. Fifth Ave.

Healing Waters

Spanning over 800 acres, **Dixon Springs State Park** offers staggering views of hills and vales, but regardless of its natural beauty and excellent hunting grounds, people have flocked here for generations because of the seven mineral springs that percolate from beneath the ground. The Shawnee Indian tribe called this the area of "Great Medicine Waters." William Dixon claimed the land for himself as the area's first white settler in 1848, but as word of the springs bubbled out to the general public, Dixon Springs became host to a rush of visitors from both the local area and faraway states. Today, the mineral bath houses are long gone, and it's the expansive views of ancient trees and breathtaking rock formations that draw visitors. The park is open year-round from dawn to dusk; admission is free; located on SR 146, Golconda; (618) 949-3394.

This is prime quilt country; Metropolis is just over twenty minutes from the National Quilt Museum in Paducah, Kentucky, which makes the two cities perfect companions for organizing a blockbuster quilting event. The **Super City/Quilt City Connection** brings national and international experts together to lecture, teach, and exhibit their work. The event is held the second week of Sept; admission depends on activities, but many are free; located at Harrah's Riverfront Event Center, 100 E. Front St., Metropolis, and in sister city Paducah, Kentucky; (877) 424-5025; www.metropolistourism.com.

When it's time to leave, stop to grab picnic supplies; then head out of town to **Fort Massac State Park** and enjoy lunch at one of the park's shelters or tables. Walk the grounds and be sure to pause at the scenic view of the Ohio River. The visitor center, museum, and reconstructed 1802 fort make this a learning opportunity, too, with site representatives ready to answer questions, videos and displays, plus several interpretive programs offered each month throughout the year. The park is open Mon through Fri from 8 a.m. to 4 p.m. and on Sat and Sun from 10 a.m. to 3:30 p.m.; admission is free; 1308 E. Fifth St.; (618) 524-4712.

Each year the park hosts the **Fort Massac Encampment,** a demonstration by reenactors who depict military life in 1814 with a mock battle, training exercises, and marching drills. Sutlers sell their wares, settlers mingle with the visitors, and music and games are part of the activities. The encampment is held the second week of Oct on Sat from 10 a.m. to 5 p.m. and Sun from 10 a.m. to 4:30 p.m.; admission is free; 1308 E. Fifth St.; (618) 524-4712.

As the self-described "Deer Capital of Illinois," **Golconda** hosts the **Pope County Deer Festival** during the first four days of hunting season. Besides a three-day hunt, there's the crowning of the Deer Queen, barbecue, and a craft fair. Be sure to dress warm. The festival is held the third week in Nov; (618) 683-9702.

For unusual lodging next to the Ohio River, arrange to stay in one of the four renovated *Lock Keepers Houses* along *Golconda Lock and Dam 51.* Built in the 1920s, each home is stocked with kitchen utensils and comfortable bedding, but you may be tempted to forget sleeping and instead sit on the screened-in porch all night to watch the boat traffic traveling on the river. The houses are located at the Golconda Marina on CR 1; (618) 683-6702.

Places to Stay in Southeastern Illinois

HARRISBURG

Comfort Inn
100A E. Seright St.
(618) 252-2442
www.comfortinn.com

Super 8 Motel
100 E. Seright St.
(618) 253-8081
www.super8.com

METROPOLIS

Baymont Inn and Suites
203 E. Front St.
(618) 524-5678
www.baymontinns.com

Comfort Inn of Metropolis
2118 E. Fifth St.
(618) 524-7227
www.comfortinn.com

Holiday Inn Express
2179 E. Fifth St.
(618) 524-8899
www.hiexpress.com

MT. CARMEL

Shamrock Motel
1303 N. Cherry St.
(618) 262-4169

Town and Country Motel
1515 W. Third St.
(618) 262-4171

OLNEY

McClure Guesthouse
215 S. Fair St.
(618) 843-6731
www.mcclureguesthouse
.com

Royal Inn Motel
1001 W. Main St.
(618) 395-8581

Shady Timbers Lodge
4560 E. Miller Lane
(618) 393-4900

Travelers Inn Motel
1801 E. Main St.
(618) 393-2186

SELECTED VISITORS BUREAUS AND CHAMBERS OF COMMERCE

Southernmost Illinois Tourism and Convention Bureau
Ullin, 62992
(618) 833-9928

Illinois Bureau of Tourism—Travel Information
(800) 2-CONNECT

Places to Eat in Southeastern Illinois

CAVE-IN-ROCK

Cave-in-Rock State Park Lodge and Restaurant
1 New State Park Rd.
(618) 289-4545
www.caveinrockkaylors
.com

LAWRENCEVILLE

Hills Hideaway Restaurant
519 12th St.
(618) 943-5212

METROPOLIS

Ace's Diner
Harrah's Metropolis Casino
100 E. Front St.
(800) 935-0050

OLNEY

Pita Place
834 E. Main St.
(618) 838-2977
www.thepitaplace.us

SOUTHWESTERN ILLINOIS

Water and Tears

Although this area of the state has its share of natural wonders, **Clinton County** also has a fair share of manufactured attractions. Start with **Carlyle Lake,** the largest engineered body of water in Illinois, with over twenty-six acres of liquid entertainment and home to all sorts of water sports, fishing, and regattas.

Nearby, in the town of **Carlyle,** there's another remarkable man-made feat. The **General Dean Suspension Bridge** was constructed for the staggering sum of $40,000 in 1859 and served as a tollway for those crossing the Kaskaskia River along the Goshen Trail. Traffic crossed here until 1920, when a replacement bridge was constructed farther up river. After years of disrepair, a restoration project converted it into a pedestrian bridge in the early 1950s, and it was renamed in honor of local Korean War veteran general William F. Dean. The span is 280 feet across the river, and the stone columns tower 35 feet high. Visitors can linger on the wood-plank walkway of this last remaining suspension bridge in Illinois. The bridge is located on Fairfax Street in Carlyle.

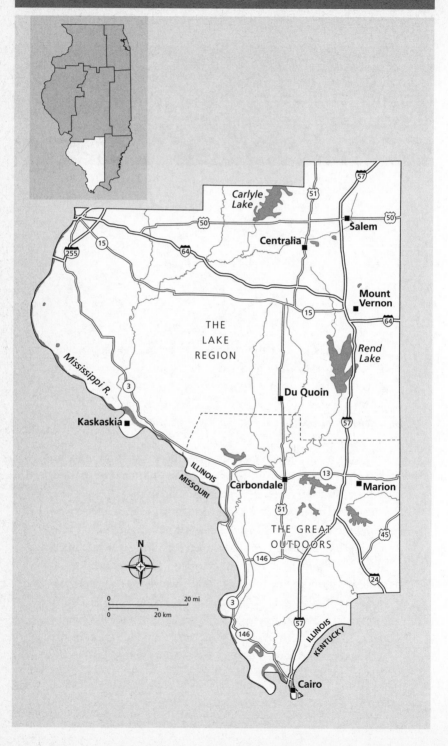

The *Clinton County Courthouse* is a modern building and it's somewhat surprising to see it in downtown Carlyle, as it seems out of character with other courthouses in neighboring counties and around the state. The courthouse is located at 850 Fairfax St.

On the other hand, the *Clinton County Historical Society Museum* is maintained in a nineteenth-century house that was once the residence of prominent judge Sidney Breese (1800–1878). After his death, the abode served as a funeral home, and the walls were altered to slide to accommodate larger gatherings. The collection includes local historical artifacts and some real oddities, such as a 1918 mousetrap, an egg-crate maker, and miscellaneous medical and church equipment. The museum is open Memorial Day to Labor Day on the second, third, and fourth Thurs of each month, from 10 a.m. to 3 p.m.; donations are requested; 1091 Franklin St.; (618) 594-4015.

During the 1920 and '30s, many of the men who lived in the tiny village of *Beckemeyer* traveled some distance to work in the area's coal mines. Tragically, in 1947 an explosion at the Centralia Coal Mine Company's No. Five Mine injured or took the lives of many of the residents. Among them was Joseph Koch Sr. Some years later, his family commissioned a life-size bronze statue of Mr. Koch to honor him and the local miners for their sacrifices. The *Coal Miner Monument* includes a replica of Mr. Koch's metal lunch box, like the one carried by millions of American workers of that era. The monument is located in the park next to the American Legion, 391 Louis St.; www.becke meyeril.gov/index.htm.

If there's the smell of sauerkraut, knockwurst, or bratwurst in the air, you must be near *Germantown* during their annual *Spassfest,* which celebrates the German heritage of its early settlers. This tradition has been going on since 1968; today it's a larger event, with an antique tractor and car show, live music,

AUTHOR'S TOP FIVE PICKS

Giant City State Park
(618) 457-4836

Fort de Chartres
Prairie du Rocher
(618) 284-7230

Du Quoin State Fair
Du Quoin
(618) 542-1515

Kaskaskia State Historic Site and Island
Ellis Grove
(618) 859-3741

Rend Lake
Benton
(618) 439-7430

The Black Fire

History records that people in this area of the state were particularly vulnerable to illnesses. Prairie life was harsh in general, and medical treatment sparse, meaning people perished from common diseases. So it's no wonder that when the cholera epidemic of 1832 hit the farmers and settlers surrounding the village of *Breese,* it quickly became a tragedy of major proportions. While entire families succumbed to the "Black Fire," the family of Joseph Altepeter was spared; legend says that Altepeter made a pact with God that if his family survived, he'd build a cross along the road in front of his farm as a witness to faith. Hence, today a white cross, called the *Cholera Cross* by locals, stands about a mile south of Breese, along the road between the hamlet and *Germantown.* This isn't the original cross; that wooden symbol decayed a long time ago, and the current owners of the dairy farm have replaced it with a stone version.

lots of contests, German food, and fireworks. Don't miss the Saturday evening Polka Mass at St. Boniface Church. The festival is held the second weekend of Aug; admission is free; located at the community park downtown; (618) 397-1488; www.germantownil.com/spassfest.htm.

In *Trenton* you can check out where the buffalo roam at the *J-H Bison Ranch,* home to some 800-plus-pound critters with cute monikers such as T-Bone and Rib-Eye. If you can visit in the spring, you might see the newborn bison calves take their bottles. The animal residents here also include llamas, alpaca, and an easy-going Sicilian donkey. Remember this is not a tourist attraction per se, but an operating ranch, so it can be tricky getting a reservation. That said, it's worth your effort and patience. Tours run ninety minutes, from 9:30 a.m. to 2:30 p.m., and require reservations, so please don't knock on their front door; admission is $17 for those age fifteen and up, $10 for children ages three through fourteen, and free for children under age three; 10802 Sunnyside School Rd.; (618) 934-3029; www.jbarhbisonranch.com.

The hot spot for eats here is the *Trenton House Restaurant,* where all-buffalo-meat burgers, buffalo meat-loaf sandwiches, and buffalo chili are popular menu items, (but don't mention this when you're visiting the J. H. Ranch). They also serve salads, salmon, chops, and regular beef selections. The restaurant is open for lunch and dinner; 2 E. Broadway St.; (618) 224-2400; trentonhouserestaurant.com.

Although this is a small town of about 2,500 residents, Trenton is into celebrating. Start with *Trentonfest,* a community get-together with a parade, live music, performances by the local drum and bugle corps, a live auction, food booths, and raffles. The festival is held the second weekend of Sept, on Fri and Sat; admission is free; located at the Trenton City Park downtown; (618) 224-7323; www.trenton-il.com/tf.htm.

As an agricultural town, residents also celebrate the fruit of the land during the *Trenton Harvest Moon Festival.* The event features live music, entertainment, and great food, and much is geared toward children, who enjoy making crafts, watching puppet shows, and participating in contests. The event is held the third Sat of Oct; admission is free; located at the Trenton City Park downtown; (618) 224-7323; www.trenton-il.com/tf.htm.

Illinois residents don't dwell much on the topic of earthquakes, since they are a rare occurrence in the Midwest. However, in 1811 a shaker along the New Madrid fault started a domino effect of migration away from the borders of Missouri and Illinois. One pioneer looking for more stable ground was Captain Samuel Young, who settled in *Salem* to build his homestead on what is now the *Marion County Courthouse* lawn of the *Salem Square.*

Oil built this county; Salem was ranked in the top ten cities nationally in oil production during the late 1930s, when the rest of the country was struggling through the Great Depression.

This is the birthplace of William Jennings Bryan (1860–1925), who served as the U.S. secretary of state from 1913–1915. Bryan joins the likes of Abraham Lincoln and Stephen A. Douglas as a nationally admired speaker from Illinois, and he was dubbed the "Silver-Tongued Orator." The *William Jennings Bryan Memorial* sits across from Salem's *Bryan Memorial Park.* The statue was sculpted by Gutzon Borglum, the artist best known for creating the faces on Mount Rushmore. The memorial is located across from Bryan Memorial Park on North Broadway.

The *William Jennings Bryan Birthplace* is listed on the National Register of Historic Places. It's a plain-looking two-story residence with a small front porch. The home provides insight into how "Billy" was raised, without

Drive-bys

There are other structures of note in Salem that warrant a drive by, as they aren't open to the public. The *Lemen-Frakes House* has a long history of famous guests, from foreign royalty to American royalty in the form of Abraham Lincoln, and rumors hint that it's haunted. The house is located at 321 S. Franklin St. The *Bachman House* is an example of a brick Craftsman bungalow, and it's listed on the National Register of Historic Places. Some locals refer to it as the "Ernst House." The house is located at 401 S. Walnut St. The *East Nation One Room School* was relocated to stand in the shadow of the Salem Community High School on East Park Street.

Secret Recipe

If you like the creamy taste of Miracle Whip, you can think about it as you drive by the building where it was invented by Max Crossett. Max's secret sandwich dressing, which he named "X-tra Fine Salad Dressing," had become a local legend when a representative of Kraft Foods approached him to sell the recipe. Economic times were looking pretty tough back in 1931, and practical man that he was, Max decided to go with the cash. Supposedly, he turned over the ingredients list and instructions for the sum of $300, and Kraft tweaked the recipe and renamed the mixture Miracle Whip. Max Crossett's Cafe was located at 100 N. Washington St. in Salem.

pretense. The house is open on Mon, Wed, and Sat from noon to 4:30 p.m.; 408 S. Broadway; (618) 548-2222.

Ironically, Bryan earned national recognition after successfully prosecuting another former Salem resident, John Thomas Scopes, for teaching the theory of evolution in his classes. The legal contest was known as the "Scopes Monkey Trial." That dot in the long line of historical dots is connected at the 1854 **Badollet House,** as this is where Scopes stayed while attending high school. Ironically, Bryan was the keynote speaker at Scopes's graduation from Salem High School in 1919, and the two were friends, despite the trial. Supposedly, Bryan offered to pay the $100 judgment that the court levied on Scopes. Today the stately Italianate brick home operates as the **Badollet House Bed and Breakfast.** The house is located at 310 N. Washington St.; (618) 548-3412.

Richard Pollard's Yard Art is an outdoor museum of sorts that features crazy old automobiles, a literal shoe tree, a crashed airplane, a giant bug, a bumper crop of bumpers, and about 300 more oddities that will occupy your time, challenge your wits, and spark your creativity. The site is open for self-guided tours from 9 a.m. to 5 p.m.; admission is free; located 1870 N. Broadway; (618)-548-1830.

If you like great music, stay for **Salem's Bluegrass and BBQ Festival** where you can not only enjoy the music, but participate too. Concerts are on Thursday and Friday evenings, but on Saturday there are mini music clinics where for a small fee, a budding blue-grasser can practice with the big guys. The highlight comes on Saturday night, when there's a Band Showdown and groups compete for over $1,000 in prizes. Now that will get those picks a flyin'! The festival is held the second week of Sept; admission runs from $3 to $10, depending on the day and events, or a flat fee of $17 for attending all days; located at Bryan Memorial Park; (618) 548-2222.

While driving through the town of **Centralia,** keep your ears open for the beautiful chimes of the **Centralia Carillon,** which lilt through the air three times a week. At 165 feet high, this bell tower is the sixth tallest in the world and requires navigating 173 steps to reach the keyboard. A carillonneur performs from the upstairs room; on the entry level, a small museum features information about carillons. **Bell Tower Park** surrounds the structure, and a wall provides seating for those wishing to pause for a concert. Performances are Wed and Fri at noon and on Sun at 2 p.m.; tours of the tower are free but require a reservation; 114 N. Elm St.; (618) 533-4381.

The **Centralia Area Historical Society Museum** features a number of displays about the local oil and coal-mining industries, including details of the tragic 1947 mine disaster. There are fun model-train and sports exhibits, too, all housed in the vintage three-story brick building that formerly contained the old Kohl and Meyer Company's grocery warehouse. The museum is open Wed, Fri, and Sat from 10 a.m. to 4 p.m.; admission is free; 240 S. Locust St.; (618) 545-0657.

As a last fling of summer, the **Centralia Chamber of Commerce and Bureau of Tourism** hosts the **Centralia Balloon Fest,** and attendees are entertained by more than forty hot-air balloons in evening glows and morning

Prairie Top Gun

Tucked away on the west side of Centralia is **Fairview Park,** a forty-five-acre city space dedicated to recreation. But there are some unusual exhibits to be discovered among the baseball and soccer fields: a 1940s U.S. Army Nike Ajax missile, an Illinois Central Railroad 2500 steam locomotive, and a collection of historic warplanes.

Centralia native son Bill Pachura, who was a U.S. Air Force lieutenant colonel, piloted both the T-33 "T-Bird" jet trainer and the F-105 Thunderchief fighter. In 1968 Pachura nicknamed the single-seat fighter the "Red River Queen" and earned two Distinguished Flying Crosses for piloting her on 129 missions over North Vietnam. They met again in 2002 when Pachura's brother-in-law, Clark Weins, located the plane at Lackland Air Force Base and arranged a reunion of pilot and machine. Unfortunately, though, his Queen arrived in Centralia after his death at age sixty-nine, so the lieutenant colonel never got to see her stationed in his hometown park. He is laid to rest in Arlington National Cemetery. But the city of Centralia greeted the "Red River Queen" with celebrations and military honors, and today young and old alike can be seen pausing from their practices and baseball games to study her camouflage mantle and remember the brave man who piloted her so many years ago.

Fairview Park is open from dawn to dusk; the park entrance is located on Illinois Route 161 just to the west of Centralia.

launches. There's live entertainment, a car and craft show, and fireworks, too. The festival is held the third weekend of Aug, Fri through Sun; admission is $2 for those over age six and free for children six and under; located at Centralia's Foundation Park at Pleasant and McCord Streets; (618) 532-6789; www .balloon-fest.com.

As the county seat of *Jefferson County,* the town of *Mount Vernon* hosts the county's *Southern Illinois Harvest Festival,* which is dedicated to American heroes. There's a terrific parade on Sat, starting at 2 p.m., but activities run all week and include bowling tournaments, a scarecrow contest, fishing with a veteran, and the taste of the town. One event, called "Guns and Hoses," pits the police department against the city firemen in a good-natured battle on the basketball court. The festival is held the second week of Oct; admission is free; located in downtown Mount Vernon; (618) 397-1488; www .silharvestfest.mvn.net.

The area's most prized art resource is a ninety-acre estate called *Cedarhurst,* which is made up of three components: the Mitchell Museum, the Cedarhurst School of Performing Arts, and the Outdoor Sculpture Garden.

The *Mitchell Museum* is based around the private collection of the late John R. and Eleanor Mitchell. Cedarhurst's permanent collection contains work from world-renowned artists such as American master Mary Cassatt. The gallery also rotates exhibits, making each visit a unique one for guests. A children's gallery displays colorful creative works and features an annual scholastic competition and exhibition.

Children will also enjoy educational but entertaining shows by the *Cedarhurst School of Performing Arts.* A chamber music concert series and

Washington Commentary

Mount Vernon is the county seat of *Jefferson County,* and if those presidential references aren't enough, the area even has its own touch of Washington, D.C., sitting in front of the local mall; the *Miniature Washington Monument* is a replica of the famous obelisk in the nation's capital.

Then, as you travel toward town, you might get the sense that this place doesn't really take itself too seriously when you spy the twisted metal mass of the *Road Sign Sculpture.* Made up of familiar signs, from route numbers and speed limits to construction warnings and street names, the display is bound to make you laugh. Maybe all the chaos is a form of silent commentary about what goes on in the nation's capital.

Both the monument and the sculpture can be seen along Potomac Boulevard, starting around the 200 block.

annual craft show have wide appeal. And perhaps the most fascinating way to spend the day is to walk the paths along the extensive **Outdoor Sculpture Garden.** Here you can ponder the work of major artists such as Martha Enzmann and Dennis Oppenheim. There are sixty large-scale works presented along winding trails that lead past a tranquil pond and through a meadow, providing a satisfying blending of art and the natural world. The garden is open Tues through Sat from 10 a.m. to 5 p.m. and on Sun from 1 to 5 p.m.; closed holidays and on Mon; admission is free except for special programs; 2600 Richview Rd.; (618) 242-1236; www.cedarhurst.org.

The year's biggest event here is the **Cedarhurst Craft Fair,** where visitors can view and purchase items from over 130 skilled artisans. Fiber, glass, jewelry, baskets, and leatherwork are just some of the offerings, and artists are on-site demonstrating their specialties, from spinning, to watercolors, to making clay pots. There are make-and-take projects for the children, as well as a Kids Store with products that will appeal to their interests. The fair is held the second weekend of Sept, from 10 a.m. to 5 p.m.; admission is $3 for adults and free for children under age ten; a round-trip shuttle is provided from the Times Square Mall for $2, with children under ten free.

The **Jefferson County Historical Society** maintains the **Jefferson County Historical Village,** where you'll find interpretive tours, displays, and demonstrations about nineteenth-century life in southern Illinois. The complex includes several historical log cabins, an 1820s jail, and a working blacksmith shop. The **Schweinfurth Museum** contains telephone equipment, military artifacts, and uniforms. There are two nature trails that provide gentle exercise, and one leads to a Civil War–era cemetery. The village is open the first weekend of May through the last weekend of Oct, on Sat from 10 a.m. to 4 p.m. and Sun from 1 to 4 p.m.; donations are requested; 1411 N. 27th St.; (618) 246-0033; www.jchs.mvn.net.

Benton serves **Franklin County** as the county seat, and besides the 1875 Italianate-style brick courthouse (don't be fooled by the modern-looking addition of wings on either side of the front of the building), there are other government buildings downtown, including both a new and the old county jail.

Today, the 1905 restored Georgian Revival building that once housed the county jail has been transformed into the **Franklin County Historic Jail Museum.** During Prohibition, this area of the state became a place of escape for gangsters, and so a secure place for incarceration was required. The stories told inside these walls revolve around the 1920s gangland Prohibition activity that swirled in this area until the final public hanging of gangster Charlie Birger ended the murders and bootlegging. The museum also features exhibits of notable county residents, including Civil War general John Logan and actor

Sleepin' Like a Log

The town of **Benton** has fostered a Grand Ole Opry star in Billy Grammer and a fairly successful homegrown grunge rock band called Revis, but it's a 1963 visit by Beatle George Harrison that locals refer to in the same terms they speak about Abe Lincoln: "George Harrison slept here." Well, he actually slept at the home of his sister, Louise. He also reportedly shopped in the area and walked the streets without notice because this was just before the Beatles took America by storm with their appearance on the *Ed Sullivan Show.*

By the time you read this, that yellow-submarine-color bungalow may or may not be standing. Ever since Louise sold the home and retired to Florida, it has faced some drama, from threats of being razed to make way for a city parking lot, to being spared for a ten-year stint as a retro lodge called the **Hard Day's Nite Bed and Breakfast.** Now rumors are that it's been auctioned off, possibly on eBay, but things change all the time with this property. Is it still standing, or is it gone? You're bound to see the next chapter in this old home's story as you drive by 113 McCann St.

John Malkovich. The **Franklin County Tourism Bureau** is also based here. The museum is open Mon through Sat from 9 a.m. to 4 p.m.; admission is free; 209 W. Main St.; (618) 439-0608; www.fctb.com.

Next, step into the year 1910 at the **Franklin County Garage.** This is a real 1910 Ford dealership that has been turned into a history museum with displays of vintage automobiles and various period machines. The museum is open Mon through Fri from 8 a.m. to 4 p.m. and on Sat from 11 a.m. to 4 p.m.; 211 N. Main St.; (618) 438-2121; www.fctb.com.

They call her the **Little Sister of Lady Liberty,** and the **Benton Public Library** is lucky to have one of the remaining vintage Statue of Liberty replicas standing proud inside. They were mass-produced from 1949 to 1951 and sold by local Boy Scout troops. Two hundred were made and purchased nationwide; today only one hundred are accounted for, and Benton is collecting funds to restore its replica to her original glorious self, with the hope she will be returned to a planned garden next to the library entrance. The library is open Mon through Thurs from 9 a.m. to 8 p.m., Fri and Sat from 9 a.m. to 5 p.m., and on Sun from 1 to 5 p.m.; 502 S. Main St.; (618) 438-7511; www .benton.lib.il.us.

Over in the town of **West Frankfort,** the **Frankfort Area Historical Society** has converted the old Logan Elementary School into the three-floor **Frankfort Area Historical Museum.** The space is cleverly used: Classrooms are full-scale vignettes of prairie life. Don't miss the mural time line painted on the walls of the auditorium. The **Red Geranium Tea Room** serves a light lunch, and a gift shop is on-site also. The museum is open Wed and Thurs from 9 a.m. to 3 p.m., and lunch is served on Wed from 11 a.m. to 1 p.m.; admission to the museum is free; 2000 E. St. Louis Street; (618) 932-6159.

The historical society has also acquired the 1912 **Old Chicago and Eastern Illinois Depot Museum,** which has been renovated and now houses artifacts from various wars. The museum is open on Sun from 1 to 4 p.m.; admission is free; 102 W. Main St., right next to the tracks; (618) 932-6159.

West Frankfort hosts the **Old King Coal Festival,** which is aptly overseen by a local gent who's crowned as Old King Coal. Besides a traditional parade, there's also a pet parade, carnival rides, live music (they've even featured an *American Idol* finalist on the main stage), and plenty of food. There's a serious side to this event, too, as the town hosts a Coal Miner's Reunion and conducts a Miner's Memorial Ceremony to remember those who've worked the backbreaking job for the benefit of all. The festival is held the second weekend of Sept, from Thurs at 4 p.m. to Sun at 5 p.m.; admission is free; located downtown; (618) 932-2181; www.old kingcoal.com.

littlesisterof ladyliberty

Benton's "Little Sister of Lady Liberty" stands 8 feet, 6 inches tall. Each of the original replicas of the Statue of Liberty varies in height, as every community built its own pedestal to suit the venue where it was to be displayed.

Southwest is the town of **Herrin,** which was incorporated in 1900 and settled by Italian immigrants who came to work in the surrounding coal mines. Today about 11,000 people live here and enjoy the great outdoors and charming hometown atmosphere. In honor of our country's veterans, Herrin has maintained a **Doughboy soldier** statue, one of only ninety remaining in the nation. The statue of a young World War I solider running with his rifle poised above his head has been relocated to a more prominent location at North Park Avenue and Adams Street. And the town demonstrates its respect for the men who helped build it with the **Coal Miner's Memorial,** a life-size statue of a miner heading to work with his young son standing nearby; behind the pair is a long wall in which the names of local miners are engraved. The statue is located at 100 N. Fourteenth St.

Each year the community parties during the **HerrinFesta Italiana,** which is a combination homecoming and celebration of the town's Italian heritage. The food is really terrific, and besides the parade, talent contest, and art and car shows, there's an internationally recognized Bocce Tournament. There's anticipation in the air during the best-sauce competition, and the pasta-eating contest is always a hit. The event is held the week leading into

Tiny Prayers

The **Roadside Chapel** is considered one of the tiniest churches in the country. It's constructed like a log cabin of weatherworn logs, but unlike the homes built by settlers in this area, this structure stands on stilts. A long, elevated wood-plank path leads the faithful inside, where a large cross awaits prayers from weary travelers. After you talk with God, stop at the convenience store next door and pick up a nice picnic lunch. The chapel is located at I-64 and SR 127 outside of Nashville.

Memorial Day weekend; admission is free for most events; located all over Herrin, but many events are at the Civic Center at 101 S. Sixteenth St. (618) 942-5163; www.herrinfesta.com.

Driving northwest, the next stop is **Nashville,** but don't expect to hear the sounds of country music; that's the other Nashville. Instead, you're liable to hear snorting, huffing, baying, and chirping coming from the **Rainbow Ranch Petting Zoo and Exotic Farm.** See zebras, a camel, peacocks, emus, zebus, fallow deer, plus all the regular farm animals at this 150-year old family enterprise. The farm is open Apr to Oct, Wed through Sat from 9 a.m. to 5 p.m. and on Sun from noon to 5 p.m.; admission is $5 per person, and children under age one are free. 9906 SR 15; (618) 424-7979; www.rainbowranchzoo.com.

Nashville is the county seat of **Washington County** and hosts the **Washington County Historical Museum,** which is located in an 1871 building that was once a home. A fine collection of vintage wedding gowns is probably this museum's most popular attraction, although there are many interesting local artifacts from early county history here. The museum is open on Sun from 1:30 to 3:30 p.m.; admission is free; 326 S. Kaskaskia St.; (618) 327-1488.

During the **Nashville Fall Festival,** more than one hundred crafts and food booths surround the town's courtyard square. Artisans demonstrate their work, and there's live music and entertainment on multiple stages. Plus, the **Fall Festival Children's Pet Parade** is always a big draw, with registration beginning at 9 a.m. and the parade following soon afterward. Check out some of the more exotic foods, such as chicken livers and gizzards, and smoked turkey legs. If those aren't to your taste, don't worry, because they serve hot dogs and chili, too. And don't miss out on the free snow cones. The festival is held the third weekend of Sept from Friday evening to Sunday afternoon; admission is free; located in downtown Nashville around East St. Louis Street; (618) 327-3700.

Since the mid-1860s, the town of **Okawville** has been known for its mineral springs. A small European-like spa hotel was built downtown, but after several iterations, the current *Original Springs Mineral Spa and Hotel* was constructed in 1892–1893. Today the forty rooms are being remodeled and restored. The massages are reasonably priced, and the facility includes a restaurant, game room, and modern spa with slides. The hotel is located at 506 N. Hanover St.; (618) 243-5458; okawvillehotel.tripod.com.

Preserved rather than restored: That's the philosophy of the Heritage House Museum group, which runs three notable historical homes in Okawville. The houses share the group's Web site at www.okawvillecc.com. The *Schlosser Home* is touted as a "different kind of museum," as it depicts the life of a 1900s working-class family. This is where Frank Schlosser lived and ran the family laundry. The giant washtubs and ironing equipment sit idle, prompting visitors to appreciate modern conveniences. Also on the property are a harness shop and two-room outhouse. The house is open Sat and Sun from noon to 4 p.m., and by appointment; admission is $2; 114 W. Walnut St.; (618) 243-5694.

TOP ANNUAL EVENTS

APRIL
Annual Sheep and Craft Festival
Waterloo
(618) 939-8536

MAY
Fruehlingfest (Springfest)
Maeystown
(618) 458-6660

JUNE
Archaeology Day
Kampsville
(618) 653-4316

AUGUST
Waterloo Homecoming
Waterloo
(618) 939-5300

SEPTEMBER
Annual Popeye Picnic
Chester
(618) 826-5114

Murphysboro Apple Festival
Murphysboro
(618) 833-9928

Applebutter Festival
Maeystown
(618) 458-6660

Wheat Fair and Festival
Okawville
(618) 243-5694

Riverboat Days
Cairo
late Sept–early Oct
(618) 734-2737

OCTOBER
Oktoberfest
Maeystown
(618) 458-6660

DECEMBER
Old-Fashioned German Christmas
Maeystown
(618) 458-6660

From the street, **Dr. Poos Home and Medical Museum** looks more like a life-size dollhouse with its pink exterior and mansard roof. Built in 1888, the Second Empire–style architecture is charming; a second building here was constructed with the intention of being a spa, but it was never employed as such. Inside, don't miss the piano that sits in the parlor; it was purchased from a vendor at the 1893 Chicago Columbian Exposition. The house is open by appointment, but if tours are running at the Schlosser Home, docents will provide tours here, too; donations are requested; 202 N. Front St.; (618) 243-5694.

The third home is the **Schlosser Brick House,** built in 1869 by Frank's brother Joseph, who was the town cobbler. The building and furnishings here seem more like they date from the late 1700s or very early 1800s—sparse with simple wood furniture, braided rugs, and primitive artifacts. The house is open by appointment, but if you're touring the Frank Schlosser Home, ask to see this one also; donations are requested; located across from the Frank Schlosser home on Walnut Street; (618) 243-5694.

If you visit the town during **Okawville Heritage Days,** you can view all of these museums and step back in time by taking a surrey ride, or watch volunteers demonstrating butter churning, soap production, and spinning. A mass yard sale is arranged on the museum grounds at Walnut Street, and there's a book fair and craft show, plus homemade ice cream, kettle corn, and lots of fair-type food. The event is held the second weekend of June; admission is free; 114 W. Walnut St.; (618) 243-5694.

The **Wheat Fair and Festival** has been an Okawville tradition since 1948. The three-day harvest celebration includes a Sunday parade, live music, kiddie rides, tractor pulls, a talent show, and displays of prized homegrown local produce. The festival is held the third week of Sept, from Fri at noon to Sun at 10 p.m.; admission is free; located at the Okawville Community Club, 511 S. Hanover St.; (618) 243-5694.

Waterloo has a long history of being the county seat of **Monroe County,** having been selected for the honor in 1825. The **Monroe County Courthouse** is a blend of old and new, as the historic structure has been preserved and expanded with a modern wing. The courthouse is located at 100 S. Main St.

There are several historic buildings in town, but two are of special note. The **Peterson House** is the last remaining stagecoach inn along the Kaskaskia-Cahokia Trail. Originally constructed in the early 1800s, it was first a general store. As time passed, additions were added and the structure was modified into a tavern and then an inn. Today the **Peterson Heritage Society** has restored the house, converting it into a museum that features the interior of an 1800s country store and 1880s-era furniture and artifacts. Two historical log cabins share the site. The house is open Sat and Sun from 1 to 4 p.m.; admission is free; 275 N. Main St.; (618) 939-5300.

The *Monroe County Historical Society* maintains the 1782 *Belle Fontaine House.* This two-story brick home was the residence of some of the area's first families, and legend says Meriwether Lewis stopped here one evening. The house is open Sat and Sun from 1 to 5 p.m.; admission is free; 709 S. Church St.; (618) 939-5300.

Each year visitors and residents flock downtown to celebrate the *Heritage Fall Festival,* when the courthouse square is transformed into party central with craft sales, food, carriage rides, a petting zoo, a big parade, and the perennial favorite, the "Best Wings in Waterloo" contest. The festival is held the second Sat of Oct; admission is free; located at the square at 100 S. Main St.; (618) 939-5300.

West of Waterloo, keep your eyes peeled for the work of true artisans: Around 1849, German stonemasons demonstrated their craft by building the beautiful *Fountain Creek Bridge.* Although it's closed to traffic, today it stands guard as the largest stone-arch bridge in Monroe County, spanning 46 feet across the waters of *Fountain Creek.* The bridge is located west of Waterloo, and just south of SR 156.

The entire village of *Maeystown* is listed on the National Register of Historic Places, and when you cross the one-lane *Stone Arched Bridge* that takes you into this special place, it not only sets the tone that you're going back

OTHER ATTRACTIONS WORTH SEEING IN SOUTHWESTERN ILLINOIS

U.S. Custom House Cairo	**Maeystown National Historic Site** Maeystown
West Walnut Historic District Cairo	**Little Grand Canyon** Murphysboro
Southern Illinois University Touch of Nature Environmental Center Carbondale	**Rainbow Ranch Petting Zoo and Exotic Farm** Nashville
Chester Riverfront Mural Chester	**Roadside Chapel** Nashville
Owl Creek Vineyard and Winery Cobden	**Richard Pollard's Yard Art** Salem

in time, but gives the impression that you've somehow magically crossed the ocean to land in Bavaria. Founded in 1852 by Jacob Maeys, Maeystown stands tucked along the Mississippi River bluffs, and old-time architectural features, such as flagstone gutters and stone walls, wind throughout the downtown. Still standing are *Jacob Maeys's Original Log House* and the 1867 *Old Stone Church,* which conducted services in German up until 1943. The *Corner George Inn Sweet Shoppe,* the *Maeystown General Store,* and various quaint novelty and antiques emporiums operate from behind the doorways of well-preserved, mostly flagstone buildings.

For an unusual lodging experience, try the *Corner George Inn Bed and Breakfast,* which from the outside gives the impression that you should be wearing your 1880s prairie bonnet and disembarking from a stagecoach. Built in 1884 as a saloon and hotel, today the inn reflects that rich heritage, and the breakfast is served in a 600-square-foot former ballroom. The B&B is located at 1101 Main St.; (618) 458-6660; www.cornergeorgeinn.com.

To discover the history of this area, visit the *Maeystown Rock Mill Museum,* which is the home to the *Maeystown Preservation Society* and town museum. The building itself has an interesting history; in 1859 a steam-powered flourmill was built on the site, but it burned to the ground in 1868. The building was reconstructed in 1880 but never used as a mill again, instead serving as space for various businesses until the preservation society purchased and renovated it in the 1980s. The museum is open on Sat from 10 a.m. to 4 p.m. and Sun from 11 a.m. to 4 p.m.; admission is free; 1113 Mill St.; (618) 458-6464.

In early spring, over forty antique and plant dealers from six states converge on Maeystown for the *Fruehlingsfest Antique and Garden Show.* Visitors purchase high-quality antiques as well as new folk art, plants, and garden accessories. A festival atmosphere takes over; there's traditional food, and local wineries participate, too. The event is held on the first Sun in May from 9 a.m. to 4 p.m.; admission is free; located downtown and along Mill Street by the Rock Mill; (618) 458-6660; www.maeystown.com.

Named after the rocks that infiltrated the ground in this area of the state, *Prairie du Rocher* was founded by the French in 1722 and settled by fur trappers, soldiers, and their families. It's said to be the oldest town in what is now the state of Illinois, and it was the proximity to the Mississippi River that first attracted French officials to this location.

One of the most notable homes here is the *Creole House.* Built in 1800 as a one-room, one-story frame home, it was expanded by its second owner, who used a post-in-ground technique, a popular method employed by the French in Creole-style architecture. The home is on the National Register of Historic

Places and is currently owned and managed by the **Randolph County Historical Society,** which also restored this gem. The home is open by appointment generally, or during special local events.

One of those events is the society's fund-raiser called the **Creole House Apple Festival.** Visitors mingle with costumed volunteers cooking homemade apple butter in giant kettles and frying batter-dipped apple fritters in antique metal skillets. Wool spinning and other colonial crafts are demonstrated, and there are carriage rides and Creole house tours, too. The festival is held the third Sun of Sept, from 10 a.m. to 4 p.m.; admission is free; 281 Market St.; (618) 397-1488; www.visitprairiedurocher.com.

Four miles east, outside of Prairie du Rocher, are the **Fort de Chartres State Historic Site, and the Fort de Chartres Rendezvous.** A stone garrison was originally built here in the 1750s by the French, who commanded the area at that time. It was thought that stone would be the strongest building material, but after the British took possession and eventually abandoned the structure in 1771, the fort fell into disrepair until the Illinois government purchased the property in the early 1900s. Today, a portion of the fort has been reconstructed, and the **Peithmann Museum** on the site provides a glimpse of life in colonial times. The perimeter of the remaining buildings and fort are outlined so visitors can gain a clear idea of the scope of the original structures. The museum is open Wed through Sun from 9 a.m. to 5 p.m.; admission is free.

The **Fort de Chartres Rendezvous** at the historic site is a "not to miss" attraction in which over a thousand reenactors perform their roles as eighteenth-century soldiers and settlers. Musical performances by the Fife and Drum Corps are always popular, and visitors can see drills by militia and demonstrations by craftsmen. The event is held the first weekend of June; admission is free; the Fort de Chartres State Historic Site is located at 1350 Rte. 155, Prairie du Rocher; (618) 284-7230; www.ftdechartres.com.

Due to the ever-present risk of fire or tornados on the prairie, creative minds often attempted to design structures that could withstand high winds and heat. One such example stands in the town of **Schuline.** It's called the **Charter Oak School** and it's the only recorded octagonal one-room school in the state, and one of only three remaining in the U.S. It was thought the "Octagon Mode" layout would maximize natural light and minimize the threat posed by high winds. The cost to build the redbrick building with a white cupola was a staggering $1,000 in 1873. It served its public purpose until 1953, when the last students matriculated there before the school district consolidated classes for economic reasons. The **Randolph County Historical Society** maintains the building, which is open for special events such as an annual fund-raiser called the **Charter Oak Corn Fest.** Visitors tour the school, peruse the craft market, and partake in an old-fashioned picnic of fried chicken, fresh vegetables, corn on the cob, and Indian pudding. The festival is held the first Sat of Aug; admission is about $10; 9272 Schuline Rd.

The county seat of **Randolph County** is **Chester,** a town of under 9,000 people who might think they're living in a cartoon world thanks to one of their native sons. That's because the creator of *Popeye the Sailorman,* Elzie Crisler Segar, was born here in 1894. It's often said that every first novel contains characters based on people the author knows. That might be the case here, too, as rumor has it that Segar's characters were caricatures of actual friends and neighbors who walked the streets of Chester when Segar was a youth.

homecookin'

The ingredients of Indian pudding were commonly found in Prairie kitchens: scalded milk, molasses, cornmeal, ginger or cinnamon, and a dash of salt. After baking, it essentially becomes cornmeal custard.

Today, you can walk among Segar's imaginary people, as they are memorialized by granite statues along the **Popeye and Friends Character Trail;** there will be twenty-one when the project is completed. It all began in 1977 when a nine-hundred-pound bronze Popeye statue was affixed to its pedestal in the center of the **Elzie C. Segar Memorial Park,** which overlooks the Mississippi River and the 1942 **Chester Bridge** on SR 51.

The **Popeye Picnic Festival** is an annual event that draws spinach lovers from around the world. There's a parade, cartooning contests, a Popeye Pet Show, and Wimpie's Wiener Dog Derby, where purebred dachshunds race for the gold. Entertainment includes comedians, live music, a midway, an official comic-book release, Sunday fireworks, great food, and giveaways and prizes. The festival is held the first weekend after Labor Day, from Fri at 9 a.m. to Sun at 8:30 p.m.; admission is free; located at various locations around town; (618) 826-5114; www.popeyepicnic.com.

The **Popeye Museum** can be found inside the **Spinach Can Collectibles** store, which has laid claim to being the world's only "shop, museum, and fan club" dedicated to Popeye. The place is chock-full of goodies, but despite the name, there's not spinach in sight, and that's probably a good thing for most of us non-spinach-eating folks. The museum is open Mon through Fri from 9:30 a.m. to 4:30 p.m. and on Sat from 10 a.m. to 3 p.m.; admission is free; 1001 State St.; (618) 826-4567; www.popeyepicnic.com.

On a more serious note, the **Randolph County Courthouse** has something unusual: a Gothic stone annex. Built in 1864, today it is the **Randolph**

County Museum, and it serves as archive space and also contains displays of artifacts pertaining to the early French settlers in Randolph County. The courthouse is open Sun, Mon, Thurs, and Fri from 12:30 to 3:30 p.m.; admission is free; 1 Taylor St.; (618) 826-2667.

Northeast of Chester is *Mary's River Covered Bridge,* the last remaining covered bridge in southern Illinois. Built in 1854, it allowed traffic to cross the necessary 90 feet over the *Mary River* until 1930, when it was closed for safety. After acquiring it, the state renovated the structure in 2005, and the bridge, noted for its Burr arch design, was saved. It's listed on the National Register of Historic Places and located between the towns of Chester and Bremen, approximately 7 miles northeast of Chester on SR 150.

Before leaving the area, consider lodging for the night at the *Stone House Bed and Breakfast.* This former Presbyterian Church, built in 1846, was transformed into a family home in 1921 after a storm damaged the roof and bell tower. The home has phenomenal views of the Mississippi River from the expansive porch, the gardens, upstairs balcony, and some of the bedrooms. Before you leave, you'll enjoy a hearty home-cooked breakfast from the Stone House's signature recipes. The Stone House is located at 509 W. Harrison St.; (618) 604-9106; www.bbonline.com/il/stonehouse.

Kaskaskia had such promise back in 1809 when it was tapped to be the capital of the Illinois Territory. The town's luck continued for two more years, from 1818 to 1820, when it was named the capital of the State of Illinois. But fate can be a harsh mistress, and politics drew the honor away when Vandalia was selected as a more suitable location for the state capital, leaving Kaskaskia a bit shocked but determined to woo the capital back. It never happened. And to add insult to the entire mess, the Mississippi finally flooded the town so badly that it became divided by water.

The west side became *Kaskaskia Island,* and today the *Kaskaskia Bell State Historic Site* operates there. The focal point here is the 1743 bell that was presented by the reigning French monarch, King Louis the XV, as a gift to the Mission of the Immaculate Conception Catholic Church. The bell is referred to as "the Liberty Bell of the West," and it's older than the Liberty Bell in Philadelphia, Pennsylvania. Curiously, it has a similar feature: A crack runs along the side of the Kaskaskia Bell, too. The site is open Memorial Day to Labor Day, daily from 9 a.m. to 4 p.m., and the rest of the year, Wed through Sun only, from 9 a.m. to 4 p.m.; admission is free; 481 Pine St.; go

allshookup

The first record of an earthquake in Illinois goes back to 1795, when Kaskaskia reported a minute-and-a-half-long trembler.

to St. Mary's, Missouri, to cross the bridge to the Illinois-side island; (618) 859-3031.

The east side of the breach is now the **_Fort Kaskaskia State Historic Site,_** which contains the stone remains of a French redoubt built in 1759, as well as the **_Garrison Hill Cemetery,_** a Mississippi River scenic overlook and a public picnic area. The site is open daily from 8 a.m. to 4 p.m.; admission is free; 4372 Park Rd., Ellis Grove; (618) 859-3741.

Nearby is the **_Pierre Menard Home State Historic Site._** This was the residence of a French-Canadian fur trader who rose to affluence and power in the Illinois Territory as the area's presiding officer. When Illinois became a state, Menard was selected as the first lieutenant governor. The home is another example of the architecture called French Creole, and it features a handsome, two-story frame structure with a sweeping front porch overlooking the Mississippi River. The grounds include reproductions of the smokehouse and springhouse, and the outside kitchen oven has been rebuilt to complete the overall picture of the good life in the Illinois Territory in the late 1700s and early 1800s. The site is open year-round, Wed through Sun from 9 a.m. to 5 p.m.; admission is free; 4230 Kaskaskia Rd., Ellis Grove; (618) 859-3031.

Waterloo, Out of the Blue

In the years immediately following the Civil War, more than twenty communities nationwide claimed to be the original location of the first U.S. Memorial Day. Mary Logan wrote in her 1913 autobiography, _Reminiscences of a Soldier's Wife,_ that it was her husband, General John A. Logan, a U.S. congressman, who conceived and authored the idea. In fact, on May 5, 1868, General Logan dictated Order No. 11 for "the first decoration of the graves of Union soldiers that ever took place in the United States." The proclamation states: "The 30th day of May, 1868, is designated for the purpose of strewing with flowers or otherwise decorating the graves of comrades who died ...." Mary explained that the date of May 30th was specifically selected because that was the "time of year when flowers would be in their greatest perfection in the different sections of the county."

The brouhaha among communities continued for ninety-eight years until President Lyndon B. Johnson settled the Memorial Day dispute in 1966 by directing the federal government to crown Waterloo, New York, as the holiday's official birthplace. The criteria he used to determine the winner was more complicated than having an official proclamation order or selecting a calendar date. Waterloo proved that its first Memorial Day celebration was held on May 5, 1866, and was a true community-wide tradition with multiple activities honoring the Civil War dead. Undoubtedly, if Mary Logan had been alive, she would have respectfully but firmly disagreed with President Johnson's choice.

Illinois and the Civil War

The people of Illinois struggled with slavery issues along with the nation. While residents in the northern part of Illinois, particularly women in the larger cities, gathered goods for shipment to the front lines, southern Illinois considered separating from the rest of the state. People living in cities like *Cairo,* nicknamed Little Egypt, found it easier to cling to their southern neighbors in Kentucky, whom they'd worked with and trusted for years, than join forces with strangers in far away northern Illinois.

More than 259,000 men joined Illinois regiments, and nearly 35,000 died of combatwounds or disease. A tax of $300 was established for those wanting to escape the conflict, but only fifty-five men paid the fee. In fact, at times volunteers were sent home because the crush to serve was too great for the state registration bureaus. Frustrated and wanting to serve, many Illinois men joined regiments from Missouri, Indiana, and Kentucky.

Murphysboro is the county seat of *Jackson County,* and people here tend to be proud of hometown native General John Logan and apples. This part of Illinois is prime apple country, and more than thirty commercial orchards provide a livelihood for area residents.

The *Murphysboro Apple Festival* draws large crowds of apple fans, who munch on all sorts of apple-laden treats while watching the parade and tapping toes to the music coming from the Appletime Stage. There are apple pie and apple-butter contests, a carnival, an arts and crafts fair, and all sorts of old-fashioned community competitions, ranging from vintage baseball and apple-core throwing to firefighter water fights. You might score some free apple cider and apple donuts on Sunday, so look for those booths. The festival is held the second weekend of Sept, from Wed at 11 a.m. to Sun at 4 p.m.; admission is free; located throughout the town; (618) 684-3200.

Civil War general John A. Logan was born in Murphysboro and served as a U.S. representative and senator. Both he and his wife were active on the Washington, D.C. circuit, helping to push legislation that had national scope. The *General John A. Logan Museum* is part of a enclave of historical homes, and a walking tour leads to each of the buildings. Since Logan's birthplace (which is also in this complex) is essentially an archaeological site, the museum is housed in the *Christopher C. Bullar House.* Visitors can tour the first floor to view Logan family memorabilia and Civil War artifacts. The museum is open June 1 to Aug 31, Tues through Sat from 10 a.m. to 4 p.m. and on Sun from 1 to 4 p.m., and Sept 1 to May 31, Tues through Sun from 1 to 4 p.m.; admission is $2 for adults and $1 for children; 1613 Edith St.; (618) 684-3455; www .loganmuseum.org.

There are other residences of note in this tract: The **Samuel H. Dalton House** was home to a freed slave and is currently undergoing renovation; the **Sheley House** is the home of the **Murphysboro Tourism Commission,** and exhibits on the town's history can be viewed here; and the **Hughes Gallery** is an artist's showroom containing works for sale. All of these properties can be toured with prior arrangements made through the Logan Museum.

In 1937 a couple of southern Illinois residents put a plan in action to build the largest cross in the Western Hemisphere, but the idea took many years and over $30,000 to become a reality. By 1959 the frame was up and waiting for the steel panels with white porcelain veneer to be installed. After four more years, in 1963 the **Bald Knob Cross of Peace** was illuminated for all passersby to see, but with no financial reserves for maintenance, the cross fell victim to the elements; the panels rusted from the weather, wind carried away portions of the exterior, and vandals did, too. Aggressive fund-raising began in earnest, and in late 2009 engineers started the renovation to save the historic cross, which is located at 3630 Bald Knob Rd., Alto Pass; www.baldknobcross.com.

The thousand or so residents of **Cobden** proudly accept the "Appleknocker Town" nickname as a reference to its plentiful apple and peach orchards. This is also the place where in 1867 local orchard owner Parker Earle created the first "refrigerated" method of shipping fruit via the Illinois Central Railroad; he called it the "ice-cooled" railroad car, and his idea meant that fruit farmers from southern Illinois could ship fresh fruit to high-demand markets.

appleknocker

Strange as it sounds, an appleknocker is someone who uses a pole to tap ripe fruit from a tree. Sometime around 1940, the Cobden High School boy's basketball team managed to win the Illinois basketball quarterfinals. The press reported a fan's surprise that "Appleknockers could win such a thing." Rather than take it as an insult, the town and school adopted the name Appleknockers, and national publications have recognized it as one of the nation's oddest mascots.

The **Cobden Peach Festival** started in 1938 and is a peachy-keen party with a Miss Peach Queen, parade, plenty of peach cobbler, games, and midway; plus many local stores host late-night sales. The festival is held the first full weekend of Aug on Fri and Sat; admission is free; located at Cobden Community Park; (618) 893-2425.

But this area isn't just fruit country. The family-run **Rancho Bella Vista** is fast becoming the place for die-hard chili-heads. That's because they grow over twenty varieties of specialty hot peppers and turn them into fine salsa and gourmet pepper jellies and jams right on premises. Fresh peppers are in season from June to mid-October and are sold at the *Darn Hot Pepper Farm Stand,* as well as the afore-mentioned pepper goods. The farm is open June to the second week of Dec, Mon through Sat from 10 a.m. to 5 p.m.; 827 Vines Rd.; (618) 893-1443; www .darnhotpeppers.com.

The *Darn Hot Pepper Festival* features walking tours of the "Fields of Fire," live music, arts and crafts, and a book sale, plus a chance to sample pepper salsa, jellies, and jams from Rancho Bella Vista and local restaurants. The festival is held the first Sat of Sept from 11 a.m. to 5 p.m.; admission to the tasting tent is $3, with children under twelve free. 827 Vines Rd.; (618) 893-1443; www.darnhotpeppers.com.

The *Union County Historical and Genealogy Society Museum* is housed in the 1892 *H. A. Dubois Building,* which is a monument in itself, being a fine example of a metal-front Mesker Brothers building. Part of the collection here is that of the former Cobden Museum, as well as memorabilia of local residents and early settlers. The museum is open Sat and Sun from 1 to 5 p.m.; admission is free; (618) 893-2865.

Since tourists are attracted to the local orchards, many wonderful bed-and-breakfast establishments offer lodging in the Cobden area. One of note is the *Water Valley Inn.* Built in 1922, the two-story farmhouse features lovely woodwork, pocket doors, a classic front staircase, and stained-glass windows. The beds are draped in comfy quits, and the many antiques will catch your attention. Sit on the back porch and gaze across the one hundred acres sprawl-ing ahead, or explore the barn and chicken coop. The inn is located at 3435 Water Valley Rd.; (618) 534-2244; www.1watervalleyinn.com.

SELECTED VISITORS BUREAUS AND CHAMBERS OF COMMERCE

Southwestern Illinois Tourism and Convention Bureau
10950 Lincoln Trail
Fairview Heights, 62208
(800) 442-1488

Carbondale Convention and Visitors Bureau
1245 E. Main St.
Carbondale, 62901
(800) 526-1500

Williamson County Tourism Board
1602 Sioux Dr.
Marion, 62959
(618) 997-3690

Places to Stay in Southwestern Illinois

CARBONDALE
America's Best Inn and Suites
1345 E. Main St.
(618) 529-4801
www.americasbestinn.com

Giant City Lodge
460 Giant City Lodge Rd.
(618) 457-4921
www.giantcitylodge.com

Holiday Inn and Conference Center
2300 Reed Station Parkway
(618) 549-2600
www.holidayinn.com

Quality Inn
1415 E. Main St.
(618) 549-4244
www.qualityinn.com

Ramada Limited
801 North Giant City Rd.
(618) 351-6611
www.ramada.com

DU QUOIN
Budget Inn
1266 S. Washington St.
(618) 542-5014
www.budgetinn.com

Francie's Bed and Breakfast Inn
104 South Line St.
(618) 542-6686
www.franciesinn.com

FAIRVIEW HEIGHTS
Drury Inn
12 Ludwig Dr.
(800) 325-0481
www.druryhotels.com

Fairfield Inn
140 Ludwig Dr.
(800) 228-2800
www.marriott.com

Four Points Sheraton
319 Fountains Parkway
(618) 622-9500
www.starwoodhotels.com/fourpoints

Hampton Inn
150 Ludwig Dr.
(800) 426-7866
www.hamptoninn.com

MARION
Comfort Inn
2600 W. Main St.
(618) 997-6221
www.comfortinn.com

Drury Inn
2706 W. DeYoung St.
(618) 997-9600
www.druryhotels.com

Hampton Inn
2710 W. De Young St.
(618) 998-9900
www.hamptoninn.com

OKAWVILLE
Original Springs Hotel
506 North Hanover St.
(618) 243-5458
www.theoriginalspringshotel.com

SALEM
Badollet House
310 N. Washington St.
(618) 548-3412

Places to Eat in Southwestern Illinois

CARBONDALE
Larry's Pit BBQ
1181 Rendleman Rd.
(618) 549-1599

Mary Lou's Grill
114 S. Illinois Ave.
(618) 457-5084

Tres Hombres
119 N. Washington St.
(618) 457-3308
www.trescarbondale.com

DU QUOIN
To Perfection
1664 S. Washington St.
(618) 542-2002

MARION
20's Hideout Steakhouse
2606 W. Main St.
(618) 997-8325
www.hideoutrestaurant.com

Sao Asian Bistro
2800 Seventeenth St.
(618) 993-2828
www.saoasianbistro.com

Index

Already "Been There, Done That"?
Then Get Off the Beaten Path!

OFF THE BEATEN PATH®

A GUIDE TO UNIQUE PLACES ➡

"For the traveler who enjoys the special, the unusual,
and the unexpected."—*The Traveler* newsletter

Alabama	Kansas	Nevada	Quebec
Alaska	Kentucky	New Hampshire	Rhode Island
Arizona	Louisiana	New Jersey	South Carolina
Arkansas	Maine	New Mexico	Southern California
British Columbia	Maritime Provinces	Metro New York	Tennessee
Colorado	Maryland & Delaware	Upstate New York	Texas
Connecticut		North Carolina	Utah
Dakotas	Massachusetts	Northern California	Vermont
Florida	Michigan	Ohio	Virginia
Georgia	Minnesota	Oklahoma	Washington, D.C.
Hawaii	Mississippi	Oregon	West Virginia
Idaho	Missouri	Pennsylvania	Wisconsin
Indiana	Montana	Philadelphia	Wyoming
Iowa	Nebraska	Puerto Rico	